THE OPTIONS COURSE

WILEY TRADING ADVANTAGE

THE OPTIONS COURSE

High Profit & Low Stress Trading Methods

George A. Fontanills

JOHN WILEY & SONS, INC.
New York • Chichester • Weinheim • Brisbane • Singapore • Toronto

Copyright © 1998 by George A. Fontanills and Richard Cawood. All rights reserved.

Published by John Wiley & Sons, Inc.

Published simultaneously in Canada.

This publication is designed to provide accurate and authoritative information in regard to the subject matter covered. It is sold with the understanding that the publisher is not engaged in rendering professional services. If professional advice or other expert assistance is required, the services of a competent professional person should be sought.

Library of Congress Cataloging-in-Publication Data:

Fontanills, George.
    The options course : high profit & low stress trading methods / by George A. Fontanills.
       p.   cm.—(Wiley trading advantage)
    Includes index.
    ISBN 0-471-24950-5 (alk. paper)
    1. Options (Finance) I. Title. II. Series.
HG6024.A3F66   1998
332.64'5—dc21   97-50522

Printed in the United States of America
10 9 8 7 6 5

To Richard Cawood,
my friend and business partner

Preface

My trading program is the result of many years of trading experience, as well as many years of research and development, all in the pursuit of developing the optimal methodologies to trade the stock, options, and futures markets. Hopefully, this book will allow you to develop a better understanding of the markets and will assist you in learning how to profitably trade. In my opinion, there is no better lifestyle than that of a successful investor.

Most new investors and traders, whether they are beginners or professionals, usually lose money for two reasons. First, they do not have a grasp of how the markets really work. Second, they are under too much stress when they trade because they fear losing money. Many times, traders liquidate good trades too quickly or have no idea when to take profits. This program has been developed to build your knowledge base of the markets to a professional level and to provide you with strategies that make money in the marketplace.

Students often ask me how I got started as a full-time investor. Perhaps like you, I was looking for an opportunity that would allow me to achieve my financial dreams after a long road of despair. After attending high school in Miami, I felt a college career was necessary to become successful. Although I questioned what success really meant to me and whether college would really bring me that success, I settled on the University of Florida in Gainesville for all the wrong reasons. It was close to home and all my friends were going there.

One day, after just a few semesters, I woke up having difficulty breathing. I went to the university clinic and was told I had a mild case of pneumonia. After a week of useless medications, my breathing troubles increased. Finally,

X rays were taken, and at the age of 18, I was diagnosed with Hodgkin's disease, a form of cancer. There is no news that can be more devastating to a young person and his family.

Perhaps the hardest thing I had to face was the loss of my physical prowess. Until that time, I was in exceptional shape, working out every day and participating in lots of sports. Over the next year, I was hospitalized and had to undergo chemotherapy treatments and radiation therapy. Throughout this dark time, I continued my studies at a community college.

At this point, I realized that life was too short to waste time, and that I needed to work as hard as I could to achieve everything I wanted. As my resolve to succeed took flight, I coined the phrase, "out of adversity comes inspiration."

I slowly recovered and went on to attend New York University, graduating with honors with a bachelor's degree in accounting. I subsequently earned my CPA license and joined a large accounting firm. However, after spending several years in public accounting, I once again felt disillusioned. I needed something more. I applied and, to my surprise, was accepted at Harvard Business School. After two grueling years (but something I would do again without hesitation), I graduated.

Here I was, a bright and energetic young man with an MBA from the finest business school in the world with countless job offers others would never dream of turning down. But somehow I just couldn't get excited about any of the positions, no matter what they paid me. I had already traveled down that road and knew that it led to a dead end. Instead, I decided to go into business for myself.

Driven by my need for a more rewarding career, I started my first business. It failed. Strike one. Undaunted, I started a second business, which never even got off the ground. Strike two. On my third attempt—an attempt to strike gold in the real estate business—I realized that I could actually be good at something. Working with some wealthy individuals in Massachusetts, I was just able to keep my head above water. I would find all these great real estate deals and they would put up the money to buy them. Subsequently, I would get a small piece of each deal.

Unfortunately, I forgot one thing: I needed to eat and pay the rent without the benefit of a consistent salary. Finally, the day came when my landlord (one of my partners) came to collect my rent and I had no money to pay it. I hedged as best I could and asked him to give me a little more time. He turned me down, adding that he was going to throw me out regardless of how much money I made him in the past. I was shocked. At first I thought he was kidding around. But with a stern look on his face, he proved me wrong, stating unequivocally, "One day you will thank me for teaching you this lesson." At the time, I cockily replied that I'd be much happier with a wheelbarrow full of money. In hindsight, I realize that he was probably referring to my favorite personal proverb about finding inspiration in adversity. However, he is still waiting for me to thank him.

Crushed and downhearted, I went to my parents to borrow money to eat and live. Being a Harvard MBA and having to borrow money from your parents is very demoralizing. Having to listen to "Why don't you get a real job?" not only from them but from others made me decide to give corporate life another shot.

Soon after, I found a consulting job that lasted a whole 30 days. It was supposed to be a permanent job. But as I was being fired, I was told I had the wrong attitude. In fact, they said much more than that, but most of it could never be printed. Unfortunately, they were right. I did have the wrong attitude. I just didn't want to work for anyone but myself. I returned to real estate and started looking for new projects, but this time I was determined to control them. In this roundabout way, I was first introduced to the concept of an option. A real estate option allowed me to control a piece of property with very little cash for a specific period of time. As I soon learned, stock and futures options are very similar.

My first deal was exciting. I found a great apartment complex going into foreclosure and convinced the owner I could buy the property. In fact, I had no cash at all. Even worse, my credit was destroyed and my shiny BMW had been repossessed. Since I was approximately $50,000 in debt, I did what I had to do: I convinced an investor to put up the option money and split the profits after the property was sold. I made a nice $35,000 profit on that deal—finally, a success.

After a series of profitable deals, the bottom fell out of the real estate market. There was no money available anywhere. Once again, I was left with a big question mark as to what I should be doing with my life. Luckily, serendipity intervened. One day, I received a small advertisement in the mail for a book on futures trading. Although I had no clue as to what futures trading was all about, I ordered the book. What struck me most were tales about making large amounts of money in a short period of time using very little cash. This sounded very similar to what I had been doing with real estate.

Why had I never learned any of this when I attended Harvard Business

School? How could the great "boot camp of capitalism" neglect to teach me about futures markets? My interest was now piqued. I picked up a few more books. I began to watch the markets. I even played with a few introductory strategies; but although I found them interesting, they were not very profitable. My first big mistake was to convince my investment partners that we should begin trading by hiring experienced professionals. In less than 30 days, these so-called professionals lost about 30 percent of our capital. This was an extremely poor way to inspire confidence in my investors. I decided to fire everyone and learn to do it myself. I knew that I could lose at least 30 percent without even trying (even more if I really tried). I was determined to make a profit, and the trick was to get a competitive edge. That much I did learn at Harvard. To be successful, you need to have an edge.

I began to analyze where I could find this edge, focusing my attention on using computers to garner information faster than others. I gained experience as a trader, even learning how to write my own computer programs. Eventually, this long and eventful journey gave birth to Optionetics. Today, I teach this system to individuals all around the world and have been able to review the performance of many of my students. Over the years, I have seen what makes some traders win and some lose.

I have been fortunate to have worked with some of this country's best traders. This has enabled me to pass on an abundance of knowledge geared to help you become a successful trader. This information comes from years of experience spanning from my first days as a novice trader through my experience running a floor trading operation at the American Stock Exchange and in the Chicago futures pits. It is my sincere hope that you can learn to develop money-making trading acumen by reading this book. Most importantly, you will be able to avoid many of the costly errors commonly made in trading and investing and ascend your own learning curve in leaps and bounds. I have confidence that you will gain significant insight into the world of investing by studying the strategies in this book. By applying this knowledge to stocks, futures, and options markets, I have no doubt that you will find trading a lucrative endeavor.

GEORGE A. FONTANILLS

Boston, Massachusetts
March 1998

Acknowledgments

I attribute my success as a trader and businessman to the incredible support I receive each and every day from my friends, family, and colleagues. I am fortunate to be able to do the job I enjoy with people that are the elite of their professions. I would like to take this opportunity to thank everyone who works for Global Investment Management Corp. and looks after me in our offices around the United States. You are all simply the best. In particular, and in no order of importance, I would like to especially thank the following:

My contributing writer, Tom Gentile, is my partner and the head trader for Global. I would like to thank him for contributing a lot of great material for this book. We work so closely together as a trading group, I cannot identify my original ideas from Tom's. Simply stated, Tom is a trading genius and his nickname "the S&P guru" is well deserved.

My editor, Kym Trippsmith, has worked with me for several years organizing my thoughts into coherent publications and allowing me to concentrate on my trading. This book would not have happened without her. I really appreciate her efforts and her inspirational catchphrase "in your next book or article you could write about . . . people really need to know that."

My partner, Richard Cawood, the CEO of Global, who maintains the lowest public profile of our group while having the highest influence on our group of companies. I am very fortunate to have his business acumen leading our team. The success of our full-time trading endeavors is only made possible as Richard takes care of all the business issues.

My thanks also go to all my trading family and friends. In particular, my appreciation goes to Tim Earnest, who has been a key member of our trading team for years. He created a lot of the risk graphs in this book and I thank him for his diligence and hard work. I am also thankful to Jon Najarian, "Dr. J.," my friend, mentor, and business partner, who has been a great supporter of my trading. Thanks to Bill and Ralph Cruz of Omega Research, who have always been of assistance in making their resources available to me and whose graphs are used throughout this publication. Finally, to *Futures* magazine, which has provided us with the opportunity to present the floor-trading secrets to the public for the past five years.

My family has supported me in all my adventures over the years. When my battle with cancer occurred, they were always at my side and their prayers were answered with my recovery. I thank God for my second lease on life. My wife, Lucy, is unique in her love, understanding, and support of my trading obsession.

People continually ask me why I publish material. For the record, I enjoy passing on my knowledge to others. However, without my team supporting me, I would probably stick to trading full time for a living. Thanks to the help of my support team, I am able to do both things that I love: trade and teach.

Finally, I would like to thank my students, who inspire me to keep writing and publishing. Over the years, we have made a lot of friends and received many great ideas from our students that have enhanced our own trading. I look forward to meeting you someday in the future at one of my many speaking engagements or at an Optionetics seminar.

G. A. F.

Contents

THE OPTIONS COURSE

1

Introduction to Options Trading

Trading is an elusive beast to the uninitiated, filled with mystery and complexity. Although trillions of dollars' worth of stocks, futures, and options change hands every day, learning to trade is a complicated puzzle that takes patience and perseverance to figure out. Perhaps you have a friend who has made money or know other friends who have lost money playing the markets. Learning to trade can be the beginning of an exciting new career, especially if you master combining options with futures and stocks.

Wall Street is the financial epicenter of the world. Even in the movies, Wall Street is portrayed as the quintessential powerhouse of wealth for the select few. Remember *Wall Street*, starring Michael Douglas? He won an Oscar for his role as Gordon Gekko, a powerful corporate raider. Then there's *Trading Places*, in which Eddie Murphy plays a down-and-out individual who, on a bet, gets to run a commodities firm and becomes a trader in orange juice futures. The final shot of the film shows Eddie Murphy and his associate, Dan Ackroyd, lounging on a Caribbean island, enjoying all the money they made in one day. These are the well-known scenes of Wall Street and the commodities pits—piles of money, lots of wealth, and huge successes. In fact, unless you are looking at scenes from the Depression of 1929 or other financially devastating periods, you rarely see the other side of the coin. The pained expressions on the faces of losing investors do not make a blockbuster Hollywood movie. However, they are the reality of investing. If you don't know what you're doing, you could lose all your investment capital and more.

Over the years, I have developed a systematic approach to trading that emphasizes risk management. I know how to spot optimal moneymaking opportunities to increase my chances of high returns from low-risk investments. I share this trading knowledge with individuals throughout the world through seminars and products designed to foster a strong foundation in options trading in the stocks and futures markets.

I have found that the most successful investors are those who do not think of trading as work. I like to call what I do "grown-up Nintendo®." I get to play an arcade game each and every day; making money is just a consequence of my daily play. A love affair with anything you do will increase your chances of success dramatically. I believe stock, futures, and options trading can provide many investors with the best opportunity to find rewards that can satisfy almost anyone's financial objectives. My investment philosophy is to make money any way we can, in any market we can. It's a matter of working with the strategies, developing a feel for trading profitably, and learning the tricks of the trade.

What separates those investors who make consistent returns year after year from those who can't ever seem to make a winning investment? Vision. Simply put, the winning investor has the vision to systematically spot good opportunities, while the losing investor has never developed this insight. Can this vision be developed? Some say that a great investor has an innate sense of how to make money. However, I believe that although there may be a few individuals with this innate sense, most great investors learn by trial and error until they find what works best for them.

For example, Warren Buffett, referred to by many as the greatest investor of all time, appears to have a knack for turning anything he touches into gold. Is it because he is just so much smarter than everyone else, or has he developed a methodology over the years that works on a consistent basis? For someone as successful as he is, I would have to say that he has *both* innate skill and a formula for success. This formula for success can be developed by anyone. The problem is that most investors don't have the persistence and drive necessary to achieve success.

First and foremost, you have to learn how to invest and trade the right way. Typically, most new investors lose money when they first begin due to their lack of understanding of what it really takes to succeed. Many may listen to their stock or commodity broker from the outset and never have an understanding of the markets. Many more lose money until they realize their main error was taking someone else's investment advice. A word of caution: Just because someone is licensed to take an order does not mean that person has the knowledge to invest your money wisely. Gaining the right kind of knowledge is critical to your success. Although there is risk in virtually all investments and trades, you can mitigate risks by learning how to protect yourself using option strategies. Once you learn how to manage risk, the rewards come much easier.

There is a big difference between investing and trading. An investor is an individual who takes a long-term perspective. For example, if I have $5000 to invest and my only objective is to place the money in a mutual fund—a pool of investments managed by a professional manager—then I am taking a passive role for the long term. If I choose to set up an IRA, it is likely that I will keep it until I retire.

A trader, on the other hand, will take a more active role. Traders may make investments that last for seconds, minutes, hours, weeks, or even years, always looking for an opportunity to move the money around to capture a greater return. Typical traders actively make investment decisions on a continuous basis, never allowing anyone else to control the funds. As a trader, you need to focus on strategies that will provide you with the best chance to create a profitable trade. Combining futures or stocks with options provides you with extra leverage; but this extra leverage is a double-edged sword. Options give you the chance to make a very high return using smaller amounts of cash than futures or stocks, but this leverage also creates an opportunity for you to lose money just as fast.

The losing traders are those who do not respect risk. For you to survive in this business and have the opportunity to enjoy the fruits of your labor, you must develop a very healthy respect for risk. Before you enter any investment, the questions you have to ask yourself should include the following:

- How much profit can I make?

- What is the maximum loss I can take?

- At what point will I get out if I am wrong?

- When should I take profits?

As you make the transition to becoming a motivated, knowledgeable, and successful trader, you will have to undertake a realistic examination of your personal goals, habits, dreams, and dislikes. This step is of utmost importance. Many individuals believe that they will enjoy a certain profession, but then give up before the opportunity to achieve success appears.

You must have a good understanding as to why you want to participate in any endeavor. Why are you taking the time to learn a new profession? What are your goals? What are your strengths? What are your weaknesses? Before you can become a serious and successful trader, you need to search for these answers. Make a list and add to it every day as more things become apparent. Try to be honest with yourself. Keep your highest goals in mind and work toward them one step at a time using your list of attributes to strengthen your willpower to succeed. The three primary reasons for developing trading savvy are:

1. *To achieve more wealth.* The number one reason that most people want to become traders in the stock, commodities, and options markets is to attain financial rewards. Stories about the large sums of money made and the successes of the rich and famous inspire a desire to achieve the same level of financial success. American Airlines wants to fly more and more passengers. McDonald's has a goal of serving more and more hamburgers. A business's objective is to produce more cash flow for the bottom line. A trader's objective is to make more money from money—that is how a trader monitors progress. Although "money doesn't buy happiness," having money does help. However, there is no need to make money the only goal in life; in fact, that would undermine your development as a well-rounded individual.

2. *To improve family life.* The ultimate goal, other than trading just to make money, is to make a better life for yourself and your family. The success I have been fortunate enough to achieve through hard work has allowed me to help my family financially when they needed it, and I have found helping family and friends very enjoyable. Once you have achieved a financial level where you can live each day without worrying about which bills need to be paid, you will have the freedom to seek what you truly want in life. As an added bonus, you can also afford the time and effort to help others. This will make your life as an investor much more fulfilling.

3. *To gain greater autonomy in the workplace or be your own boss.* The third most common reason is the desire to break away from a day-to-day job that has been emotionally and/or financially unfulfilling. This is why I started to trade. I needed more than real estate offered. As I like to ask my seminar students, "How many of you are here to try to get out of a real job?"

More often than not, it's better to describe the day-to-day grind most people subject themselves to as an *unreal* job, since many cannot believe they have to do it each day. It has become a nightmare.

Whether you enjoy what you are doing today and just want to supplement your income, or you are looking to become your own boss, there is no better profession than that of a trader. For example, I travel extensively and live in various locations. With a small laptop computer, an FM receiver, and a telephone, I can conduct my business from almost anywhere, which maximizes my freedom. For me, trading is a dream come true.

THE ROAD TO SUCCESSFUL TRADING

Achieving trading success is not easy. Just getting started can be an overwhelming process. The road to wealth can take many paths. To determine your trading approach, you will have to make an honest assessment of your financial capabilities. Successful options traders only use funds that are readily available and can be invested in a sound manner. It is also critical to accurately assess your time constraints to determine the style of trading that suits you best. If you want to trade aggressively, you can do so using a certain strategy. If you want to take a hands-off approach, you can structure trades to meet that time frame. All of these choices are less difficult to make if you follow certain trading rules.

Gain the Knowledge to Succeed for the Long Run

You have to have knowledge to succeed. Most new investors and traders enter this field expecting to immediately become successful. However, many have spent tens of thousands of dollars and years in college learning a specific profession and still do not make much money. Why should they be able to enter this field and immediately make money? If you start your journey on the right path, you have a much better chance of reaching your destination. Learn as much as you can by increasing your knowledge base systematically and by knowing the value of low-risk techniques.

Gather enough tools in your trading arsenal to be competitive in the markets. I have used the word "arsenal" purposely. I believe that as an investor or trader, you need to recognize that each and every day in the marketplace is a "war." You must be ready to strategically launch an attack with all the resources in your arsenal. Your first weapon is knowledge that will allow you to make fast and accurate decisions regarding the probability of success in a specific investment. Is it incongruent to suggest that trading is war and also that to trade successfully one must reduce one's level of stress? I believe not. Wars are won by the most composed and well-armed opponents. The same is true for trading. A war between equally well-armed combatants will be won by the opponent with the better strategies. In most cases, the winner will be more comfortable (less stressed) regarding their ability to win. Knowledge provides confidence. If you are well armed, you will be confident as you go off to fight the battle of the markets. Increased confidence leads to lower stress and higher profits.

Start with Acceptable Trading Capital

Many investors start with less than $10,000 in their trading account. However, it is important to realize that the less you have in your account, the more cautious you have to be. Perhaps the toughest problem is to establish a sufficient capital base to invest effectively. If you begin investing or trading with very little capital, you will assure yourself of failure. Making money in the markets requires a learning curve, and incurring loss is part of the trading process. When it comes to trading, "you have to pay to play." You don't need to be a millionaire, but trading does require a certain amount of capital to get started. In many cases, the brokerage firm you choose will determine how much is required to put you in the game. However, no matter how much you begin with, it is a good idea to start out by trading conservatively. If you invest smartly, you can make very good returns and your financial goals will be realized.

Establish a Systematic Approach to the Markets

The third key to successful moneymaking in the markets is to develop a systematic approach that combines all the weapons in your arsenal to compete effectively in the marketplace. Then, and only then, will you be able to reduce your stress enough to believe in the plan and stick with it. A systematic approach diffuses the inherent madness of the marketplace allowing you to make insightful trading decisions.

Be Alert for Trading Opportunities at All Times

By opening your opportunity receptivity, you will be able to find many more opportunities than you thought possible. Where do you find opportunities? Everywhere. When you begin to train yourself to automatically look for trading opportunities in everything you do, you are on your way to being an up-and-coming successful trader. See Chapter 5 for ideas.

Develop the Fine Art of Patience

Patience is one of the most difficult aspects of trading and investing and extremely hard to teach. I have to work at applying patience conscientiously each and every day, even after years of trading.

As a professional trader and investor, I have the opportunity to sit in front of computers all day long, day after day. This is another double-edged sword. Yes, I do have a chance to look for trading opportunities, because I have lots of information in front of me; however, I also have the opportunity to second-guess great trades due to fluctuations in the market that may be unimportant. Therefore, I have learned that the best investments are those in which I have thoroughly studied the risk and reward and have developed a time frame for the trade to work. For example, if I place a trade with options six months out, I try to stay with the trade for that period of time. This takes patience. Of course, if I reach my maximum profit level before that time, I get out.

Do not feel that you are at a disadvantage if you cannot trade and invest full-time. This allows you to avoid the "noise" in the market that occurs each and every trading day. Many of my successful students make more money by not watching the markets too closely.

Build a Strong Respect for Risk

You must respect risk if you are to survive as an investor or trader. Before you ever place an order with your broker, make sure you calculate the maximum potential risk and reward of the trade. This will help you stay in the game so you can achieve your goals.

Develop a Delta Neutral Trading Approach

Delta neutral trading is composed of strategies in which a trade is created by selecting a calculated ratio of short and long positions that balance out to an overall position delta of zero. (Delta refers to the degree of change in option price in relation to changes in the price of the underlying security.) This approach reduces risk and maximizes the potential return. To effectively apply these strategies in your own personal trading approach, four steps must be taken:

1. Test your trading systems by paper trading. Paper trading is the process of simulating a trade without actually putting your money on the line. You will probably need to practice strategies by placing trades on paper rather than with cash. Although it may not feel the same as putting your money on the line, it will help you develop practical experience which will lead to confidence in your abilities. This will come in very handy in the future. Since there is no substitute for personal experience, test all ideas *and* your ability to implement them properly prior to using real money.

2. Discuss opening a brokerage account with several brokers. Make sure you have a broker who is knowledgeable and fairly priced. Brokers can be assets or liabilities. Make certain your broker is an asset who will help make you richer, not "broker." Do not sacrifice service by selecting the broker with the lowest cost. Shop around for the right person or firm to represent your interests. Your broker will play a crucial role in your development as a successful trader. Take your time, and if you are not satisfied, find someone else.

3. Open a brokerage account. It is best to consider a brokerage firm that specializes in stocks, futures, and options. Then you can easily place trades in any market using the same firm. When it comes to trading, flexibility and precision are equally important.

4. Start small. Any mistakes you make early in your trading career will obviously cost you money. If you start with small trades in the beginning, you will be able to gain the knowledge, experience, and confidence necessary to move on to bigger trades. The bottom line is that a mistake made in a small trade means a smaller loss of capital, which can help keep you in the game.

Reduce Stress

Successful traders have to find ways to reduce the stress commonly associated with trading. I reconstructed my trading style after experiencing more stress than I had thought I could ever handle. In a typical trading day with the S&P 500 (Standard & Poor's 500 Index, which represents the 500 largest companies in the United States), I found myself buying close to the high of the day. Immediately the market started to tumble so fast that I was down 100 points even before I got my buy filled (executed order). I finally was able to gain my composure enough to pick up the phone with a panic to sell as fast as possible. By then the market had tumbled almost 200 points. Worst of all, I had purchased too many contracts for the money I had in my account; and, to top it all off, it was my first trade ever in the S&P.

In just over three minutes, I lost more than one month's pay as an accountant. That was the point in my trading career that I experienced the panic and stress of losing over 40 percent of my account in three minutes. I did not trade again for over two months while I tried to figure out whether I could really do this for a living. Luckily, I did start trading again; however, I reduced my trading size to one contract position for over a year.

Many professional floor traders and off-floor traders have had similar experiences. However, these kind of stressful events must be overcome. They are lessons that need to be learned. Simply put, stress produces incomplete knowledge access. Stress, by its nature, causes humans to become tense in not only their physical being but also their mental state. For years, physicians have made the public aware that stress can lead to many illnesses including hardening of the arteries with the possibility of a heart attack or other ailments. Reducing stress leads to bigger rewards and can be accomplished by building a low-stress trading plan. To create your own plan, examine the following three-point outline:

1. *Define your risk.* As a trader you have the ability to make large profits with the risk of potentially large losses. This is no secret. Unfortunately, that old maxim "cut your losses and let your profits run" is easier said than done. By defining your risk, you are assured that you cannot lose more money than the amount you have established as being the maximum position loss. You will also be able to develop strategies that create the potential for large reward by predefining your acceptable risk parameters and by applying strategies that combine futures and options on futures or stocks and options on stocks.

2. Develop a flexible investment plan.   The second step in reducing risk and stress is to develop an investment plan that is flexible. Flexibility allows a trader to cultivate a matrix of strategies with which to respond to market movement in any direction. Erratic market movement can change your position dramatically in seconds. Each price move (tick) rearranges everyone's assumptions about what the market is about to do. This dynamic environment borders on schizophrenia, where the bulls and bears do battle trying to outguess each other. This, in turn, creates profitable opportunities for the knowledgeable investor with a smart and flexible investment plan and creates nightmares for the uninitiated trader without a plan, only a hunch as to where the market appears to be going. Investors and traders have to be entrepreneurial by nature to survive. One of the greatest attributes of entrepreneurs in any industry is the ability to change direction when a roadblock is reached. Traders must also exhibit this flexibility if they are to survive in the marketplace.

3. Build your knowledge base systematically.   The third step to creating a successful investment plan is to build your knowledge base systematically. You then have a solid base of creative strategies from which to invest wisely. Most investors start the same way. They read a few books, open a small account, and lose everything very quickly. However, there is one way to differentiate the winners from the losers. Winners persist at learning as much as they can by starting slow and collecting tools to beat the market consistently. Successful futures traders first learn to walk, then run. Usually traders begin with simplistic strategies such as going long or shorting the market, and using stops to limit loss. Some just listen to their brokers and follow their trading ideas. Once initiated, traders accelerate their learning at the right time to become successful. Successful traders usually specialize in one or just a few areas. This specialization allows the trader to develop strategies that consistently work in certain recognizable market conditions.

A successful investor realizes that, in all likelihood, these situations will reoccur and the same strategies can be used profitably over and over again. At my alma mater, Harvard Business School, the same systematic approach is used. I never realized what the school was attempting to accomplish until after graduation when I had time to apply this approach to the real world—all those case studies on businesses I had no interest in fostered my ability to learn how to think in any environment. This systematic building of knowledge has allowed me to quickly get up and running as a successful trader in the marketplace.

CONCLUSION

As you build experience as a trader, you will become more confident in your strategies. This will help you to develop the perseverance necessary to stay with the winning trades and exit losing positions quickly. In the long run, you will be successful if you start with a solid foundation of the basics. Keep a journal of every trade you make, especially your paper trades. This book becomes your road map of where you've been and will guide you on the road to wealth. Remember, patience and persistence will help you to succeed.

2

The Big Picture

Trading involves the buying and selling of three basic elements: stocks, futures, and options. These three instruments can be assembled in an infinite number of combinations. Let's take a closer look at the fundamental components of each of these important trading instruments.

STOCKS

For those of you just starting in the field of investment, the one instrument you have likely heard about is a stock. In its most basic form, a stock is a unit of ownership in a company. The value of that unit of ownership is based on a number of factors, including the total number of outstanding shares, the value of the equity of the company (what it owns less what it owes), the earnings the company produces now and is expected to produce in the future, and demand for the shares of the company.

For example, if you and I form a company together and decide that there will be only two shareholders (owners) with only one share each, then we have two units of ownership. If our company has only one asset of $10,000 and we have no liabilities (we don't owe any money), our shares should be worth $5000 each ($10,000 ÷ 2 = $5000). If the company was sold today, we would have a net worth of $10,000 (assets = $10,000, liabilities = 0).

However, if it is projected that our company will make $100,000 this year, $200,000 next year, and so on, then the value goes up on a cash flow basis as we will have earnings. Investors would say that we have only $10,000 in net worth now, but they see this growing dramatically over the next five years. Therefore, they value us at $1 million—in this case, 10 times next year's projected earnings. This is very similar to how stocks are valued in the stock market.

Stocks are traded on organized stock exchanges and through the computerized market of the National Association of Securities Dealers Automated Quotations (NASDAQ), also referred to as the over-the-counter (OTC) market. The stock price moves due to a variety of factors including assets, expected future earnings, and the supply of and demand for the shares of the company. Accurately determining supply of and demand for a company's shares is very important to finding good investments. This is what creates momentum, which can be either positive or negative for the price of the shares of stock.

For example, public companies—those traded on an organized exchange—have to file quarterly reports with the Securities and Exchange Commission (SEC), which monitors stock exchanges and fair trading practices. These reports follow a certain format to allow investors to inspect the financial position of a company and can cause major fluctuations in the price of a stock.

Scores of analysts from brokerage firms follow certain industries and companies. They have their own methods of determining the value of a company and its price per share. They typically issue earnings estimates and reports to their clients. Street expectation will drive the value of the shares before the report is issued. If more investors feel the company will beat the street expectation, then the price of the shares will be bid up as there will be more buyers than sellers. If the majority of investors feel that the company's earnings will disappoint the street, then the price will decline (also referred to as "offered down"). As stated earlier, the stock market is similar to an auction. If there are more bidders (buyers), prices will rise. This is referred to as "bidding up." If there are more people offering (sellers), prices will fall.

For example, let's say IBM is expected by analysts to report earnings of $1 per share. If news starts to leak that the earnings will be $1.25 per share, the stock price will jump up in anticipation of the better-than-expected earnings. If, however, IBM reports only $.75 per share, then the stock price will fall dramatically, as the actual earnings do not meet initial expectations and are well below the revised expected earnings. The investors who bought IBM in anticipation of the better-than-expected earnings will sell the stock at any price to get out. This happens quite often in the market and causes sharp declines in the value of companies. It is not uncommon to see stocks decline in price 25 percent to 50 percent in one day. Conversely, it is also common to see stocks rise in value in a similar fashion.

In addition, a company may periodically declare cash and/or dividends on a quarterly or yearly basis. This is done to provide the shareholders—otherwise referred to as stockholders—an income stream that they can rely on. This is quite similar to a bank paying interest on certificates of deposit (CDs) or savings accounts. There are a number of companies that boast that they have never missed a dividend or have always increased dividends. Companies that distribute their income are usually in mature industries. You typically will not find fast-growing companies distributing dividends, as they may need the capital for future expansion and may feel they can reinvest the funds at a higher rate of return than the stockholders. As a trader of common stock, you need to know how this process affects your long or short investment. Basically, a company's board of directors will decide whether to declare a dividend, and whether it will be a periodic dividend. Also, some companies will declare a special dividend from time to time. This dividend is paid out and distributed to shareholders on a date set by the company, referred to as a payable date.

In order to qualify for a dividend, you must be a shareholder on record as of the record date (the date you are "recorded" as the owner of the shares) of the dividend. Since most stocks settle in three days, you must buy the stock at least three days before the record date of the dividend. You can also sell the stock as soon as the next day and still receive the dividend.

A beginner may think this is a profitable way to buy and sell stock: Buy the stock three days before the payable date and sell the stock the day after the payable date. Before you run out and open a stock brokerage account, you may want to consider that, in most cases, the stock prices will be trading lower on the day that the dividend is payable. That's because on the dividend payable date, the stock should trade at its regular price minus the dividend. For example, if IBM declared a $1 per share dividend payable on June 30, and closed at $50 on June 29, then on June 30, IBM would open at $49. The date on which you get paid the dividend is referred to as the payable date. As a stock trader, it is important to be aware of dividends and how they can affect a stock. You can find stocks declaring dividends by looking in the newspaper financial pages. The payable dates are marked by an "X" directly adjacent to the stock.

There are approximately 8500 stocks available to trade. Many traders judge a company by its size which can be a determinant in price and risk. In fact, there are three unofficial size classifications—blue chip, mid-caps, and small-caps. Blue chip is actually a term derived from poker where blue chips in a card game hold the most value. Blue-chip stocks symbolize those stocks which have the most market capitalization in the marketplace. Typically they enjoy solid value and good security, with a record of continuous dividend payments and other desirable investment attributes. A dividend is a share of a company's profits paid directly to shareholders on a per share basis. Mid-cap stocks usually have a bigger growth potential than blue-chip stocks but they are not as heavily capitalized. Small-cap stocks can be potentially difficult to trade because they do not have the benefit of high liquidity. However, these stocks, although quite risky, are usually relatively inexpensive and big gains are possible. Some traders like to trade riskier stocks that have the potential for big price moves while others prefer the longer-term stability of blue-chip stocks. In general, the stocks you choose to trade depend on your time availability, stress threshold, and account size.

Officially, there are two kinds of stocks, common stocks and preferred stocks. Common stocks are initially sold by a company to investors. Obviously, most investors hope to make money by deriving a profit from buying the stock at a lower price and selling it at a higher price. This profit is called capital gains. However, if the company falters, the price of the stock may plummet and shareholders may end up holding stock that is practically worthless. Common stock holders also have the opportunity to earn quarterly dividend payments as the company profits. For example, if a company announces a $1 dividend on each share and you own 1000 shares, you can collect a healthy dividend of $1000.

In contrast, preferred stock holders receive guaranteed dividends prior to common stock holders, but the amount never changes even if the company triples its earnings. Also, the price of preferred stock increases at a slower rate than common stock. However, if the company loses money, preferred stock holders have a better chance of receiving some of their investment back. All in all, common stocks are riskier than preferred stocks, but offer bigger rewards if the company does well.

There is also a name for stocks derived from what they do with their profits. If a company reinvests its profits to promote further growth, then it is known as a growth stock. If it regularly pays dividends to its shareholders, then it is regarded as an income stock. Usually only large, fully established companies can afford to pay dividends to their shareholders. Growth stocks are more risky than income stocks but have a greater potential for big price moves.

Stock market activity is reported each day by certain indexes which reflect the general health of the economy. Everyone has seen the Dow Jones Industrial Average (DJIA) mentioned on the nightly news as a key indicator of the day's trading performance. But what is the Dow Jones and how did it get started? In 1884, Charles Dow surveyed the average closing prices of nine railroad stocks and two manufacturing companies which in his opinion represented the general trends in the national economy. He printed the results in his newspaper, a forerunner of today's *Wall Street Journal*. Over the next 12 years, he honed that list until he finally settled on 12 industrial stocks. In 1896, Charles Dow began to publish this list and the overall average every day. Today's DJIA reflects the performance of 30 major companies representing key manufacturing, energy, financial, and service industries worth approximately 25 percent of the total value of all stocks listed on the New York Stock Exchange. It is widely regarded as an accurate assessment of the daily trends in the American economy, although the S&P 500 (Standard & Poor's 500) Stock Index is followed very widely as it represents a more diversified portfolio with 500 different companies. Many investors believe the DJIA is too narrow with only 30 stocks in the index. However, if you track the performance of the DJIA to the S&P 500 you will find that they are highly correlated (prices move very similarly).

Although there are many indexes that reflect stock performance, stock market direction has a highly unpredictable nature. Trying to accurately forecast it can be a nightmare for the uninitiated. Usually only hindsight is 20/20.

There is a wide variety of stock sectors from which to choose. The following list is a general outline of the most popular ones.

STOCK SECTORS

- Technology:
  Computers (e.g., Dell Computer, Compaq Computer)
  Internet-related (e.g., Netscape, Yahoo!)
  Software-related (e.g., Microsoft, Oracle)

- Health-related:
  Pharmaceuticals (e.g., Merck, Glaxo)
  Hospitals (e.g., Kaiser Permanente, Oxford Health)

- Defense industry (e.g., Rockwell, General Dynamics)

- Consumer products:
  Clothing (e.g., Gap, Gucci)
  Sportswear (e.g., Nike, Reebok)
  Auto (e.g., Chrysler, General Motors, Ford)

- Retail (e.g., Kmart, Sears)

- Financial services (e.g., Citicorp, Wells Fargo)

This list was not meant to be an exhaustive list; rather, it is meant to reflect the diverse range of fields and individual stocks within each sector. This may very well be why many prospective investors shy away from making their own investment decisions. The plethora of opportunities can be overwhelming to many people.

FUTURES

Futures markets consist of a variety of commodities (i.e., gold, oil, soybeans, etc.), financial trading instruments (i.e., bonds, 10-year notes), and indexes (i.e., S&P 500). A futures contract is the agreement to buy or sell a uniform quality and quantity of physical or financial commodities at a designated time in the future at a specific price. The contracts themselves are traded on the futures market.

Futures markets gave rise to two distinct types of traders: hedgers and speculators. Hedgers consist primarily of farmers and manufacturers. Since futures are directly driven by consumer supply and demand which is dependent on events and seasonal factors, futures were initially used by farmers and manufacturers to protect themselves or lock in prices for a certain crop or product cycle. Hedgers are primarily interested in actually selling or receiving the commodities themselves.

For example, if I am a farmer who grows wheat, soybeans, and corn, I can sell my products—which have not yet been farmed—prior to doing so. If the price of corn is at a level that I like, I can sell a corresponding number of futures contracts against my expected production. An oil company can do the same thing, locking in the price of oil at a point to guarantee the price it will receive. For instance, British Petroleum (BP) may sell crude oil futures one year away, to lock in that specific price. To make a profit, a company has to know the price of its production and plan accordingly.

The other players are the speculators. These traders play the futures markets to make a profit. Speculators do not expect to take delivery of a product or sell futures to lock in a crop price. Most contracts are now traded on a speculative basis. In other words, most people are in the futures market to try to make money on their best judgment as to the future expectation of the price movement of the futures contract. For example, if you believe corn prices will rise in the next three months, you would buy—go long—the corn futures three months out. If you believe corn prices will fall during this same period, you will sell—go short—the corn futures contract three months out.

Hedgers and speculators have a symbiotic relationship. They need one another for futures trading to work. Hedgers try to avoid risk while speculators thrive on risk and reward. Together they keep the markets active enough for everyone to get a piece of the action. Unlike stocks, where profits depend on company growth, futures markets are a zero-sum game—for each buyer there is a seller and vice versa.

Physical commodities are raw materials which are traded on futures exchanges; examples include grains, meats, metals, and energies. Financial commodities include debt instruments (such as bonds), currencies, and indexes. In these markets, money is the actual commodity being traded, and price depends on a variety of factors including interest rates and the value of the U.S. dollar.

Physical Commodities

There is a wide variety of commodities that can be profitably traded. Some are seasonal in nature, such as agriculturals, metals, and heating oil. Some fluctuate due to seasonal changes in climate. Others may change due to world events, such as an Organization of Petroleum Exporting Countries (OPEC) meeting. Each market is unique.

Physical commodity markets include the following:

- Agricultural products (e.g., corn, soybeans, wheat)

- Metals (e.g., gold, silver, copper)

- Energies (e.g., crude oil, natural gas, heating oil)

- Foods (e.g., coffee, cocoa, sugar)

- Meats (e.g., live cattle, lean hogs, pork bellies)

Financial Commodities

Debt Instruments.   Just as there are instruments to trade stocks, either individually or collectively as an index, there are numerous instruments available to trade interest rates. The first response I usually get when I talk about trading interest rates is, "Who would want to trade interest rates?" The simple answer is banks and other lending institutions that have loans outstanding, as well as investors who have a great deal of exposure in interest rate investments.

Originally, the futures markets were primarily used to hedge—offset or mitigate—risk. Today, financial commodities, including all the interest rate instruments, are growing at a faster rate than traditional commodities. The interest rate markets have participants from all over the world trading interest rates for hedging purposes and speculation. If you have interest rate risk or you just want to speculate on the direction of interest rates, there are plenty of markets and opportunities awaiting you. The Chicago exchanges abound with individuals trading these instruments. These markets are also traded extensively in off-exchange markets such as those created by banks and securities trading firms (also referred to as the over-the-counter or OTC market).

Bonds are one of the most popular forms of financial instruments. A bond is a debt obligation issued by a government or corporation that promises to pay its bondholders periodic interest at a fixed rate and to repay the principal of the loan at maturity at a specified future date. Bonds are usually issued with a value of $1000 to $100,000, representing the principal or amount of money borrowed. Other popular financial instruments include the following:

- *Treasury bill (T-bill).*   These short-term government securities have maturities of no more than one year. Treasury bills are issued through a competitive bidding process at a discount from par; there is no fixed interest rate.

- *Treasury bond (T-bond).* This marketable, fixed-interest U.S. government debt security has a maturity of more than 10 years. The most often quoted T-bond is the 30-year bond.

- *Treasury note (T-note).* This is a marketable, fixed-interest U.S. government debt security with a maturity of between one and 10 years.

- *Eurodollars.* Eurodollars are dollars deposited in foreign banks. The futures contract reflects the rates offered between London branches of top U.S. banks and foreign banks.

Currency Markets. The currency markets are another very large market. Each country has its own currency. These currencies go up or down relative to each other based on a number of factors such as economic growth (present and future), interest rates, and supply and demand. Most major currencies are tied to the U.S. dollar. Therefore, there will typically be an inverse relationship between the dollar and other currencies. The major currency futures traded at the Chicago Mercantile Exchange include the following:

- Japanese yen.
- British pound.
- German deutsche mark.
- Swiss franc.
- Canadian dollar.

If the U.S. dollar goes up, then the Japanese yen will drop along with the mark, franc, or pound. (The Canadian and U.S. dollars move similarly due to the proximity and closeness of our economies.) Each of these currencies will then have a rate relative to each of the others. This cross-reference is referred to as the cross rate. The mark/yen, yen/pound, mark/franc, and so on will have their own rates at which they may be traded.

Why are currencies traded? As you are probably aware, many products are sold across borders. IBM may sell $100 million worth of computer equipment in Germany, and will likely be paid in deutsche marks. If IBM wants to be paid in dollars, it can go into the futures market or cash market—traded from bank to bank—to change its deutsche mark purchase. By selling deutsche mark futures contracts, IBM can lock in its profits in U.S. dollars. Trillions (yes, trillions) of dollars are traded each day in the currency markets, 24 hours a day.

Index Markets

An index is an indicator that is used to measure and report value changes in a specific group of stocks or commodities. There are a variety of indexes tailored to reflect the performances of many different sectors of the marketplace. The indexes are usually tracked according to today's high and low, today's performance in relation to yesterday's close, over the past year (365 days), and since December 31. Other details include volume and volatility. Each measurement signals a possible trend in whichever sector the index represents.

The most popular indexes include the following:

- *Dow Jones Industrial Average (DJIA).*   Most widely followed index. It represents 30 blue-chip stocks on a one share to one share basis.

- *Standard & Poor's 500 Index (S&P 500).*   A benchmark of U.S. common stock performance, this index includes 500 of the largest U.S. stocks—400 industrial companies, 40 utilities, 40 financial corporations, and 20 transportation companies. This index is favored by large investors and can be an expensive investment.

- *NYSE Composite Index.*   This index is composed of all the stocks traded on the New York Stock Exchange.

- *NASDAQ Composite Index.*   This index tracks the performance of all stocks traded on the NASDAQ stock market. NASDAQ stands for the National Association of Securities Dealers Automated Quotations and is a computerized system that provides brokers and dealers with price quotations for securities traded over-the-counter as well as for many New York Stock Exchange–listed securities.

- *AMEX Market Value Index.*   This index tracks the performance of the more than 800 companies traded on the American Stock Exchange, which handles approximately one-fifth of all securities traded within the United States.

- *Wilshire 5000.* This market value–weighted index monitors 7000 U.S.-based equities traded on the New York Stock Exchange, the American Stock Exchange, and the NASDAQ stock market, and is a popular indicator of the broad trend in stock prices.

- *Commodity Research Bureau Futures Price Index (C.R.B. Futures).* This index tracks the commodity markets and is closely monitored as an indicator of economic inflation.

As you can see from the wide variety of indexes listed, you can trade in virtually any type of futures market that interests you. However, it is important to specialize in just one to begin with and then continue learning various risk management techniques. There is a vast amount of information that everyone needs to sort out, and that's what makes investing so interesting. It is exciting to find the "needle in the haystack"—you just need to know where to begin looking and what to look for. Buying (going long) and selling (going short) are the most simplistic forms of trading in futures markets. They are also the most popular strategies because many individuals are not familiar with the more creative aspects of trading. However, by learning to combine futures with options, you can create trades which limit your risk and maximize your potential profits.

OPTIONS

Options are probably the most versatile trading instrument ever invented. They provide a high leverage approach to trading that can significantly limit the overall risk of a trade, especially when combined with stocks or futures. Simply put, option buyers have rights and option sellers have obligations. Option buyers have the right, but not the obligation, to buy or sell a stock or futures contract at a predetermined price until a predefined expiration date. In contrast, option sellers have the obligation to buy or sell the underlying instrument if the option is exercised by an option holder.

Options contracts differ greatly from futures contracts. A futures contract is a legally binding agreement that gives the holder the right to actually buy or sell a commodity at a specific price. Purchasing an option is the right, *but not the obligation*, to buy or sell the underlying instrument at a specific price. The key here is that buying an option is not a legally binding contract. In contrast, shorting an option obligates the seller to provide the underlying instrument at the agreed upon price if and when someone buys and exercises his or her right to take delivery.

Using our corn example, if you felt the price of corn was going to rise over the next three months, instead of buying a corn futures contract you could buy a corn call option. The corn call option will give you the right, but not the obligation, to buy a corn futures contract for a specific price until a specific point in time. For this right you have to pay a price; this is called the option premium.

Options on stocks and options on futures are very similar. However, it is essential to understand trading terms and their utilization in the process of making successful trades. For example, every option has a strike price—a price at which the stock or futures can be bought or sold until the option's expiration date. Options are available in several strike prices depending on the current price of the underlying. Once you have purchased an option, you have the right to buy or sell the underlying at the strike price you chose until the option's expiration date regardless of how high or low the price of the underlying rises or falls as long as the option is in-the-money (has value). Therefore, the profitability of an option primarily depends on the rise or fall in the price of the underlying instrument. An option's premium also depends on several other factors including probability and volatility, which will be discussed later in this book.

In general, options have the following characteristics:

1. Options give you the right to buy or sell an underlying instrument.

2. If you buy an option, you are not obligated to buy the underlying instrument; you simply have the right to exercise the option.

3. If you sell an option, you are obligated to deliver the underlying asset at the price at which the option was sold if the buyer exercises his or her right to take delivery.

4. Options are good for a specified period of time after which they expire and you lose your right to buy or sell the underlying instrument at the specified price.

5. Options when bought are done so at a debit to the buyer.

6. Options when sold are done so by giving a credit to the seller.

7. Options are available in several strike prices representing the price of the underlying instrument.

8. The cost of an option is referred to as the option premium. The price reflects a variety of factors including the option's intrinsic value and time value.

9. There are two kinds of options: calls and puts. Calls give you the right to buy the underlying asset and puts give you the right to sell the underlying asset.

10. All the options of one type (put or call) which have the same underlying security are called a class of options. For example, all the calls for IBM constitute an option class.

11. All the options which are in one class and have the same strike price are called an option series. For example, all the IBM calls with a strike price of 105 and various expiration dates constitute an option series.

There are a variety of options available, including options on stock, futures, and indexes.

Stock Options

Not all stocks have options available to be traded. Currently, there are approximately 2730 stocks that have tradable options. This number grows daily. Each stock option represents 100 shares of a company. Therefore, if I buy one IBM stock option, it represents 100 shares of IBM stock. If IBM shares are trading at $100 per share, then I am controlling $10,000 worth of shares with one option ($100 per share × 100 shares). I may be controlling this $10,000 amount with only $1000 depending on the price of the option's premium. This would give me a 10 to 1 leverage.

Futures Options

Most futures markets have tradable options, including gold, silver, oil, wheat, corn, soybeans, orange juice, Treasury bonds, and so on. However, unlike stocks, each contract represents a unique quantity.

An option on a futures contract—also known as a futures option—gives you the right or obligation to go long (buy) or go short (sell) the underlying future by a certain time at a specified price. For example, if I buy a December gold call, at a strike price of $285, and gold moves up to $300, then I can exercise my call and force the seller to deliver a gold futures contract to me at the $285 price. I would have an unrealized profit of $1500 per contract at that time [(300 − 285) × 100 = $1500].

Options on futures have the futures contract as the underlying instrument that is to be delivered in the event an option is exercised. Each futures contract represents a standardized quantity of the commodity. As you begin to trade futures, you have to become familiar with the specifics of each futures market. (If you have any questions, you may always call your broker.) For example, a gold futures contract is equal to 100 ounces of gold. With gold trading at $290 per ounce, the futures contract is worth $29,000 (100 ounces × $290 per ounce). Each futures contract has its own unique specifications which can be confusing to a novice futures trader.

Index Options

An index option is an option that represents a specific index—a group of items that collectively make up the index. Options on indexes of stocks are designed to reflect and fluctuate with market conditions. Broad-based indexes cover a wide range of industries and companies. Narrow-based indexes cover stocks in one industry or economic sector.

Index options allow investors to trade in a specific industry group or market without having to buy all the stocks individually. The index is calculated as the average change of the stock price of each stock in the index. Each index has a specific mathematical calculation to determine the price change, up or down. An index option is an option that is tied directly to the change in the value of the index. You will not receive a percentage of each stock, but the index will have a cash value.

Index options make up a very large segment of the options that are traded. Why are so many options traded on indexes? The explosive growth in index trading has occurred in recent years due to the increase in both the number of indexes and the number of traders who have become familiar with index trading. The philosophy of an index is that a group of stocks—a portfolio—will diversify the risk of owning just one stock, and an index of stocks will better replicate what is happening in an industry or the market as a whole. This allows an investor or trader to participate in the movement of a specific industry, both to the upside and to the downside.

It appears that index options will continue to proliferate and trading volume will increase in many of the instruments. A word of caution: A number of these instruments do not have much liquidity. However, used wisely, indexes can be an important instrument in your trading arsenal.

LIQUIDITY AND VOLATILITY

Profitable markets are those markets that provide opportunity for making good returns on investments. Obviously, some markets are more trader-friendly than others. Opportunity in a market is contingent on a number of factors. The most important factors are liquidity and volatility. A plentiful number of buyers and sellers and an elevated volume of trading activity provide high liquidity, which gives traders the opportunity to move in and out of a market with ease. Illiquid markets can make the process much more difficult and more costly.

Volatility measures the amount by which an underlying stock or future is expected to fluctuate in a given period of time. Volatility is used as a primary determinant in the valuation of options' premiums and time value. There are two basic kinds of volatility—implied and historical (statistical). Implied volatility is calculated by using the actual market price of an option and an option pricing model (Black-Scholes for stocks and indexes and Black for futures). Overpricing and undervaluing an option's premium can be caused by an inaccurate perception of the future movement in the price of an asset. If the premium of an option increases without a corresponding change in the underlying, the option's implied volatility will have increased also. In contrast, historical volatility gauges price movement in terms of past performance. It is calculated by using the standard deviation of underlying asset price changes from close to close of trading going back 21 to 23 days (or any other predetermined time frame). Delta neutral trading requires a trader to pay close attention to implied volatility and a variety of nondirectional strategies to take advantage of implied volatility changes. Calculating volatility is a complex computation best tackled by using a computer or by visiting the Optionetics Web site at www.MarketScoreboard.com.

CONCLUSION

Although option trading provides knowledgeable traders with a great deal of moneymaking opportunities, the option universe you can trade is exhaustive. New traders are usually scared away from options markets due to the difficulty associated with options trading. Learning to make money from the options markets can appear to be an imposing task. Traders pick up a newspaper and see thousands of options listed with different months and different strike prices. In addition, most books written about options have a menagerie of mathematical calculations guaranteed to scare anyone away. Getting the big picture is critical to a well-rounded understanding of trading. Although learning to trade options can be overwhelming at first, if you approach it as a science, you will be able to build on the basic fundamentals until you are adept at applying a variety of strategies that will empower you to make money.

3

Elements of a Good Investment

To be a successful trader, you have to know the fundamentals of finding a profitable investment. You will have to decide, probably by trial and error, which of the many analytical techniques and market-forecasting methods work well for you. I find many investment tactics to be irrelevant to profit making, preferring to use strategies that are nondirectional in nature. However, there are a few basic guidelines that will enhance your ability to increase your account size consistently.

DESIRABLE INVESTMENT CHARACTERISTICS

Involves Low Risk

First and foremost, a good investment must be low risk. What does low risk really mean? The term's significance may vary with each person. You may be able to accept a risk level of $5000 per trade based on the capital you have available. However, an elderly person on a fixed income may find $100 to be too much to risk. Acceptable risk is based on your available investment capital as well as your tolerance for uncertainty. You should trade only with money you can afford to lose, as there is risk of loss in all forms of trading.

Has a Favorable Risk Profile

Every time you contemplate placing a trade, you need to create a corresponding risk profile. Whether you trade stocks or commodities, invest in real estate, or put your money in the bank, every investment has a certain potential risk and reward profile. Some are more favorable than others. Studying a risk profile can show you the potential increasing or decreasing profit and loss of a trade relative to the underlying asset's price over a specific period of time. As the variables change, the risk curve changes accordingly.

In order to find the best investment, you have to look for trades that offer optimal ratios of risk to reward. For example, which of the following investment choices has the better risk to reward ratio?

- Trade A: potential risk of $1000, potential reward of $1000.

- Trade B: potential risk of $1000, potential reward of $5000.

Anyone would rather make $5000 than $1000. However, to actually make a good decision, you must also have enough knowledge to discern which trade has the greater probability of working. Another key ingredient is time frame—the time it takes to make the money. If Trade A can make me $1000 in one month with a 75 percent chance of winning, and Trade B takes a year to make $5000 with a 75 percent chance of winning, I would rather go with Trade A. In one year, I could potentially make $9000 [(12 × $1000) × .75] repeating Trade A, and only $3750 ($5000 × .75) using Trade B. This is referred to as an expected value calculation.

The risk/reward profile of any investment must take into account the following elements:

- Potential risk.

- Potential reward.

- The probability of success.

- How long the investment takes to make a return.

Offers High Potential Return

Risk comes hand in hand with reward. A trader cannot be expected to take a risk unless reward is also in the equation. Believe it or not, I have seen countless investors make foolish investments where the risk outweighs the reward many times over. Why would they do such a thing? Usually because they simply haven't taken the time to verify the potential risk and reward of the trade or they are taking advice from someone who doesn't know any better.

The best investments have an opportunity for high reward with acceptable risk. In addition, the good trades have a high probability of winning on a consistent basis. I consider 75 percent an acceptable winning percentage. This means I win three out of four times I place a trade. A baseball player who could do this would have a .750 batting average—which is unprecedented in baseball history.

Meets Your Time Requirements

The process of locating and monitoring your investments must meet your time constraints if you are to be successful. In other words, if you do not have the time to sit in front of a computer day in and day out, then your best investments will not be day trades (entering and exiting a position in the same day). If you don't even have the time or inclination to look at your investments over a one-week period, then you have to take this into consideration. The time you have available for making investment decisions and monitoring those investments will affect the types of investments you should make. If you don't have enough time to pay attention to a trade that needs to be closely monitored, chances are you'll lose money on it. The best investments will match your time availability.

Meets Your Risk Tolerance Level

Your risk tolerance level is directly proportional to your available investment capital. Risking more than you can afford to lose creates stress that impairs your ability to make clear decisions. Some people have the ability to handle uncertainty better than others. It is important to accurately assess your own risk tolerance levels and stay within those boundaries as you progress up your own trading learning curve. As experience in the markets naturally develops your confidence level, your risk tolerance level will increase.

Can Be Understood by You, the Trader

One of my most basic investment rules is as follows: if you don't know how hot the fire is, don't stick your hand into it. This rule is broken on a consistent basis by many beginning and intermediate traders. In addition, many seasoned traders singe their fingers as well. Basically, if you don't understand the exact characteristics of a trade, it is better to walk away from it.

It is imperative that you familiarize yourself with the trades you place. Each trade has a unique personality. Your personality and your trade's personality have to match for you to be successful over the long run.

Meets Your Investment Criteria

Your personal investment criteria can come in many shapes and sizes. Each individual has personal goals, expectations, and objectives when making investments. When I ask my students what they want out of their investments, the typical response is to make money. However, there are a number of related issues that also must be evaluated, including the following:

- *Capital gains (stocks—medium- to high-risk securities).* What are the tax implications of your investing and trading practices?

- *Interest income (fixed income securities—medium-risk bonds and lowest-risk U.S. government securities).* Is your objective to earn interest income?

- *Security (government securities—lowest-risk securities).* Do you want to invest in only low-interest, low-return investments such as U.S. government securities (e.g., Treasury bonds)?

Meets Your Investment Capital Constraints

Does the investment requirements match your capital available for investment? Just as your investment strategy must meet your personality and time constraints, the capital you have available will have a major impact on what you invest in, how often you invest, and the amount you can afford to invest. For example, if you have a small account (less than $10,000), you will invest very differently from someone with $1 million. In addition, if you're trading commodities with a small account, you should trade in markets that have low margin requirements and good return potential. You should stay away from the high-margin markets such as the S&P 500 stock index futures.

No matter how much money you have to invest, start small. I have taught a variety of people over the years with a very wide range of capital available for investment. I advise them all to start by trading small until they figure out what they're doing. Whether you have $1000 or $1 million, you have to learn to walk before you can run. In the beginning, I recommend risking only 5 percent of your account on any one trade. In this way, you can afford to learn from your mistakes as a novice trader.

Oftentimes, having too much money as a beginner can be detrimental. The more money you have, the greater the chance of overinvesting and making costly mistakes. I find that the best long-term investors are very cautious early on. However, they systematically increase the size of their trades based on the increase in capital in their accounts. For example, you may begin with $5000 and choose to invest 100 shares at a time, then not increase to 200 shares until such time as your account has doubled to $10,000.

CONCLUSION

Each of these investment elements will guide you on the road to success. Trading can be a humbling experience. It can also be highly profitable. Perhaps it is human nature to get a little overconfident and cocky when the money starts rolling in. But that's the time when you need to fight against your own bravado. Remember, it takes only one big mistake to send you back to zero. Start small and let your account grow consistently. There's always more to be learned and a better trade down the road.

4

A Short Course in Investment Economics

Forecasting market direction is never a sure thing. However, there are a few economic interrelationships that can enable you to make consistent profits. One of the most important of these is the relationship between interest rates and bond prices. The following chart illustrates the typical interrelationship of the change in interest rates to the price of a bond and the subsequent effect on the stock market.

Interest Rates	Bond Prices	Stock Prices
Up	Down	Down
Down	Up	Up
Sideways	Sideways	Up

Although these relationships are relatively stable, occasionally there are deviations from typical economic behavior, referred to as divergences. This chart, however, illustrates the *normal* expected action based on economic theory.

A bond is a debt instrument sold by governments or corporations to raise money for various reasons. The bond most widely considered by investors and traders is the 30-year Treasury bond. It has a corresponding futures contract that is traded at the Chicago Board of Trade and reflects one very important aspect of many people's lives—mortgage interest rates.

INTEREST RATES AND BOND PRICES

Bonds are rarely held by the same buyer until maturity. Instead, they are traded at a price that fluctuates according to interest rates and inflation. Since a bond's interest rate stays the same until maturity, its real value at maturity depends on inflation's actual value of the dollars at repayment. In general, interest rates are also tied to inflation.

According to economic theory, if interest rates go up, bond prices go down; and if interest rates go down, bond prices rise. Why does this inverse relationship hold true? Let's say that you decide you are going to lend me $1000 for a five-year period. I agree to pay you interest at a rate of 8 percent each year, which happens to be the market rate for interest charges. Therefore, I will pay you $80 per year interest. The very next day, interest rates jump to 10 percent. Now you could lend $1000 and receive 10 percent interest, which would bring in $100 per year, but you have lost the opportunity of lending that first $1000 at the higher rate of interest. Did the value of the first loan go up or down with the rise in interest rate? The first loan's value went down. If you want to sell that 8 percent loan as an investment to someone else, you will find that its value has decreased. A loan with a 10 percent interest rate has a greater value than one with 8 percent. Therefore, when interest rates go up, bond (loan) prices fall.

Let's examine the converse situation: When interest rates go down, bond prices rise. If interest rates drop from 8 percent to 5 percent, an investor could receive only $50 on the $1000 investment. A previous loan with an 8 percent interest rate would now increase in value, because it would make the investor $80 a year instead of just $50. In general, fluctuations in interest rates stimulate the bond market. Trading bond options can also be quite lucrative if you pay close attention to interest rates and inflation.

It is also a good practice to monitor certain bond markets' yield to maturity. This measurement predicts a bond's return over time by assessing its interest rate, price, par value, and time until maturity. To access this information, please consult our Web site: www.MarketScoreboard.com.

INTEREST RATES AND THE STOCK MARKET

In general terms, the same inverse relationship exists between interest rates and stocks as between interest rates and bond prices. Thus, bond prices and the stock market usually move in the same direction. Assume your company has to buy $10,000 worth of equipment. You don't want to pay cash for the equipment; therefore, you have to finance the purchase. In this case, you will pay 8 percent interest—$800 per year. Interest is an expense that gets subtracted from what you earn. Therefore, if you earn $20,000 before interest, you will have earned $19,200 after interest is paid. If the interest rate were 10 percent for the same $10,000 loan you would pay $1000 per year and your earnings would drop to $19,000 after you subtracted interest. Once again, we see an inverse relationship, this time between interest rates and earnings—the higher your interest rate, the less money flows to your earnings. If your company has reduced its earnings due to a higher interest expense, then your company's value decreases. This affects your company's stock price. Therefore, an interest rate increase (bond prices fall) usually decreases stock prices.

This inverse relationship does not *always* hold. There are periods when a divergence will occur and a company's earnings will increase regardless of whether interest rates go up or down. However, these divergences are generally short-term in nature. You can usually count on the market coming back, reacting to the change in interest rates.

If you watch the day-to-day price changes in the stock market, you may find that investors and traders are watching bond prices and interest rates very closely. Changes in either may determine whether it is a good time to buy or to sell bonds. In addition, if you see interest rates increasing quickly, you don't want to be a buyer of stocks. An increase in interest rates signals a time of caution due to the negative bias for individual stocks and the stock market in general. However, if you find that interest rates are stable or decreasing, being a buyer of stocks is a good idea because the stock market has an upward bias.

Historically, the general bias of the stock market is to rise. Investors usually push markets up. Even after the stock market crash of 1987, the market rebounded extremely strongly. The stock market's cyclical movement is directly related to economic, social, and political factors, with bull markets lasting longer than bear markets—dropping quickly and then rising slowly but steadily. However, when it comes to the stock market, there are no absolutes. Since no one has a crystal ball with which to see the future, I prefer to create trades that are nondirectional in nature using delta neutral strategies that reap consistent profits.

CONCLUSION

Paying close attention to interest rates can help you to forecast market direction. Although many delta neutral strategies are not dependent on market direction, it never hurts to be able to anticipate movement. Since prices have extremely erratic fluctuation patterns, monitoring interest rates is a relatively consistent method that can help you to find profitable trading opportunities.

5

How to Spot Explosive
Opportunities

Locating exceptional investment opportunities is the key to successful trading. The main objective is to discover opportunities that:

- Meet all the criteria for a good investment.

- Use your investment capital in the most efficient manner.

- Produce substantial returns in a relatively short time.

Throughout the years I have been investing and trading, I have thought of myself as being fairly successful, while in the eyes of others, I have been perceived as extremely successful. However, contrary to popular belief, I knew deep down inside that I had more room to grow. Over the past few years, I have been able to accelerate my profitability by being patient (as much as I could be) and by being *selective* when I made an investment.

I have to admit that I love the day-to-day excitement and the financial rewards of trading. However, I make a great deal more money by looking for opportunity intelligently. In other words, instead of being in the markets just because I feel I need to be, now I wait like a cheetah in the jungle, looking for a wounded animal to pounce upon. Although the cheetah can catch any animal, wounded or not, it preys on the sure thing. I have learned that this is the best way to trade—wait for everything to look right, then attack with speed and confidence.

Initially it may not be easy for you to do the same. However, this confidence and patience will come over time as you build up experience and increase your investment account through successful trades. How do you spot explosive profit opportunities? I will show you how to make 100 percent on your money, sometimes in minutes, hours, or days, not years.

How do you find the growing money trees hidden deep within the information forest? Simply use the vast amounts of information available to you; learn to filter the data and find the best investments. The problem is that there is so much information. This can be overwhelming and quite confusing. Many would-be investors pick up a newspaper, look at the financial section, quickly decide that they can't make heads or tails out of the information, and promptly give up. The general feeling is that anything this complicated must be extremely difficult to succeed in.

What if you gave up the first time you fell off a bicycle? What if you gave up the first time you sat behind the wheel of a car to learn to drive? What if you gave up on anything halfway challenging? You wouldn't get anywhere—which is why many people never succeed. Successful individuals persevere. This also is true in learning the financial markets. It may seem difficult at first; but once you know the basics about how to ride the bike, it gets easier. After a while, you're cruising down the road yelling, "Look, Mom—no hands!"

Recognizing an excellent trade when you see it is just half the battle. As a trader, you must know how to go about finding explosive profit opportunities. There are an overwhelming number of methods used by the investment community to evaluate trading opportunities. I will not attempt to impart an exhaustive study of analysis techniques—there are far too many of them, and most do not work on a long-term basis. However, there are two basic categories that should be included as fundamental components of a trader's arsenal.

FUNDAMENTAL ANALYSIS

Fundamental analysis is research that is used to predict future price movements of a market based on the underlying factors that contribute to the supply and demand of the stock or commodity. Various economic data, including income statements, past records of earnings, sales, assets, management, products, and markets aid in predicting the future success or failure of the company. Supply and demand is paramount in the futures markets. This type of analysis is often used to determine whether a stock, future, or index is overvalued or undervalued at the current market price.

A fundamental analyst studies the fundamentals of a business—its products, customers, consumption, profit outlook, management strength, and supply of and demand for outputs (i.e., oil, soybeans, wheat, etc.). Fundamental analysts use this data to anticipate price transitions. They see a company or market as it is now in the present, and they attempt to forecast where it is going in the future. Entire industries are built around fundamental analysis. Every major brokerage firm has armies of analysts to review industries, companies, and commodities markets. The majority of what you see and hear on television or read in the newspapers is fundamental analysis.

For example, you may hear that a company's product is selling like hotcakes, or perhaps there has been a management change. Maybe the weather is killing the orange juice crop. Fundamental analysis comes in many shapes and forms. It's up to you to learn how to apply this information to making money in the markets. Typically, I don't listen to others, because too often they are wrong. On the other hand, I love to find opportunities to do the opposite of everyone else. This is known as the contrarian approach—when all the information is too positive, look for an opportunity to sell, and when it is too negative, look for an opportunity to buy. Moral of the story: Listen to the market. It will tell you a great deal. Use a discerning ear when listening to anyone else.

TECHNICAL ANALYSIS

Technical analysis consists of methods for evaluating securities by analyzing statistics generated by market activity, such as past prices and volume. Technical analysis is built on the theory that prices display repetitive patterns. These patterns can be utilized to forecast future price movement and potential profit opportunities.

Technical analysts study the markets using numerical calculations to determine strength, weakness, and many other factors. The analysis of price action is built up from certain fundamental issues. Never forget that price is the determinant of all factors and perceptions of market participants. A technical analyst will look primarily at the price of the stock or commodity—as it is trading now and as it has traded in the past—to try to determine price patterns that will forecast future price movements.

Do I believe in technical analysis? Absolutely. I believe a good technician can look at many factors and determine future price action with a certain degree of accuracy. However, no person or computer can predict the future 100 percent of the time. We need to use all the information available about the markets in the past and present to attempt to forecast the future. Although many a profit has been made from complex technical charts, there are no crystal balls.

The simplest and most widely used technical analysis tool is a moving average. A moving average is the analysis of price action over a specified period of time on an average basis. This typically includes two variables (more can be used). For example, we may look at the price of gold trading right now and how that price compares to the average over the past 10 days and the average price over the past 30 days. When the 10-day average goes below the 30-day average, you sell; and, conversely, when the 10-day average goes above the 30-day average, you buy. Technicians go to great lengths to fine-tune which time spans and averages to use. When you find the right time frames, the moving average is probably the simplest and most effective technical tool.

Another technique is to use a momentum indicator. This technical market indicator utilizes price and volume statistics for predicting the strength or weakness of a current market and any overbought or oversold conditions, and can also note turning points within the market. This can be used to initiate momentum investing, a strategy in which you trade with (or against) the momentum of the market in hopes of profiting from it. It's one of my favorite ways to trade because I can spot stocks, futures, and options with the potential to make money on an accelerated basis. Finding these explosive profit opportunities is the key to highly profitable trading.

Briefly, a momentum investor looks for a market that is making a fast move up or down at a specific point in time, or there is an indication of an impending movement. Like a volcano about to erupt, a great deal of pressure starts to build, followed by an explosion for some time, with a calm thereafter. A momentum investor might miss the eruption but be able to catch the market move right after the eruption. Different techniques are used in each case. To catch the first move (another example is that of a surfer trying to ride a wave), you have to see the signs, place the appropriate strategy, and then get ready to get off when the momentum (or eruption, or wave) fizzles. This can be hours, days, or weeks. If you miss the first move, it's best to wait until the movement fizzles and then look to place a contrarian trade. If you wait until there is a slowdown, you can then anticipate a reversal. If you employ a contrarian approach, you will be trading against the majority view of the marketplace. A contrarian is said to fade the trend (which suits me just fine). Very fast moves up lead to very fast moves down, and vice versa.

Trading, investing, and price action are driven by two elements—fear and greed. If you can learn to identify both, you can profit handsomely. Momentum investing plays off of these two human emotions perfectly: greed not to miss a profit opportunity and fear that profits made will be lost if the market reverses course, thus intensifying the reversal in many cases.

There are hundreds of technical analysis tools out in the marketplace. Be very cautious with those that you decide to use. Make sure you thoroughly test these systems over a long period of time (i.e., 10 years or more).

Both fundamental and technical analysis have their proponents. Some traders swear by one and hold great disdain for the other method. Other traders integrate both methods successfully. For example, fundamental analysis can be used to forecast market direction while technical analysis prompts profitable trading entrances and exits. Most investors have had to use trial and error to determine which methods work best for them. Ultimately, it depends on what kind of trading you are more inclined to use, and which methods you are most comfortable employing.

When you begin to select investment methods, try to determine why they work, when they work best, and when they are not effective. Test each method over a sufficient period of time and keep an accurate account of your experiences. If possible, you should always back-test systems as well. You can use trading software to back-test almost any technical analysis technique available. Inevitably, as the markets change, suitable methods of analysis will change also. The key is to remain open-minded and flexible so that you can take advantage of what works.

NONANALYTICAL METHODS

There are many other ways to find a good investment. However, the two most common are probably the most unreliable. It is important that you use discretion as you make investment decisions.

Reliance on Others

The biggest mistake most people make in the field of investing is relying on others. This includes consulting brokers, listening to friends, receiving tips, or even calling psychic hot lines. Professional money managers (mutual fund managers) also must be selected with care. Be careful whom you listen to. The only person who is ultimately responsible for your profitability is yourself.

Religious Experience

After contemplating it for a while, I realized that prayer is truly the method most often used by traders and investors. Most traders and investors do very little analysis and have no idea as to what is going on; still they go ahead and trade. Then, they just pray that they will be right. Even when their initial position goes against them, they just stay in the bad trade praying the market will come back. They continue to pray until they can't take the loss anymore or they lose all their money.

Nick Leeson, the trader who allegedly lost $1 billion for Barings Bank— a loss that brought down the 200-year-old institution—got himself into a bad position and kept adding to that bad position praying that the market would indeed turn around and make him right. It never happened.

CREATING A TRADING FILTER

After years of investing and trading, I came to the realization that to become good at this business I only had to keep my eyes and ears open. I then set myself up to be able to accept both visual and audio information and to filter out all useless information. Peter Lynch, former manager of the Fidelity Magellan mutual fund, is one of the best money managers of our time. In his books, he clearly states this principle of accepting all available information. Although the Magellan Fund, like many other funds, has longer-term investments, the principles stated in his books—as well as books by other great investors—can be applied on a short-term trading basis also. I focus my attention on these principles of "intelligent investing" for both a long-term and short-term perspective.

Many investors may be satisfied with a 10 percent return on their money compared to 4 percent interest for a CD. I prefer to work a little harder in order to get a much higher percentage return. After all, this is the business I choose to be in. I want my trades and investments to make me a very good living no matter how much money I started with. Remember, the only way to build your account up quickly is to spot the best opportunities and to use your money efficiently.

Most investors and traders have very little idea how to find explosive opportunities. It's not that they're not smart enough. It's just that they haven't been made aware of the effectiveness of these techniques. During each trading day, I can work as little as five minutes and still make more money (with a much higher return) than investors who work all day. This is not to say that I spend only five minutes a day trading. I enjoy this business way too much. In fact, I don't even see what I do as work. I am typically disappointed when the trading day is over. Believe it or not, weekends are my most difficult periods.

However, explosive opportunities can be found every day. To gain true opportunity insight, open yourself up to receive information from the perspective of a trader. Don't let important information slip through your fingers as most people do. Filtering information correctly can be the key to making money. Years of experience have shown me that megasuccessful investors have developed unique approaches to finding opportunities others may be missing. Let's take a closer look at where these chances to make a very high return on your money in the short term—minutes, hours, or days—can be found.

Learn to Use the Contrarian Approach

We've all heard the saying, "What goes up must come down." Applying this phrase to trading can be quite profitable. Likewise, "What goes down may come up." I believe that the contrarian approach to investing is one of the best ways to make explosive trading profits. The majority of people who trade lose money. That's because there's a serious herd mentality. Most traders don't have the knowledge to be successful by thinking for themselves, so they follow the trend. The problem is that by the time most traders know that there is a trend, the trend is usually about to reverse. This provides the contrarian with a great deal of opportunity. A trend is your friend if you catch it early.

If you do the opposite of what everyone else is doing, oftentimes you make money faster. The main reason most investors and traders lose money is because they do what others do. Look for opportunities to sell when everyone is buying and look to buy when everyone is selling. Always use hedging techniques to minimize your risk.

Remember That Stocks Follow Bonds

If you keep your eyes on how interest rates are moving, you can determine where stocks are likely to go. When interest rates are going up, bond prices are going down and stocks will likely go down also. Conversely, if interest rates are decreasing, then bond prices are rising and stocks should also be rising. If interest rates are stable, stocks will have a tendency to go up. You can use these insights to create consistent profits in your account. There are points in time when this relationship does not hold; then it is your job to understand what has affected this relationship. For example, in 1998 there was turmoil in the Asian markets which changed this relationship as foreign investors bought bonds, increasing the price of bonds and lowering yields while the stock market moved downwards.

Stay Informed on Seasonal and Event-Driven Markets

Event-driven markets are exactly that: markets that are driven by events—seasonal, political, or otherwise. Obviously, timing is everything. For instance, the energy markets are seriously affected by Organization of Petroleum Exporting Countries (OPEC) meetings. The agriculturals are directly impacted by seasonal weather changes. Bonds are tied to changes in interest rates and the monthly release of the government's *Unemployment Report*. In essence, look for markets that have an event that triggers a specific trade strategy once or twice a month, or maybe once every three months.

To keep up with these important market factors, you must keep abreast of daily news by watching television and reading newspapers and magazines. It can also be important to listen to what key people in specific markets have to say. Typically, you need to come home from work and study what the markets are doing from many angles. In the beginning, it can be empowering to keep a journal of daily events and their effect on the markets. If a market's going to move, then it's more likely that you can make money from it. By studying the daily reactions of specific markets to events, you can begin to forecast which strategy can be used to make the largest potential profit.

Always keep an eye on markets that are dependent on the weather (oil, soybeans, wheat, etc.). See how they are reacting to seasonal factors. The tougher the winter, the higher the price of heating oil. The longer the drought, the higher the price of soybeans. This information can be used to place highly profitable trades.

Walk Around Retail Stores

You can even make money while you are spending it. Just open your eyes and ears when you are shopping and see if you can spot an interesting investment.

- Find out what products are "hot."

- Notice which products have the most store shelf exposure.

- Ask a clerk which products are literally flying off the shelf.

On a shopping trip to a Toys " Я " Us at Christmastime, I noticed that the store I was in was filled to capacity. I also noticed that people were fighting over the last items of one obviously "hot" product. Instead of jumping into the battle to fight for a toy, I picked up a box to find out the manufacturer. In addition, I asked a clerk at the store about the frenzy over this one product. He stated that this was almost a daily occurrence and then told me about a number of other items which were also flying off the shelf.

This is not to say that everyone will be this helpful, but I was able to spot some particular potential investment opportunities by just asking questions of a store clerk. I then called my broker and investigated whether these particular companies were doing well. The next time you are shopping, take a look around and see if you can spot hot products or hot companies.

Look for Opportunities When Driving

Even when you're driving your car, you can spot opportunities. Once again, all you have to do is keep your eyes and ears open. For example, in my area, I found a new restaurant—at least it was new when I found it—by the name of

Boston Chicken. I first visited the place because I was hungry. However, when I saw the food and tasted the meals, I realized that this was a different kind of fast-food restaurant. I was given large portions of delicious food at a good price. I was not only satisfied with the food quality, but I felt that I got a good deal as to price and quantity as well. I returned on several occasions with others and everyone had the same impression. In addition, the counters displayed information on franchise opportunities. Although I was not interested in becoming a franchisee, it was clear this concept had to explode. Sure enough, these restaurants started popping up all over Boston and the list of franchises exploded nationwide. When the company went public, I knew I had to get in on this. The company's public offering was a smash success. Now the company is known as Boston Market with stores all over the country.

When driving, always look for trends. For example, I recently spotted a number of cars and trucks that had interesting designs. It surprised me that they were Dodge products—I had never been a big fan of Dodge or any U.S. manufacturer's automobiles. However, I kept seeing television commercials about the "new Dodge." Well, I knew the old Dodge was not very exciting; but as a car fan—I love sports cars—I kept reading about their newest "super car," the Dodge Viper.

Luckily for me, a friend ended up buying one and I had the privilege of driving the Viper in the Nevada deserts. If you've ever driven in the desert, you know you can drive quite fast out there. After all, there's really nothing there but hard-packed sand. I won't tell you how fast I was going; but, I was beyond merely being impressed with this car. At that time, I owned some other sports cars (Porsche and Ferrari). Believe it or not, I found the Dodge Viper to be much more exciting and fun to drive. Thereafter, I sold the Ferrari and bought the Viper, remaining to this day one of the Viper's biggest fans. Almost two years later, I still get a thrill out of driving this car and so does anyone I know who drives one. It is, by far, the best sports car I have ever owned and I have owned a lot of very expensive cars.

This very positive impression of the car—a Chrysler product—led me to change my opinion of Chrysler products and American automobiles in general. Since then, I have bought two other Chrysler products (Jeep Cherokees), and I love them just as much. Such a positive experience on my part and the number of Dodge Ram pickups I saw on the road led me to believe that Chrysler had nowhere to go but up. Just recently, the company reported record earnings. Indications are that this trend will continue and the stock will be a good long-term investment.

Critique That Which You Already Own

If you like a certain product, others probably do also. You can then look at this product as a potential investment. In addition, if you have a problem with a product and you feel dissatisfied, then others will likely have the same opinion. This may be a good selling opportunity for the stock (use a strategy that makes money when the price drops). Most of us have had a lot of both good and bad experiences. It is up to you to figure out how to translate these experiences into profit opportunities.

If you buy an item and then are dissatisfied, can't get anyone to help you, or can't exchange the product, you're probably not the only one. This happened to me recently. I kept hearing about a certain computer product and how great it was. I subsequently purchased it and found installing it to be extremely difficult. The product was supposed to be easily installed, especially for a computer-literate person like myself. I contacted the customer support line and was put on hold for 20 minutes. I hung up out of frustration and called a second time determined to get through. After being kept on hold for 45 minutes (a very expensive long-distance call), I finally got a representative who knew less about the hardware and computers than I did. I asked for someone else, who ended up giving me information that crashed my computer.

I quickly returned the product and went back to a reliable company that I have never had any problems with, Hewlett Packard. I figured that everyone was having the same problems I was and that the product would flop as the hype about the product fizzled. The stock of this overhyped company was trading at around $50—it had made a very fast move up from around $5 in less than a year. I immediately put on a bearish position to make money when the stock went down. The stock fell in less than four months to around $15, and I smugly changed my dissatisfaction and frustration with the company into cash.

I didn't have to be a genius to figure this one out. All I had to do was translate a personal experience into what other people's experience was likely to be and calculate a way to make money from this information. You can do this on a daily basis with items you own or have purchased and returned.

Ask Your Children

Yes, even children can be a good source of spotting new trends. What new movie do they want to see? What new toys do they want to purchase? What clothes styles are "all the rage"? What sports are popular?

There is a wealth of information that you can receive from your own and other children. Children are influenced greatly by what other kids are doing as well as what they see on television, in the movies, or anywhere. They can alert you to new trends that can affect the bottom line of a company. These pieces of information are valuable when you are establishing an investment perspective.

Look Around Where You Work

Opportunities can also be spotted directly from where you work, your spouse works, or a friend works. For example, my wife, who was working at a pharmacy, told me that one of her favorite customers sadly has AIDS. One day, he came into the pharmacy looking much better. He credited a new experimental drug from a company called Nexstar Pharmaceutical with helping him feel better than he had in years—this new drug was a godsend.

My wife had an article from the local newspaper that her customer had shown her (he was in the article). I called my broker to ask about the stock. It was trading around $9 a share. I bought some stock in the company and within a few months it was well over $20 per share. (I'll give my wife credit for this one.) I sold the stock for a large return, and now I keep asking pharmacists what they consider to be exciting products. By going directly to the people (the pharmacists) who know a lot about a particular industry, I can leverage their years of education and experience into a profit-making opportunity.

Subscribe to a Data Service Provider

Data service providers can furnish you with current prices on stocks, futures, and options. In addition, you can receive up-to-the-minute news and market analyses. This information comes in a variety of ways, including cable, FM radio, satellite, and wireless networks, and can be received real-time (as the prices change on the exchanges they are transmitted to you), delayed (typically 15 to 20 minutes after the prices change), or end-of-day (after the markets close).

Your service fees are based on what kind of service you choose to receive. The faster you get your data, the more costly it will be to obtain; however, it will also be more accurate for making your investment decisions. If you are not going to sit in front of a computer all day long, then you don't really need real-time feeds; you can easily get away with delayed or end-of-day quotes. Subscribing to only what you need keeps your cost as low as possible—you can upgrade later as your trading progresses. Depending on the data you want and the exchanges you sign up to, data feeds can cost you from $20 per month to $400 per month. For instance, a basic real-time subscription that gives you access to all exchanges starts at approximately $180 per month. It goes up from this price depending on a variety of criteria, including how you want to receive the data. There are even feeds used by the large institutional firms (big trading firms) that can run thousands of dollars per month. If you want to place longer-term trades, delayed or end-of-day quotes should be sufficient for your needs. Remember, if you are just starting out, keep your overhead as low as possible. Request information on only the markets you initially want to trade. Too much information can be overwhelming if you don't know how to use it. It is essential to start small and build your profits systematically. A detailed account of data providers can be found in the Appendixes.

Watch Television with an Investor's Eye

Television is one of the best sources of beneficial investment ideas. Commercials can give you a greater awareness as to who is doing what, and who is competing with whom. Television is not just a source of daily entertainment; it is an exceptional medium for distributing information, much of which is useful for spotting investment opportunities. Specifically, you should watch commercials to discover which products you see over and over again and which products have been newly introduced.

However, you can also use this powerful medium in other ways. CNBC and CNN Business are shown in many areas on cable. These are the primary channels watched by traders and investors throughout the trading day. CNBC was born from the Financial News Network (FNN), which was watched widely by the investment community. Before, during, and after trading hours, CNBC broadcasts market information on many issues, including stocks and futures. Expert commentators and guests give market summaries and opinions throughout the day.

As a professional trader, I leave CNBC on with just enough volume to overhear any piece of information that might have a bearing on an investment decision. I typically do not watch any particular show unless something strikes me as intriguing, but I do listen to the commentary all day long. As with any news organization, they report on stories they believe to be interesting to their target audience—the investment community. They talk about what is "hot" and what is "not." They focus on the most market-moving information they can find, because that's the business they are in.

What kind of information do I listen for? Extremely good news and extremely bad news. This is where you can make explosive profits. For example, one day CNBC reported about a company that had a drug use test using a string of hair. My broker informed me the stock was trading around $6 per share. I bought some shares knowing the news would get out overnight and create buying interest in the stock. As I predicted, the stock opened the next day at around $9.50. I sold my shares immediately, because stocks with this kind of run-up can come down quickly. The stock closed that day at around the same level I bought it, leaving me with a 50 percent profit on my investment overnight.

To give you another example, CNBC reported about a stock that had dropped from around $12 per share to about $3.50 overnight due to "accounting irregularities." I called my broker and found that there were options available on the stock to trade. Seeing less risk in the options than the stock, I bought out-of-the-money (OTM) call options at $50 each. These I sold 27 days later at $150 apiece for a 200 percent profit in less than a month.

My mother used to complain that I watched too much television. Well, watching TV for me now has become a profitable experience. Looking at CNBC or CNN Business, one can have a 15-minute delay of price quotes all at the touch of a remote (some prices are actually real-time). But what does this TV ticker tape tell me? Let's forget for the moment about the men and women at the anchor desks in the flashy studio, and concentrate on the bottom of the screen. This is referred to as a ticker tape.

Before the market opens, you will see a recap of stocks—the closing prices of the day before. Also, futures prices are mixed in every few minutes. At 8:30 A.M., after a government or economic report, bond prices are shown in the lower-right-hand corner for 10 minutes or so. Beginning at 9:30 A.M. and until 9:45 A.M. Eastern Standard Time (EST), the market averages run real-time across your screen. The top line usually represents the NYSE stocks, and from time to time futures will appear. The bottom line represents the AMEX and OTC stocks as well as real-time market averages that appear about every minute. Throughout the day, from 9:45 A.M. until 4:15 P.M., stock prices are quoted on the screen. These are displayed as the ticker symbol, followed by shares traded, followed by the last trade and the change in price since yesterday's close (on some stations)—for example:

$$\text{IBM } 10000.00 \; 98 \; +{}^{1}/_{2}$$

The stock symbol is IBM, which last traded 10,000 shares at $98 each, up $.50 from yesterday. If you see only the symbol and the price, then that was the last quoted price of the stock, no shares having been traded. Averages that are quoted include the Dow Jones Industrial Average (DJIA) and the Standard & Poor's 500 Cash Index (S&P 500 Cash Index), followed by the daily change of the index. This information is useful to anyone who has the time to watch the markets on a daily basis.

There are many more examples of how I've been able to use television, especially CNBC, to make money. You can do the same. In some cases, I have been able to apply the contrarian approach to accelerate my profits even further.

Local television programming is certainly not as concise as CNBC; however, you can pick up information on local companies and futures markets that are pertinent to the local community. There are also several national television shows that have segments on investing and trading, such as CNN and nightly business news reports. Unfortunately, most of them lack a great deal of specialized information; either they do not focus on the investment community or they intersperse business news with general news stories.

Read Newspapers Attentively

The first task is to learn how to read a newspaper efficiently and intelligently. A successful investor can scan a newspaper in about five minutes and spot potential opportunities. You must be able to pass by all the fluff and get to the meat of the information.

You can start by picking up copies of newspapers that specialize in financial news, such as *Investor's Business Daily* and the *Wall Street Journal*. (See Appendixes for a breakdown of investment terms found in these two papers.) It's also important to keep tabs on what is happening locally by scanning the local papers that highlight regional companies. This gives you an opportunity to get a better understanding of these potential investments. For example, if you live in the San Francisco Bay Area, you will find a great deal of news about the Silicon Valley companies (e.g., Intel, Oracle, Hewlett Packard, Yahoo!, etc.). These companies employ a great many individuals in the region, so both good and bad news often leaks out. If you don't live in the Bay Area, you can locate information about Silicon Valley's high-tech companies by using the various resources found on the Internet, including our Web site (www.MarketScoreboard.com).

Since local newspapers are in the business of finding and reporting news that has an impact on the people in the area, they look for any chance to report on developments both positive and negative on major companies. Therefore, you can usually find a much wider variety of pertinent information in local papers than in a national newspaper. It is a wise practice to research the major employers in your area and then look for news that can directly affect the performance of these companies' stocks.

A number of periodicals and magazines are also available to help you spot good investment opportunities and educate yourself further regarding stocks, options, and futures including *Futures* magazine, *Technical Analysis of Stocks and Commodities*, and *Commodity Price Charts*. However, make no mistake, both the *Wall Street Journal* and *Investor's Business Daily* are essential weapons in the battle to locate investment opportunities. When looking at the first page of the *Journal*'s Money & Investing section, you can scan the left-hand side of the page to gauge what the markets look like. Focus on the interest and stock charts. See if they are moving in the same direction, or if interest rates are stable and stock prices are moving up, down, or sideways. See if the interrelationship follows what is expected.

In addition to reviewing the tables in the *Wall Street Journal* and *Investor's Business Daily*, I like to look at the charts—graphical representations of price movement—found in the *IBD*. These charts are almost like looking at an electrocardiogram (EKG) of your heart. This EKG-like analysis does not require you to overstudy the chart. With a quick glance, a knowledgeable investor or trader can visualize the health or weakness of a stock or a commodity. New investors can look at a chart and find one of three scenarios:

- Is the price of the security (stock or future) going up?

- Is the price of security going down?

- Is the price of the security going sideways?

The best investments will have momentum. This momentum should be monitored over both a short and long period of time. You want to make short-term investments by looking at short-term price momentum (daily or weekly) and long-term investments by looking at the investment from a long-term perspective (each quarter or yearly). If a stock's volume is low, it isn't likely to go anywhere. Look for increasing volume in a stock to signal movement. The best investments will have a reasonable price-earnings ratio (P/E) compared to the industry average. All of this information can be obtained by studying the investment sections in the *Wall Street Journal* or *Investor's Business Daily*, or by consulting your broker or our Web site.

To locate the best potential investment opportunities in a newspaper, you should focus on the following information for stocks:

- Stocks with greatest percentage rise in volume.

- Stocks with an increase in price greater than 30 percent.

- Stocks with a decrease in price greater than 30 percent.

- Stocks with strong (buying) or weak (selling) earnings per share (EPS) growth.

- Stocks with strong (buying) or weak (selling) relative strength.

- Stocks making a new 52-week high or new 52-week low.

Many people think that it takes years of practice to become a good chart reader. Some experts on technical analysis—the study of price movement through numerical analysis—tend to make the process look more difficult than it really is, so that many individuals give up in their quest to be good investors or traders before they have given themselves a chance to succeed. Many times, information from traders and analysts with accurate knowledge often gets lost in the abundance of useless investing debris.

I have often mentioned that sometimes the best investment to make is to use the contrarian approach by doing the opposite of the crowd. You may find local newspapers (depending on where you live) reporting on a number of issues that can affect commodity prices. For example, if you live in the farm belt of the United States, you will read many articles on the weather, crop expectations, and livestock outlooks. These tidbits of information get filtered to the investment community. Investors and traders then make investment decisions based on their perceptions of the impact of these tidbits of information on the prices of the various commodities.

For example, on a trip to the farm belt, I noticed that everyone was talking about the skyrocketing prices of wheat and soybeans. I heard this in stores and restaurants, and it was front-page news in the local papers. I could tell—even though I wasn't from the area—that there was a feeling of frenzy. No one thought prices could fall. When people who probably don't monitor investment prices make them a topic of conversation, I sense a frenzy. That's when I know the end is near for that movement. I sold both contracts, knowing that on a very fast move up in prices, on any sign of weakness all those who thought the markets were shooting up to the moon will realize the party is over and have to sell in a panic. The same holds true for markets that move quickly to the downside. Sellers will become "panic buyers."

One of the most successful trading techniques is to look for markets that have made very fast moves to the upside or downside and watch for the momentum to change; then place a trade that benefits from a reversal. This accelerates profits, as a frenzied movement in one direction will move even faster (in many cases) in the opposite direction when the move is over.

Look for Good and Bad News Concerning Specific Companies

Explosive opportunities can often be found when specific companies are the subject of extremely good or bad news. There is tremendous financial loss for millions of stockholders when stocks drop like a rock. When such a stock dropped to around $4 per share overnight from $12 (not to mention a previous high of $35 about nine months earlier), this signaled a buying opportunity. With the stock this low, I bought call options that would make money when the stock moved back up. They cost only $25 apiece, and they doubled in value in a day. I sold my position a few days later for a profit of over 400 percent. You can find extreme examples almost daily and super investment opportunities at least twice a week. If you wait for these opportunities, you can become much more successful.

For example, keep an eye out for bad earnings reports or news from a company that the earnings will not be as had been expected. As mentioned earlier, the value of a company's stock is determined by many factors. However, the most significant factor is expected future earnings as forecast by brokerage company analysts. If a company begins to give these analysts any information that is viewed as hurting a company's next earnings release, then they will quickly downgrade their forecasts. This turn of events can trigger a major selling frenzy.

Take Medaphis Corporation in August 1996. This leading provider of management services to physicians and hospitals let out that there was a significant underperformance of the quarterly results compared to analysts' expectations. The stock price, which had been steadily advancing over the previous year and was trading at around $36 the day before, dropped overnight to around $12. That was a $24 drop—representing two-thirds of the value—lost overnight. If you owned the stock, how would you feel? Devastated. I would feel the same way. If I had invested $1000 in this supposedly safe stock, I would have only $333 the next day. I would jump ship just like the other owners that day. However, after a fast move down like this there is usually a bounce back in price (which happened) for a short period of time. Then the stock usually continues down until a new support level is reached.

After many years of trading, you learn that reactions are very similar in extreme situations. A good trader and investor will immediately react to this situation and place a trade that will benefit from this situation. What would I do? I'd buy out-of-the-money (OTM) calls and OTM puts—a spread—at a cheap enough price so that I would risk very little, with enough time for me to be proven right (three months or so).

Watch for New Product Developments

There can be numerous investment opportunities when pharmaceutical companies and biotech research and development companies announce successful trials of new drugs and approvals from the Food and Drug Administration (FDA). If you ask your broker to notify you of these types of situations, this alone can present tremendous opportunities.

Bet on Smart People

This is an easy one that many people overlook. Why not invest your money with smart, successful people? My theory is that someone who has been successful in the past will be successful in the future. There are many examples of this around you. Why not let a billionaire invest your money for you? Billionaires do not become billionaires without investing their money very wisely. Jump on the bandwagon and join them. Let Bill Gates of Microsoft invest for you. How do you do this? Just invest money in Microsoft stock.

Many of you may not know his name yet, but let me tell you, he can make you wealthy. I am referring to Wayne Huzienga. Perhaps you have heard of two companies—Waste Management and Blockbuster—he built and sold successfully. I am sure you have spent a few nights in front of a television set after visiting one of his stores. After selling Blockbuster, he now uses Republic Industries as his investment vehicle. The stock went from $3 to $60 in less than a year (it now trades around $25 after a two for one stock split). He has already built Republic Industries faster than the other two, having taken the new company from around $150 million in revenues to over $1 billion in one year.

There are a number of other individuals you might want to follow. Guess where I put my longer-term investment dollars? I just ride the wave with other successful people.

Look for Low-Priced Stocks

I define low-priced stocks as those trading at $20 or less. It's a lot easier to make a high return on a low-priced stock than a high-priced stock. If I buy a stock that is trading at $100 per share, how long will it take to double my money? Although anything can happen in this business, most likely a high-priced stock like this could take years to double in value. In addition, there is a greater chance of losing a lot of money. If I take a stock that is $10 per share, how long might it take for this stock to double in value? Many times I have seen it happen in a day. Also, if the stock becomes worthless, I lose only $10. Bottom line: Placing a low-priced stock trade gives you the following benefits:

- You can make a high return faster.
- You have less money invested to lose.
- You can play more stocks with $100 (10 different stocks if they average $10 each).

This last point is very important. If I have $100 to invest, I will—in many cases—pick a few stocks that allow me to average my risk. This is referred to as a portfolio. A broad portfolio is the basis of a mutual fund. The basic theory is that a larger group of stocks will even out the chances of winning in the long run. This, in turn, reduces your risk.

If I put my $100 into one stock, there is a 50 percent chance of the stock losing money (50 percent up, 50 percent down). If I buy 10 stocks (average price of $10), then if one stock loses 100 percent of its value, I have nine stocks to carry the portfolio and can still make money. A mutual fund may have hundreds of stocks. Some may be terrible investments, but overall the fund may still do very well as it diversifies its risk. Let's take another example: If I feel that a particular $100 stock may make a large move up in price, instead of buying the stock, I would buy a $4 OTM call option giving me control of 100 shares for $400. If the stock now moves up from $100 to $105 (a 5 percent price increase), these options may go up 50 percent in price to $600, because a move in the price of a stock will typically have a magnified effect on the price of the options. This magnification is due to a number of factors, including the leverage the options provide you. Therefore, it's a lot easier to make a 100 percent return on your money using options on stocks (as well as options on futures). However, I have to caution you: It is also easier to *lose* 100 percent of your investment with options. If you want to trade options, never underestimate how important it is to learn as much as you can about them.

Look for Price Increases or Decreases of Over 20 Percent in the Past 60 Days

Momentum creates opportunities for both buying and selling. Momentum investors are very widespread; however, they are a very fickle group. When a stock (or future) gains momentum and then starts to lose momentum, there is usually a flurry of activity to take the market in the other direction. I like to invest when the momentum is strengthening or weakening, because these are the best short-term opportunities and they often create longer-term opportunities.

Momentum investors are much shorter-term-oriented than mutual fund investors or money managers. A momentum investor may be looking for momentum over the previous few seconds, minutes, days, weeks, or even months. This creates many different time frames in which investors and traders are viewing the market. When a market starts to move quickly, then all these players may jump aboard. The momentum may last, but usually, on a short-term basis, prices will reverse as investors become disappointed when the market dies.

How do I measure momentum? I look for a change in price of a stock over the previous 60 or 90 days. I use this as my long-term indicator. If I am building a longer-term portfolio of stocks, I want stocks that are showing a minimum of 60-day strength.

As previously mentioned, many technical analysts use momentum indicators. These indicators are very specific. They might show the change in stock price relative to a set prior period (i.e., five minutes, one day, etc.). Perhaps they use a moving average to locate a change in momentum. When the current price moves below the moving average, they sell; when it moves above, they buy.

Look for Price Increases or Decreases of More than 30 Percent since Yesterday

This is the most important indicator I use for momentum investments. The 30 percent rule is the minimum. I prefer a much higher number to show even stronger momentum. Typically, the higher the percentage, the stronger the momentum. How does this work? You can either look at the price percentage gainers and losers lists from the newspapers or check out our Web site to access this information from your computer terminal. If you are receiving real-time or delayed quotes, then you can get this information from your data feeds during the day.

When I look at the lists, I look for the stocks that have gone up the most in price over the previous day's closing price—the basis for the percentage gain or loss. However, it is important to note that stocks with the highest percentages do not necessarily have the most interest or momentum. Sometimes a stock that was trading for only $1 moves up to $1.75. Although that's a 75 percent increase, it doesn't always mean high profits.

In order to get a better understanding of a stock's profitability, I also look at price range and trading volume. I typically trade only stocks starting at $5; however, sometimes I do trade lower-priced stocks if they show significant trading volume. Generally, I trade in stocks that have increased in volume significantly. If a stock trades less than 300,000 shares a day, I avoid it.

Maybe it will make a move, but there is not enough interest from other investors for me to believe the trade will be profitable. I like to see over one million shares trading. This shows commitment on the part of the investors. Once again, the more volume the better. When buying stocks, I want them to be on the price percentage gainers list.

I consult the price percentage losers list to find stocks that have made major moves down (30 percent or more) and then look for a rebound. This is when I find buying opportunities. This may sound strange, as most investors may think this shows more weakness coming, but remember that I like the contrarian approach. Also, understand that when a stock moves so far down so fast there is usually negative news regarding the company. Perhaps the quarterly financial results are disappointing Wall Street, or the company has presented information that future earnings will be disappointing. Most importantly, this usually creates a panic and what is called a blow-off bottom. This means that the fast move down has made every potential seller panic. After the sellers have all sold, buyers tend to produce a rebound.

How often does this occur? Sometimes on a daily basis I find at least one stock that has dropped at least 30 percent (50 percent or more is even better). These declines appear to come in spurts, especially around the time in each fiscal quarter when companies are reporting earnings. When the market opens, I watch these stocks closely and wait for them to start gaining momentum to the upside before buying. I wait for a movement of at least a 20 percent price move off the lows, with heavy volume of at least 300,000 shares. I like to see large blocks (5000 shares or more) increasing, as this shows the institutions are buying.

When this scenario occurs, I look to buy the stock, but prefer to buy the call options (if there are options available). Remember, I get more leverage with options and also have the benefit of limited risk. All I can lose is the amount I paid for the options.

Let's take an example of a recent trade. The stock price of Syquest Technology, Inc., was increasing on heavier-than-average volume. Syquest's stock had had an average volume of around 200,000 shares trading daily. One day, the stock moved from $5 to $6 (a 20 percent increase) on volume of over one million shares trading. This was an obvious clue that something was happening that was creating a great deal of interest. I contacted my broker to see if there was any news to account for this movement. There was none.

The stock price had been much higher before dipping to trade just around $5 for the past few months. I considered buying the stock. However, 2000 shares would cost me $12,000. I decided to buy the $7\frac{1}{2}$ (i.e., strike price of $7.50) call options instead with plenty of time left to expiration (I like to buy options with at least three months remaining on momentum investments). I paid $87.50 for each option representing control of 100 shares of stock. In comparison, buying 100 shares of the stock would have cost $600.

Although the options did not represent the shares on a one-to-one basis, any move up in the price of the stock would double the value of the options quickly. Approximately four days later, the stock had doubled in value (a 100 percent move) and I sold all the options I had bought for $87.50 for $537.50. That was more than a 500 percent return in four days by trading the options versus a 100 percent return if I had purchased the stock.

Let's review this trade:

Trade Initiation

Current stock price:	$6 per share
Previous stock close:	$5
Percent increase:	20 percent
Average daily trading volume:	200,000 shares
Most recent day's volume:	1,000,000+ shares
Margin required:	Zero (cost of options)
Option price:	$7/8 ($87.50)

Note: I used a 20 percent rule in this example due to the dramatic increase in trading volume.

Trade Closing

Stock price:	$12
Option price:	$5^3/_8 ($537.50)
Stock price up:	100 percent
Option price up:	500+ percent

This simple technique can provide you with profits greater than you ever imagined could be made in such a short period of time.

Look for Stocks Reaching New Highs or Coming Off New Lows

When used in conjunction with lists of price percentage gainers and losers, this is one of the most powerful indicators. When a stock is on one of the gainers lists and it's making new highs as calculated over the previous 52 weeks, then it may be a buy (especially if it's making new historical highs). Also, when the stock has made new lows and is coming off new lows, the blow-off bottom may have occurred.

Buy a Small Number of Shares

Until you have the experience to make money consistently in the markets, start off as a small investor. Regardless of whether you have $1000 or $1 million, while you learn what you're doing, you'll be much better off with small investments. How small is small? This question is virtually impossible to answer. Just be cautious when you start out, until such time as you are a consistent winner. Then build up slowly.

Build Your Confidence

It is important to earn your confidence through winning investments. However, be vigilant that you do not build a false sense of confidence. Although I have been investing for many years, I still spend considerable time figuring out ways to improve my trading. If you develop a sense of temperate confidence, you will most likely be a survivor. That means you'll actually be around to enjoy the benefits of this business.

Oftentimes, when a trader starts to make a little money in the markets, a false sense of confidence drives them to make much bigger trades. This is a big mistake. As they say on Wall Street, "Pigs get fat, hogs get slaughtered."

When You Make a Good Return, Sell

What is a good return? Every trader or investor will probably tell you something different. I like to make 100 percent on my money when trading stock options, and a minimum of 20 percent when making commodity trades. With stocks you usually have to settle for a lower return (10+ percent). These are the numbers I use based on my experience with winning trades; however, these are benchmarks, not hard-and-fast rules. My exit strategies are usually based on momentum shifts, which means that some of my trades have returns much higher than 100 percent.

I also have losing trades (nobody's perfect). However, a disciplined trader will get out of losing trades quickly and learn how to stay with the winners. It's very much like being a surfer waiting for the big wave. A wave might approach that has the characteristics of a winner but then starts to look like a loser. Instead of wasting time riding the loser to shore, the experienced surfer will get off that wave and look for another opportunity. You too are looking for the big winners. So don't forget to get out of the losers quickly so that you can use your capital in the most efficient manner possible.

CONCLUSION

Profitable trading opportunities come from an infinite number of sources. The trick is to foster the growth of your own personal trading antennae through cultivating a variety of sources. Remember, you will never have as much time as you would like to study the markets. You have to use your time efficiently to find the best possibilities for profitable trades.

Trading might as well be a foreign country to the uninitiated. It has its own language and its own customs. It's up to you to find your favorite haunts by exploring the territory and finding out what suits you best. If fundamental analysis feels comfortable and fits in with the rest of your lifestyle, then read all you can about it. If you prefer to study the *Wall Street Journal* from front to back page, make it a part of your daily morning ritual. Whatever you choose, make sure you really understand it. Familiarity may breed contempt, but when it comes to trading, familiarity breeds prosperity.

6

Option Basics

When I first started trading, I learned how to profit from the upward movement of a stock. That was easy enough. I thought I was well on my way to financial success. Next, a friend treated me to a taste of shorting a stock. It was a surprise to learn that I could sell stock I didn't own by simply borrowing it from a brokerage firm in the hope that the stock would go down in price and then buying it back later at a less expensive price to make a profit. It took me more than a few days to really understand this concept, though to date I still have a problem short-selling companies. It must be the "bullish on America" in me. I was then introduced to the futures market and how with a small amount of capital I could increase my leverage and control much more of a particular commodity using less. What I did not fully understand was the potential risk. Shortly into my futures trading career, what could happen to an account when one was on the wrong side of a market move became evident. This resulted in a temporary setback referred to by many in the business as a margin call in which I was required to give additional money to my broker as a guarantee to stay in the trade. Later that year, I returned to the futures market with a more disciplined approach that included options trading.

As a trader, I find options to be the most effective way to maintain consistent trading profits. They have become vitally important weapons in my trading arsenal. However, like any weapon, they are most effective when used properly and dangerous if not respected. Options don't lose money; people do.

Most of my favorite trading strategies use put and call options to act as insurance policies in a wide variety of trading scenarios. You probably have insurance on your car or house because it is the responsible and safe thing to do. Options provide the same kind of safety net for your trades. They also allow you to control more shares of a certain stock without tying up a large amount of capital in your account.

Did you ever miss a big profit on a declining stock because you didn't know how to execute a short sale? Or, perhaps you've been afraid to take the high risk associated with short sales. After all, by itself, shorting has unlimited risk. But, if you combine it with the appropriate option strategy, you can minimize your risk and thereby maximize your profits. Understanding how to trade put and call options strategically is the key to making great returns on your investments regardless of market direction.

In order to grasp the complex nature of trading options, you need to have a strong foundation in option basics. Let's start at the very beginning and work our way from simple definitions to some of the strategies that will enable you to make consistent trading profits.

The purchase of an option gives a trader the right, but not the obligation, to buy or sell a specified number of shares or contracts of the underlying security or derivative at a predetermined price for a set period of time. In its most basic form, an option gives you the right, but not the obligation, to do something. There is an infinite number of examples of options. Perhaps you are looking for a house to rent; but, you are also interested in buying a house in the future. Let's say I have a house for rent and would be willing to sell the house. A 12-month lease agreement with an option to buy the house at $100,000 is written. As the seller, I may charge you $1000 extra just for that 12-month option to buy the house. You now have 12 months in which to decide whether to buy the house for the agreed price. You have purchased a call option which gives you the right to buy the house for $100,000, but you are in no way obligated to do so.

A variety of factors may help you decide whether to buy the house, including appreciation of the property, transportation, climate, local schools, and the cost of repairs and general upkeep. Housing prices may rise or fall during the lease period, which could also be a determining factor of your decision. Once the lease is up, you lose the option to buy the house at the agreed price. If you decide to buy the house, you are exercising your call option agreement. That's basically it.

Let's now apply this in the stock, index, and futures markets. An option gives you the right to buy a specified number of shares or contracts of the underlying security at a predetermined price within a specific time period. Options are available on most futures, but not every stock. To determine whether options are traded on a market you are interested in, you should consult your broker.

In general, options have the following seven characteristics:

1. Options give you the right to buy or sell an instrument.

2. If you buy an option, you are not obligated to buy or sell the underlying instrument; you simply have the right to exercise the option.

3. If you sell an option, you are obligated to deliver—or to purchase— the underlying asset at the predetermined price if the buyer exercises his or her right to take delivery—or to sell.

4. Options are good for a specified period of time, after which they expire and you lose your right to buy or sell the underlying instrument at the specified price.

5. Options are bought at a *debit* to the buyer.

6. Options are sold by giving a *credit* to the seller.

7. Options are available at several strike prices representing the price of the underlying instrument.

The premium is the total you have to pay to buy an option or the total credit you receive from selling an option. It reflects a variety of factors including the option's intrinsic value and time value, primarily due to the fact that the longer the period of time until expiration, the greater the chance the option has of being profitable by the expiration date.

Another important feature of an option is the strike price, the predetermined price at which the underlying asset is bought or sold. When you buy a call on a stock, you get the right (but not the obligation) to buy 100 shares of this stock at a certain price. That certain price is called the strike price. Generally, options are available at several strike prices. Strike prices for stocks usually come in multiples of five, but not always. Stocks that trade for less than $25 will have strikes at each $2\frac{1}{2}$ strike. The relationship of the strike price to the current price of the underlying asset determines whether the option is in-the-money (ITM), at-the-money (ATM), or out-of-the-money (OTM). You lose your option to buy or sell the underlying instrument at the strike price if you do not exercise the option by its expiration date or the option has expired worthless. A call option is in-the-money if the strike price of the option is below where the underlying security is trading and out-of-the-money if the strike price is above the price of the underlying security. A put option is in-the-money if the strike price is greater than the price of the underlying security and out-of-the-money if the strike price is below the price of underlying security. A call or put option is at-the-money if the strike price is the same as the price of the underlying security.

Price of Underlying Asset = 100

Strike Price	*Call Option*	*Put Option*
102	OTM	ITM
101	OTM	ITM
100	ATM	ATM
99	ITM	OTM
98	ITM	OTM

Most of the options traded on exchanges in the United States are called American exercised options. This means that they can be exercised at any time on or before their expiration dates. European options, on the other hand, can be exercised only on (not before) their expiration dates.

Each option is a contract that gives the holder (the option buyer) the right, but not the obligation, to buy or sell a fixed amount of the underlying asset at a specific price from or to the writer (the option seller). The writer of the option contract (the seller) receives a payment for the option in the form of an option premium. The seller must deliver the underlying security at the strike price if the buyer exercises his or her right. The underlying asset is a stock, commodity, or other financial instrument on which the option contract is based. However, the option contract is a wasting asset, unlike the financial instrument it is based on, because it has value only until its expiration date. At that time, it will expire and become worthless, be exercised by its owner, or be assigned. An option is exercised when its holder implements his or her right to buy or sell the underlying instrument at the specified price. If the writer receives an exercise notice, the option has been assigned and the writer is obligated to buy or sell the specified amount of underlying assets at the strike price to the holder.

A stock option represents the right to buy or sell 100 shares of the underlying stock. The expiration date is always the third Friday of the expiration month. Strike prices for stock options come in increments of $5, except lower-priced stocks that have strike increments of $2.50. The strike price and expiration date of futures options, however, differ depending on the underlying instrument they represent. To be successful at trading, it is essential to thoroughly research every market you trade in to determine the correct expiration dates, strike prices, and various other important contract variables. If you are unsure about any of this, you can obtain the necessary information by contacting the futures exchange, by asking your broker, or by using a reliable Internet source (such as www.MarketScoreboard.com).

Many traders do not understand how an option's price changes relative to the stock or futures price. To fully comprehend this relationship, you must understand the delta—the rate of change of the price of an option relative to the price change of the underlying instrument. It is not enough to simply buy calls when you expect a market to move up or purchase a put when you anticipate a drop in a market. It is essential to know how fast an option will make or lose money. The option's delta provides the clue to this paradox. An option with a delta of 50 will move twice as fast as an option with a delta of 25. The calculations are discussed in depth later in this book.

In addition, an option's price changes as a result of a number of variables that are handled capably by options pricing models such as Black-Scholes. Most options software can determine these calculations as well.

TYPES OF OPTIONS

There are two types of options—calls and puts. These two types of options make up the basis for an infinite number of trading scenarios. Successful options traders can effectively use both kinds of options in the same trade to hedge their investment creating a limited-risk trading strategy.

Call Options

Call options give the buyer the right (but not the obligation) to buy the underlying futures or stock contract. In order to familiarize you with the basics of call options, let's explore an informal example. A local newspaper advertises a sale on portable compact disc players for only $49.95. Knowing a terrific deal when you see one, you cut out the ad and head on down to the store to purchase one. Unfortunately, when you arrive you find out all of the advertised portable CD players have already been sold. The manager apologizes and says that she expects to receive another shipment within the week. She gives you a rain check entitling you to buy a portable CD player for the advertised discounted price of $49.95 for up to one month from the present day. You have just received a call option. You have been given the right, not the obligation, to purchase the portable CD player at the guaranteed strike price of $49.95 until the expiration date one month away.

Later that week, the store receives another shipment and offers the portable CD players for $59.95. You return to the store and exercise your call option to buy it for $49.95, saving $10. Your call option was in-the-money. But what if you returned to find the portable CD players on sale for $39.95? The call option gives you the right to purchase it for $49.95—but you are under no obligation to buy it at that price. You can simply tear up the rain check coupon and buy the portable CD player at the lower market price of $39.95. In this case, your call option was out-of-the-money and expired worthless.

Let's take a look at another scenario. A coworker says her portable CD player just broke and she wants to buy another one. You mention your rain check. She asks if you will sell it to her so she can purchase the portable CD player at the reduced price. You agree to this; but, how do you go about calculating the fair value of your rain check? After all, the store might sell the new shipment of portable CD players for less than your guaranteed price. Then the rain check would be worthless. You decide to do a little investigation on the store's pricing policies. You subsequently determine that half the time, discounted prices are initially low and then slowly climb over the next two months until they start over again. The other half of the time, discounted prices are just a onetime thing. You average all this out and decide to sell your rain check for $3. This price is the theoretical value of the rain check based on previous pricing patterns. It is as close as you can come to determining the call option's fair price.

This simplification demonstrates the basic nature of a call option. All call options give you the right to buy something at a specific price for a fixed amount of time. If the market price is more than your strike price, your call option is in-the-money (ITM). If the market price is less than your strike price, your call option is out-of-the-money (OTM). If the market price is the same as your strike price, your call option is at-the-money (ATM). The price of the call option is based on previous price patterns that only approximate the fair value of the option.

If you buy call options, you are "going long the market." That means that you intend to profit from a rise in the market price of the underlying instrument. If bullish (you believe the market will rise), then you want to buy calls. If bearish (you believe the market will drop), then you want to "go short the market" by selling calls. If you buy a call option, your risk is the money paid for the option (the premium) and brokerage commissions. If you sell a call option, your risk is unlimited unless hedged in some manner.

A call option is in-the-money (ITM) when the price of the underlying instrument is higher than the option's strike price. For example, a call option that gives the buyer the right to purchase 100 shares of IBM stock for $100 each is ITM when the current price of IBM stock is greater than $100, because the option can be used to purchase stock for less than the current market price. A call option is at-the-money (ATM) when the price of the underlying security is equal to its strike price. For example, an IBM call option with a strike price of $100 is ATM when IBM stock can be purchased for $100. A call option is out-of-the-money (OTM) when the underlying security's market price is less than the strike price. For example, an IBM call option with $100 strike price is OTM when the current price of IBM stock is less than $100. No one would want to exercise an option to buy IBM at $100 if it can be bought directly for less. That's why call options that are out-of-the-money by their expiration date expire worthless.

Price of IBM = 100

Strike Price	Call Option	Option Premium
120	OTM	$\frac{1}{2}$
115	OTM	1
110	OTM	$2\frac{1}{4}$
105	OTM	$4\frac{3}{4}$
100	ATM	$6\frac{1}{2}$
95	ITM	10
90	ITM	$13\frac{3}{4}$
85	ITM	$17\frac{1}{2}$
80	ITM	$20\frac{3}{4}$

Purchasing a call option is probably the simplest form of options trading. A trader who purchases a call is bullish, expecting the underlying asset to increase in price. The trader will most likely make a profit if the price of the underlying asset increases fast enough to overcome the option's time decay. Profits can be realized in one of two ways if the underlying asset increases in price before the option expires. The holder can either purchase the underlying stock for the lower strike price, or, since the value of the option has increased, sell the option at a profit. In general, purchasing a call option has a limited risk because all you risk is the premium paid for the option and the commissions paid to the broker for placing the trade.

Let's review the basic fundamental structure of buying a standard call on a stock using IBM. If you buy a call option for 100 shares of IBM stock, you get the right but not the obligation to buy 100 shares of the stock at a certain price. The certain price is called the strike price. Your right is good for a certain amount of time. You lose your right to buy the stock at the strike price on the expiration date of the call option.

Generally, calls are available at several strike prices, which usually come in increments of five. In addition, there normally is a choice of several different expiration dates for each strike price. Just pick up the financial pages of a good newspaper and look at the options for IBM. Looking at this example, you will see the strike prices, expiration months, and the closing call option prices of the underlying stock, IBM.

Price of IBM = 105

Strike Price	January	March	May
100	$6^3/_8$	$7^1/_2$	$8^1/_4$
105	2	$3^7/_8$	$4^3/_4$
110	$^3/_8$	$1^9/_{16}$	$2^3/_4$

The numbers in the first column are the strike prices of the IBM calls. The months across the top are the expiration months. The numbers inside the table are the option prices, called option premiums. For example, the premium of an IBM January 100 call is $6^3/_8$. Each $1 in premium is equal to $100 per dollar. Looking at the IBM January 100 call, a premium of $6^3/_8$ indicates that one contract trades for $637.50 [(6 × $100) + ($^3/_8$ × $100) = $637.50].

The table also shows that the last transaction for the day in the January 105 calls are at a premium of 2 per 100 shares of IBM. Since a call contract is an option on 100 shares, you would have to pay $200 plus brokerage commissions to buy one IBM January 105 call. A May 100 call trading at $8^1/_4$ would cost $825 ($8^1/_4 \times 100) plus commissions:

- Cost of IBM January 105 call = $2 \times $100 = $200 + commissions.

- Cost of IBM May 100 call = $8^1/_4 \times $100 = $825 + commissions.

All the options of one type (put or call) that have the same underlying security are called a class of options. For example, all the calls on IBM constitute an option class. All the options that are in one class and have the same strike price are called a series of options. For example, all of the IBM 105 calls with various expiration dates constitute an option series.

Put Options

Put options give the buyer the right (but not the obligation) to sell the underlying futures or stock contract. Once again, let's look at an informal example to become familiar with the basics of put options. You've decided to set up a small cottage industry manufacturing down jackets. Your first product is a long-sleeved jacket complete with embroidered logos of the respective ski resorts placing the orders. The manager of the pro shop at a local ski resort agrees to purchase 1000 jackets in November for $40 each, if you can deliver them. In effect, you've been given a put option. The cost of producing each jacket is $25, which gives you a $15 profit on each item. You have therefore locked in a guaranteed profit of $15,000 for your initial period of operation.

This guaranteed order from the resort is a put option. You have the right to sell a specific number of jackets at a fixed price (strike price) by a certain time (expiration date). However, just as November rolls around, you find out that a large manufacturer is creating a very similar product for ski resorts for $30 each. If you didn't have a put option agreement, you would have to drop your price to meet the competition's price, and thereby lose a significant amount of profit. Luckily, you exercise your right to sell your jackets for $40 each and you enjoy a prosperous Christmas season. Your competitor made it advantageous for you to sell your jackets for $40 using the put option because it was in-the-money.

In a different scenario, you get a call from another ski resort that has just been featured in a major magazine. The resort needs 1000 jackets by the beginning of November to fulfill obligations to its marketing team and is willing to pay you $50 per jacket. Even though it goes against your grain to disappoint your first customer, the new market price of your product is $10 higher than your put option price. Since you are under no obligation to sell the jackets for $40, you elect to sell them for the higher market price.

These examples demonstrate the basic nature of a put option. All put options give you the right to sell something at a specific price for a fixed amount of time. If the market price is less than your strike price, your put option is in-the-money. If the market price is more than your strike price, your put option is out-of-the-money. If the market price is the same as your strike price, your put option is at-the-money.

Put options give the buyer of puts the right to "go short the market" (sell stock). If bearish (you believe the market will drop), then you could go short the market by buying puts. If bullish (you believe the market will rise), then you could "go long the market" by selling puts. If you buy a put option, your risk is the money paid for the option (the premium) and brokerage commissions. If you sell a put option, your risk is unlimited until the underlying asset reaches zero unless you hedge the sale.

A put option is in-the-money (ITM) when the price of the underlying instrument is lower than the option's strike price. For example, a put option that gives the buyer of the put the right to sell 100 shares of IBM stock for $100 each is ITM when the current price of IBM is less than $100, because the option can be used to sell the stock for more than the current market price. A put option is at-the-money (ATM) when the price of the underlying stock is equal to its strike price. For example, an IBM put option with a strike price of $100 is ATM when IBM stock can be purchased for $100. A put option is out-of-the-money (OTM) when the underlying security's market value is greater than the strike price. For example, an IBM put option with a $100 strike price is OTM when the current price of IBM stock is more than $100. No one would want to exercise an option to sell IBM at $100 if it can be sold directly for more. That's why put options that are out-of-the-money by their expiration date expire worthless.

Price of IBM = 100		
Strike Price	Put Option	Option Premium
120	ITM	$20^{3}/_{4}$
115	ITM	$17^{1}/_{2}$
110	ITM	$13^{3}/_{4}$
105	ITM	10
100	ATM	$6^{1}/_{2}$
95	OTM	$4^{3}/_{4}$
90	OTM	$2^{1}/_{4}$
85	OTM	1
80	OTM	$^{1}/_{2}$

Purchasing put options is generally a bearish move. A holder who has purchased a put option benefits when there is a decrease in the price of the underlying asset. This enables the holder to buy the underlying asset at a lower price on the open market and sell it back at a higher price to the writer of the put option. A decrease in the underlying asset's price also promotes an increase in the value of the put option so that it can be sold for a higher price than was originally paid for it. The purchase of a put option provides unlimited profit potential (to the point where the underlying asset reaches zero) and a limited risk of the put option's premium plus commissions to the broker placing the trade.

CONCLUSION

Put and call options create a matrix of strategic trading opportunities when combined. The trick is to understand the markets well enough to be able to use them to limit your risk and maximize your profits. In the beginning, start small and keep a record of every trade you place. As your option trading experience increases, you will discover market patterns that offer familiar opportunities for the same option strategy.

7

Introduction to Delta Neutral Trading

Delta neutral trading strategies provide traders with a variety of opportunities to take advantage of market movement while maximizing trading profits and minimizing potential risk. This unique trading approach combines stocks or futures with options, or options with options in such a way that the sum of all the deltas in the trade equals zero. An overall zero position delta when managed properly can enable a trade to make money within a certain range of prices regardless of market direction. Before placing a trade, the upside and downside break-evens can be calculated to gauge the trade's profit range. A trader may also calculate the maximum potential profit and loss to assess the viability of the trade. As the price of the underlying instrument changes, the overall position delta of the trade moves away from zero. In some cases, additional profits can be made by adjusting the trade back to zero (or delta neutral) through buying or selling more options, stock shares, or futures contracts.

Delta neutral trading has been used on stock exchange floors for many years. Some of the most successful trading firms ever built use this type of trading. When I ran a floor trading operation, I studied what traders did. In most cases, floor traders think in 10-second intervals. I soon realized that we could take this trading method off the floor and change the time frame to make it successful for off-floor traders.

In general, it is extremely hard to make any money competing with floor traders. These individuals pay large sums of money for the privilege of moving faster and paying less per trade than off-floor traders. However, changing the time frame enabled me to compete with those with less knowledge. After all, 99 percent of the traders out there have very little concept of limiting risk, including money managers in charge of billions of dollars. They just happen to have control of a lot of money so they can keep playing the game for a long time. For example, a friend once lost $10 million he was managing. Ten minutes later I asked him, "How do you feel about losing all that money?" He casually replied, "Well, it's not my money." That's a pretty sad story; but it's the truth.

If you are trading with your own hard-earned cash, limiting your risk is an essential element of your trading approach. That's exactly what delta neutral trading strategies do. They use the same guidelines as floor trading but apply them in time frames that give off-floor traders a competitive edge in the markets.

Luckily, these strategies don't exactly use rocket science mathematics. The calculations are really quite simple. You're simply trying to create a trade that has an overall delta position as close to zero as possible. I can look at a newspaper and make delta neutral trades all day long. I don't have to wait for the S&Ps to hit a certain number, or confuse myself by studying too much fundamental analysis. However, I do have to look for the right combination of factors to create an optimal trade.

An optimal trade uses your available investment capital efficiently to produce substantial returns in a relatively short period of time. Optimal trades may combine futures with options, stocks with options, or options with options to create a strategy matrix. This matrix combines trading strategies to capitalize on a market going up, down, or sideways.

To locate profitable trades, you need to understand how and when to apply the right options strategy. This doesn't mean that you have to read the most technically advanced books on options trading. You don't need to be a genius to be a successful trader. You simply need to learn how to make consistent profits. One of the best ways to accomplish this is to pick one market and/or one trading technique and trade it over and over again until you get really good at it. It's just like McDonald's. The franchises sell hamburgers over and over again and make big bucks. If you can find just one trade that works, you can make money over and over again until it's so boring you just have to move on to another market. After a few years of building up your trading experience, you will be in a position where you are constantly re-defining your strategy matrix and markets.

Finding moneymaking delta neutral opportunities is not like seeking the Holy Grail. Opportunities exist each and every day. It's simply a matter of knowing what to look for. Specifically, you need to find a market that has two basic characteristics—volatility and high liquidity—and use the appropriate time frame for the trade.

VOLATILITY

Volatility measures market movement or nonmovement. It is defined as the magnitude by which an underlying asset is expected to fluctuate in a given period of time. As previously discussed, it is a major contributor to the price (premium) of an option. Usually, the higher an asset's volatility, the higher the price of its options. This is because a more volatile asset offers larger swings upward or downward in price in shorter time spans than less volatile assets. These movements are attractive to options traders who are always looking for big directional swings to make their contracts profitable. High or low volatility gives traders a signal as to the type of strategy that can best be implemented to optimize profits in a specific market.

I like looking for wild markets. I like the stuff that moves, the stuff that scares everybody. Basically, I look for volatility. When a market is volatile, everyone in the market is confused. No one really knows what's going on or what's going to happen next. Everyone has a different opinion. That's when the market is ripe for delta neutral strategies to reap major rewards. The more markets move, the more profits can potentially be made.

Volatility in the markets certainly doesn't keep me up at night. For the most part, I go to bed and sleep very well. In fact, perhaps the only problem I have as a 24-hour trader is waking up in the middle of the night to sneak a peek at my computer. If I discover I'm making lots of money, I may stay up the rest of the night to watch my trade.

Highly volatile markets can be found everywhere. The S&Ps, bonds, currencies, and certain high-technology stocks are just a few of the markets with high volatility these days. There are also a few event-driven markets that move a lot during specific periods. Obviously, timing is everything. For instance, the energy markets are seriously affected by OPEC meetings. The agriculturals are directly impacted by seasonal weather changes. Bonds are tied to changes in interest rates and the monthly release of government employment reports. In essence, look for markets with events that trigger a specific trade strategy once or twice a month, or maybe once every three months.

In the beginning, it can be empowering to keep a journal of daily events and their effect on the markets. Why? Simply put, the more media attention a market receives, the more likely that market is to move. If a market's going to move, then it's likely that you can make money from it. By studying the daily reactions of specific markets to events, you can begin to forecast which strategy can be used to make the largest potential profit.

For example, gold prices have been wildly fluctuating for the last 30 years. The United States abandoned the use of the gold standard in the early 1970s. By January of 1980, gold surged to an all-time high of $850 an ounce. It has slowly been declining ever since. In fact, today's gold market is trading around $300 and shows few signs of a major reversal. In the past, international adversity prompted people the world over to invest in gold because of its reputation for safety and stability. However, these days as the Asian markets flounder and international conflicts rage, the financial world is turning to the stability of the U.S. dollar. Many countries, such as Australia and Canada, have been drastically selling off their gold reserves, flooding the market and driving prices down. This has contributed to the closure of gold mines worldwide, which may someday produce a shortage that will eventually drive the prices back up.

Although chaotic trends in the supply and demand of gold have radically changed the gold market, it still exhibits the characteristics of a range-bound or sideways market. Range-bound markets rise to a specific resistance level which triggers a sell-off and then fall to a certain support level triggering a buying trend. In this way, these markets gravitate to a center point between two equal and opposing prices to a specific equilibrium level. It's very much like stretching a length of elastic. The center point is the equilibrium level— the point at which price pressures to the upside and the downside are at rest. Movement in either direction exerts pressure causing a corresponding movement back to the center point.

The gold market is a sideways to down market and continues to exhibit high volatility. Up until 1996, gold maintained a support level around $370 and a resistance level of approximately $400 to create an equilibrium level of $385. During January and February of 1996, gold broke through the resistance level to $420. Then the market fell like a rock in 1997. Price fluctuations continued through 1997 with support being around $280 and resistance about $300 by year's end. This moves the equilibrium price to $290. Gold will have to remain above $300 for several months to establish a new equilibrium level.

Range-bound markets are a perfect example of the unusual physics of trading. Traders can use the price range to bid the market up or down, always looking at the equilibrium level as the place where the market wants to rebound to. For example, when a market reaches the upside resistance level, you can employ a strategy that benefits from a drive down to the support level. Conversely, when a market's price hits its support level, you can place a trade which profits from a rise back to the equilibrium level. There are a number of delta neutral strategies that take advantage of this kind of sideways market activity that will be reviewed later in this book.

HIGH LIQUIDITY

Liquidity is the ease with which a market can be traded. It can be defined as the volume of trading activity that enables a trader to buy or sell a security or derivative and receive fair value for it. A high volume of people trading a market is needed to make it rewarding. Liquidity provides the opportunity to move in and out of positions without difficulty. For example, at-the-money (ATM) options have excellent liquidity because they have a better chance of being profitable than out-of-the-money (OTM) options. Therefore, they are easier to trade.

How do you avoid illiquid markets? When I first started trading, I visited the exchanges. A friend who was a floor trader walked me from one pit to another. In one pit, there were two guys sitting around reading the newspaper. Is there a lot of opportunity there? I didn't think so. I figured when an order hits that pit, everyone probably starts laughing at the poor sucker who placed it. Then I checked out the bond pit. There were 500 people fighting for an order. I quickly recognized that the bond market had high liquidity and plenty of opportunity. I went to the natural gas pit at the New York Mercantile Exchange. It was a madhouse. There were 200 people in a pit 10 feet wide (prior to moving to their new state-of-the-art building), yelling and screaming. I couldn't understand a thing they were saying, but once again I recognized high liquidity. To this day, I look for pits where there are plenty of people playing the game because people playing the game equals opportunity.

If you don't have the ability to actually visit an exchange, you can still check out the liquidity of a market by reviewing the market's volume to see how many shares or contracts have been traded. It's hard to quantify just how much volume is enough to qualify a market as one with liquidity. However, as a rule of thumb, always look for stocks that are trading at least 300,000 shares every day. Futures markets vary widely and it is best to monitor activity daily and pick a market that trades many more contracts than you trade. Since there are no absolutes, there are situations when this rule can be tossed out the window in exchange for common sense. But until you have enough experience, this may be a good rule of thumb to follow.

APPROPRIATE TIME FRAME

The next step is to select the appropriate time frame for the kind of trade I want to place. Since I am no longer a day trader, I'm usually in the 30- to 90-day range of trading. For the most part, I prefer 90 days. Since I don't want to sit in front of a computer all day long at this point in my trading career, I prefer to use delta neutral strategies. They allow me to create trades with any kind of time frame I choose.

Delta neutral strategies are simply not suitable for day trading. In fact, day trading doesn't work in the long run unless you have the time and the inclination to sit in front of a computer all day long. Day trading takes a specific kind of trader with a certain kind of personality to make it work. My trading strategies are geared for a longer-term approach.

If you're going to go into any business, you have to size up the competition. In my style of longer-term trading, my competition is the floor trader who makes money on a tick-by-tick basis. But I choose not to play that game. I've taken the time frame of a floor trader—which is tick-by-tick—and expanded it to a period floor traders usually don't look at. Applying my strategies in longer time frames than day-to-day trading is my way of creating a trader's competitive edge.

THE DELTA

To become a delta neutral trader, it is essential to have a working understanding of the Greek term delta and how it applies to option trading. The
delta can be defined as the change in the option premium relative to the
price movement in the underlying instrument. Almost all of my favorite option strategies use the calculation of the delta to devise managed-risk trades.

A rough measurement of an option's delta can be calculated by dividing
the change in the premium by the change in the price of the underlying asset. For example, if the change in the premium is 30 and the change in the
futures price is 100, you would have a delta of 30. Now, if your futures contract advances $10, a call option with a delta of 30 would increase only $3.
Similarly, a call option with a delta of 10 would increase in value approximately $1.

One contract of futures or 100 shares of stock has a fixed delta of 100.
Long futures are +100 and short futures are −100. Buying 100 shares of
stock equals +100 and selling 100 shares of stock equals −100 deltas. All
options have adjustable deltas. Long option strategies have positive
deltas; short option strategies have negative deltas. Long strategies include long futures or stocks, long calls, or short puts. These positions all
have positive deltas. Short strategies include short futures or stocks, short
calls, or long puts; these have negative deltas. To summarize the plus or
minus delta possibilities:

Market Up (Positive Deltas)	Market Down (Negative Deltas)
Buy calls.	Sell calls.
Sell puts.	Buy puts.
Buy stocks.	Sell stocks.
Buy futures.	Sell futures.

As a rule of thumb, the deeper in-the-money your option is, the higher the
delta. Remember, you are comparing the change of the futures or stock price
to the premium of the option. In-the-money (ITM) options have higher
deltas. A deep ITM option might have a delta of 80 or greater. ATM options—these are the ones you will be probably working with the most in the
beginning—have deltas of approximately 50. OTM options' deltas might be

as small as 20 or less. Again, depending how deep in-the-money or out-of-the-money your options are, these values will change.

When an option is very deep in-the-money, it will start acting very much like a futures contract or a stock as the delta gets closer to plus or minus 100. The time value shrinks out of the option and it moves almost in tandem with the futures or stock. Many of you might have bought options and seen huge moves in the underlying asset's price but hardly any movement in your option. When you see the huge move, you probably think, "Yeah, this is going to be really good." However, if you bought the option with a delta of approximately 20, even though the futures or stock had a big move, your option is only moving at 20 percent of the rate of the futures in the beginning. This is one of the many reasons that knowing an option's delta can help you recognize profitable opportunities. In addition, there are a number of excellent computer programs geared to assist traders to determine option deltas.

Let's try an example using December gold at 290 (Figure 7.1). In this example, we are very bullish on the price of gold and we have $1250 to spend. Let's go ahead and buy a December gold 290 call at $12\frac{1}{2}$. The strike prices in gold are every $5. A dollar move in gold is worth $100. The tick value on the premium is worth $100. The profit on this trade is unlimited. The risk is limited to the option premium of $1250 ($12\frac{1}{2}$ = 12.50 × $100 = $1250). The break-even occurs at 302.50 (290 + 12.50 = 302.50).

Let's say that an individual by the name of Peter thinks gold is going to make a big move to the upside. As it turns out, Peter is right: Surprisingly, gold goes to $460 an ounce. At expiration, that $1250 call option when exercised is now worth about $17,000 [($460 – $290) × $100 = $17,000]. That's a profit of $15,750—a pretty nice return on a $1250 investment. Peter is feeling quite proud of his tidy profit until he meets Sarah, who was also very bullish on gold. The difference is that Sarah is a delta neutral trader. She expected a large rise in the gold market and decided to buy five OTM 310 calls at $250 apiece for a total of $1250. How did she calculate this trade? She calculated the delta on the 310 calls to be about 20 percent. She bought five calls because that equals the movement of a futures contract. When gold goes to $460 an ounce she makes 150 points on each option when exercised, which is $15,000 [($460 – 310) × $100 = $15,000] per option or $75,000 (5 × $15,000 = $75,000). That's a profit of $73,750 on her original $1250 investment. Meanwhile, poor Peter is no longer feeling quite so plucky about his paltry $15,750 profit. This example, although clearly an exaggeration of

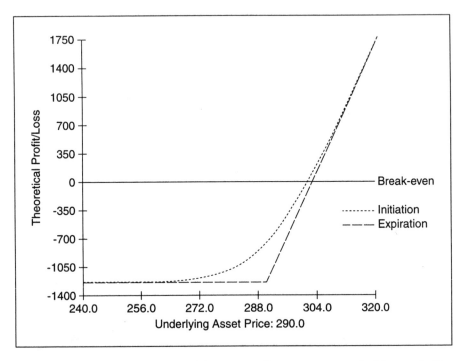

Figure 7.1   Risk Profile—Gold Long Call (Long 1 Dec Gold 290 Call @ 12.50)

price movement, shows the vast range of profits that can be made from using different delta-based strategies.

What happens if Peter and Sarah are both wrong and gold falls? If gold goes down to $280 an ounce, they both lose the same $1250. The only time that Peter would come out better would be if the price of gold stays somewhere between $290 and $310. In that range, Peter would either make some money or at least get his money back, whereas Sarah would lose her $1250, since she bought five options that subsequently expired worthless.

Obviously, you want to cover the cost of your premium. However, if you are really bullish on something, then there are times you need to step up to the plate and go for it. If you are just moderately friendly to the market you still want to use deltas to determine your best trading opportunity. Now, perhaps you would have said, "I am going to go for something a little further out-of-the-money so that I can purchase more options." Unless the market makes a big move, chances are that these OTM options will expire worthless. No matter what circumstances you encounter, determining the deltas and how they are going to act in different scenarios will foster profitable decision making.

When I first got into the business, I would pick market direction and then buy options based on this expected direction. Many times, they wouldn't go anywhere. I couldn't understand how the markets were taking off but my options were ticking up so slowly they eventually expired worthless. At that time, I had no knowledge of deltas. To avoid this scenario, remember that knowing an option's delta is essential to successful delta neutral trading. In general, an option's delta:

- Estimates the change of the option's price relative to the underlying security. For example, an option with a delta of 50 will cost less than an option with a delta of 80.

- Determines the number of options needed to equal one futures contract or 100 shares of stock to ultimately create a delta neutral trade with an overall position delta of zero. For example, two ATM call options have a total of +100 deltas; I get to zero by selling one futures contract or 100 shares of stock (–100 deltas).

- Determines the probability that an option will expire in-the-money. A 50 delta option has a 50 percent chance of expiring in-the-money.

- Assists you in risk analysis. For example, when buying an option you know your only risk is the premium paid for the option.

To review the delta neutral basics: The delta is the term used by traders to measure the price change of an option relative to a change in price of the underlying security. In other words, the underlying security will make its move either to the upside or to the downside. A tick is the minimum price movement of a particular market. With each tick change, a relative change in the option delta occurs. Therefore, if the delta is tied to the change in price of the underlying security, then the underlying security is said to have a value of 1 delta. However, I prefer to call the value of 1 delta 100 deltas instead because it's easier to work with.

Let's take an example using Treasury bond (T-bond) futures options. The T-bond futures contract has a value of 100 deltas.

- Long one T-bond futures contract = +100 deltas.

- Short one T-bond futures contract = −100 deltas.

Simple math shows us that going long two futures contracts equals +200 deltas, going long three futures contracts equals +300 deltas, going short 10 futures contracts equals −1000 deltas, and so on. On the other hand, the typical option has a delta of less than 100 unless the option is so deep in-the-money that it acts exactly like a futures contract. We will not typically deal with options that are deep in-the-money as they generally cost too much and are illiquid.

All options have a delta relative to the 100 deltas of the underlying security. If one futures contract is equal to 100 deltas, then the options must have delta values of less than 100. An Options Delta Value Chart can be found in the Appendixes outlining the approximate delta values of ATM, ITM, and OTM options.

CONCLUSION

Delta neutral trading combines options with futures, options with stocks, and options with options to create trades with an overall position delta of zero. To set up a balanced delta neutral trade, it is essential to become familiar with the delta values of ATM, ITM, and OTM options. Deltas provide a scientific formula for setting up trading strategies that give you a competitive edge over directional traders. Experience will teach you how to use this approach to take advantage of various market opportunities while managing the overall risk of the trade efficiently. I cannot stress enough the importance of developing a working knowledge of the deltas of options.

8

The Greeks and Option Pricing

To create a delta neutral trade, you need to select a calculated ratio of short and long positions that together create an overall position delta of zero. To accomplish this goal, it is necessary to be able to determine a variety of risk exposure measurements. The option Greeks are a set of measurements that can be used to explore the risk exposures of specific trades. Since options and other trading instruments have a variety of risk exposures that can vary dramatically over time or as markets move, it is essential to understand the various risks associated with each trade you place.

Each risk measurement except vega is named after a different letter in the Greek alphabet—delta, gamma, theta, and zeta. In the beginning, it is important to be aware of all of the Greeks, although understanding the delta is the most crucial to your success. Comprehending the definition of each of the Greeks will give you the tools to decipher option pricing as well as risk. Each of the terms has its own specific use in day-to-day trading by most professional traders as well as in my own approach to trading.

- Delta: Change in the price (premium) of an option relative to the price change of the underlying security.

- Gamma: Change in the delta of an option with respect to the change in price of its underlying security.

EXTRINSIC VALUE

- Theta: Change in the price of an option with respect to a change in its time to expiration.

- Vega: Change in the price of an option with respect to its change in volatility.

- Zeta: The percentage change in an option's price per 1 percent change in implied volatility.

Each of these risk measurements contains specific important trading information. As you become more acquainted with the various aspects of options trading, you will find more and more uses for each of them. For example, they each contribute to an option's premium. The two most important components of an option's premium are intrinsic value and time value (extrinsic value).

INTRINSIC VALUE AND TIME VALUE

Intrinsic value is defined as the amount by which the strike price of an option is in-the-money. It is a very important value to determine, since it is the portion of an option's price that is not lost due to the passage of time. For a call option, intrinsic value is equal to the current price of the underlying asset minus the strike price of the call option. For a put option, intrinsic value is equal to the strike price of the option minus the current price of the underlying asset. If a call or put option is at-the-money, the intrinsic value would equal zero. Likewise, an out-of-the-money call or put option has no intrinsic value. The intrinsic value of an option does not depend on how much time is left until expiration. It simply tells you how much real value you are paying for. If an option has no intrinsic value, then all it really has is time value, which decreases as an option approaches expiration.

Time value (theta) can be defined as the amount by which the price of an option exceeds its intrinsic value. Also referred to as extrinsic value, the time value of an option is directly related to how much time the option has until expiration. Theta decays over time. For example, if a call costs $5 and its intrinsic value is $1, the time value would be $5 – $1 = $4.

Let's use the following table to calculate the intrinsic value and time value of a few options.

Price of IBM = 106

Strike	January	March	May
100	$6^3/_8$	$7^1/_2$	$8^1/_4$
105	2	$3^7/_8$	$4^3/_4$
110	$^3/_8$	$1^9/_{16}$	$2^3/_4$

Here are the calculations for the IBM March 105 calls if the price of IBM is now trading at 106:

- Intrinsic value = underlying price minus strike price; $106 – $105 = $1.

- Time value = call price minus intrinsic value; $3^7/_8 – $1 = $2^7/_8$.

Now let's look at the intrinsic value of each option relative to its time value.

- The January 100 call has a minimum value of 6; therefore, you are paying $^3/_8$ point of time value for the option.

- The March 100 call has a minimum value of 6; therefore, you are paying $1^1/_2$ points of time value for this option.

- The May 100 call has a minimum value of 6; therefore, you are paying $2^1/_4$ points of time value for this option.

As you can see, the intrinsic value of an option is the same, no matter what time is left until expiration. Now let's look at some options within the same month, but with different strike prices:

Price of IBM = 106

Strike	January
90	$16^1/_4$
95	$11^1/_2$
100	7

- The January 90 call has 16 points of intrinsic value (106 – 90 = 16) and $^1/_4$ point of time value ($16^1/_4 – 16 = ^1/_4$).

- The January 95 call has 11 points of intrinsic value (106 – 95 = 11) and $^1/_2$ point of time value ($11^1/_2 – 11 = ^1/_2$).

- The January 100 call has 6 points of intrinsic value (106 – 100 = 6) and 1 point of time value (7 – 6 = 1).

Obviously, an option with three months till expiration is worth more than an option that expires this month. Theoretically, the option with three months till expiration has a better chance of ending up in-the-money than the option expiring this month. That's why an OTM option consists of nothing but time value. The more out-of-the-money an option is, the less it costs. However, since it has no real (intrinsic) value, all you are paying for is time value (i.e., the time to let your OTM option become profitable due to a swing in the market). The probability that an extremely OTM option will turn profitable is quite slim. To confirm this, just go to your local library and look up some options' prices in previous copies of a financial newspaper, such as *Investor's Business Daily*. Compare the present-day price of a particular option to prices in back issues of the same publication.

Since you can exercise an American-style call option anytime you want, its price should not be less than its intrinsic value. An option's intrinsic value is also called the minimum value primarily because it tells you the minimum the option should be selling for (i.e., exactly what you are paying for and how much time value you have left). What does this mean? Most importantly, it means that the cheaper the option, the less real value you are buying. Intrinsic value acts a lot like car insurance. If you buy a zero-deductible policy and you have an accident, even a fender bender, you're covered. You pay less for a $500-deductible policy but if you have an accident, the total damage must exceed $500 before the insurance company will pay for the remainder of the damages.

The prices of OTM options are low, and get even lower further out-of-the-money. To many traders, this inexpensive price looks good. Unfortunately, OTM options have only a slim probability that they will turn profitable. The following table demonstrates this slim chance of profitability.

Call Strike	Price of IBM = 106		
	January	*Intrinsic Value*	*Time Value*
90	17	16	1
95	$13\frac{1}{2}$	11	$2\frac{1}{2}$
100	$10\frac{3}{4}$	6	$4\frac{3}{4}$
105	$6\frac{1}{2}$	1	$5\frac{1}{2}$
110	3	0	3

With the price of IBM at 106, a January 110 call would have a price (premium) of 3. To be 3 points above the strike price, IBM has to rise 7 points to 113 in order for you to break even. If you were to buy a January 95 call and pay $13\frac{1}{2}$ for it, IBM would have to rise to $108\frac{1}{2}$ in order to break even. As you can see, the further out-of-the-money an option is, the less chance it has of turning a profit.

Theta (time value) correlates the change in the price of the option with respect to the time left until expiration. The passage of time has a snowball effect as well. Those of you who have bought options and sat on them until the last couple of weeks before expiration might have noticed that at a certain point the market stopped moving anywhere. Option prices are exponential—the closer you get to expiration, the more money you're going to lose if the market doesn't move. On the expiration day, an option's worth is its intrinsic value. It's either in-the-money, or it isn't.

Early in my options career, I realized that as you go deeper in-the-money with calls or puts, the options have less time value and more intrinsic value. This means that you are paying less for time; therefore, the option moves more like the underlying asset. This is referred to as the delta of an option. As previously discussed, the delta is the key to creating delta neutral strategies and we will delve deeply into its properties and functions as we explore more advanced trading techniques throughout this book. Let's now explore various strike price trends.

Price of IBM = 106

Strike	*January*	*March*	*May*
100	$6\frac{3}{8}$	$7\frac{1}{2}$	$8\frac{1}{4}$
105	2	$3\frac{7}{8}$	$4\frac{3}{4}$
110	$\frac{3}{8}$	$1\frac{9}{16}$	$2\frac{3}{4}$

Looking at the expiration months for IBM, notice that in the January column, the price (premium) of a call is higher for lower strike prices. For example, the price of an IBM January 100 call ($6\frac{3}{8}$) is higher than the price of the IBM January 105 call (2). That makes sense since the IBM January 100 call allows you to buy a $106 stock (IBM) for $100 a share, while the IBM January 105 call allows you to buy it for $105. Also notice that the price of a call is lower for closer expirations. The same principle applies to puts. Less time to expiration means lower prices. The buyer has less time for the put to move in-the-money or to decide what to do with the option. For example, the price of the IBM May 105 call ($4\frac{3}{4}$) is higher than the price of the IBM January 105 call (2). This makes sense since the May 105 call allows you to buy IBM at $105 until the third Friday of May (a period of about four months from January). With the IBM January 105 call, your right expires the third Friday of January. The only difference between these options is the amount of time the trader has to make a decision on the option and its probability of closing in-the-money.

COMPONENTS OF OPTION PRICING

There are seven main components that affect the price of an option:

1. The current price of the underlying financial instrument.

2. The strike price of the option.

3. The type of option (put or call).

4. The amount of time remaining until expiration.

5. The current risk-free interest rate.

6. The dividend rate, if any, of the underlying financial instrument.

7. The volatility of the underlying financial instrument.

Each of these variables plays a unique part in the price of an option. While the first four are easy to figure out, the other three are often either forgotten in the equation, or are confusing enough to be overlooked when determining a strategy.

The risk-free interest rate is what you would have received on an investment based on the rate for 90-day Treasury bills. Higher prevailing interest rates can increase option premiums, while lower interest rates can lead to a decrease in option premiums.

Dividends act in a similar way, increasing and decreasing an option premium as they increase or decrease the price of the underlying asset. It is interesting to note that if a stock were to pay a dividend, a short seller would be responsible for that payment. (A short seller in securities not only has unlimited risk of the stock rising, but is also responsible for the dividends paid.)

VOLATILITY

Volatility can be defined as a measurement of the amount by which an underlying asset is expected to fluctuate in a given period of time. It is one of the most important variables in options trading, significantly impacting the price of an option's premium as well as contributing heavily to an option's time value.

As previously mentioned, there are two basic kinds of volatility: implied and historical (statistical). Implied volatility is computed using the actual market prices of an option and one of a number of pricing models (Black-Scholes for stocks and indexes and Black for futures). For example, if the market price of an option increases without a change in the price of the underlying instrument, the option's implied volatility will have risen. Historical volatility is calculated by using the standard deviation of underlying asset price changes from close to close of trading going back 21 to 23 days or some other predetermined period. In more basic terms, historical volatility gauges price movement in terms of past performance. Implied volatility approximates how much the marketplace thinks prices will move. Understanding volatility can help you to choose and implement the appropriate option strategy. It holds the key to improving your market timing as well as helping you to avoid the purchase of overpriced options or the sale of underpriced options.

In basic terms, volatility is the speed of change in the market. Some people refer to it as confusion in the market. I prefer to think of it as insurance. If you were to sell an insurance policy to a 35-year-old who drives a basic Honda, the stable driver and stable car would equal a low insurance premium. Now, let's sell an insurance policy to an 18-year-old, fresh out of high school with no driving record. Furthermore, let's say he's driving a brand-new red Corvette. His policy will cost more than the policy for the Honda. The 18-year-old lives in a state of high volatility!

The term vega represents volatility. It is the measurement of the change in the price of the option in relation to the change in the volatility of the underlying asset. As the option moves quicker within time, we have a change in volatility. Volatility moves up. If the S&P's volatility was sitting just below 17, perhaps now it's at 17.5. You can equate that .5 rise to an approximate 3 percent increase in options. Can options increase even if the price of the underlying asset moves nowhere? Yes. This frequently happens in the bonds market just before the government issues the employment report on the first Friday of the month. Before the Friday report is released, demand causes option volatility to increase. After the report is issued, volatility usually reverts to its normal levels. In general, it is profitable to buy options in low volatility and sell them during periods of high volatility.

When trading options, you can use a computer to look for some sort of indicator that an option's price is abnormal when compared to the movement of the underlying asset. This abnormality in price is caused mostly by an option's implied volatility, or perception of the future movement of the asset. Implied volatility is a computed value calculated by using an option pricing model for volume, as well as strike price, expiration date, and the price of the underlying asset. It matches the theoretical option price with the current market price of the option. Many times, option prices reflect a higher or lower option volatility than the asset itself.

The best thing about implied volatility is that it is very cyclical; that is, it tends to move back and forth within a given range. Sometimes it may remain high or low for a while, and at other times it might reach a new high or low. The key to utilizing implied volatility is in knowing that when it changes direction, it often moves quickly in the new direction. Buying options when the implied volatility is high causes some trades to end up losing even when the price of the underlying asset moves in your direction. You can take advantage of this situation by selling options and receiving their premium as a credit to your account instead of buying options. For example, if you buy an option on IBM when the implied volatility is at a high you may pay $6\frac{1}{2}$ for the option. If the market stays where it is, the implied volatility will drop and the option may then be priced at only $4\frac{3}{4}$ with this drop in volatility.

I generally search the computer for price discrepancies that indicate that an option is very cheap or expensive compared to its underlying asset. When an option's actual price differs from the theoretical price by any significant amount, I take advantage of the situation by buying options with low volatility and selling options with high volatility, expecting the prices to fall back in line as the expiration date approaches.

To place a long volatility trade, I want the volatility to increase. I look for a market where the implied volatility for the ATM options has dropped down toward its historic lows. Next, I wait for the implied volatility to turn around and start going back up.

In its most basic form, volatility means change. It can be summed up just like that. Markets that move erratically—such as the energy markets in times of crisis, or grains in short supply—command higher option premiums than markets that lag. I look at volatilities on a daily basis and many times find options to be priced higher than they should be. This is known as a volatility skew. Most option pricing models give the trader an edge in estimating an option's worth. Computers are an invaluable resource in searching for these kinds of opportunities.

For example, deeply OTM options tend to have higher implied volatility levels than ATM options. This leads to the overpricing of OTM options based on a volatility scale. Increased volatility of OTM options occurs for a variety of reasons. I used to intentionally buy inexpensive OTM options. Many traders prefer to buy two $5 options than one $10 option because they feel they are getting more bang for their buck. What does this do to the demand for OTM options? It increases that demand, which increases the price, which creates a volatility skew. These skews are another key to finding profitable option strategy opportunities.

Although I strongly recommend using a computer to accurately determine volatility prices, there are a couple of techniques available for people who do not have a computer. One way is to compare the S&P against the Dow Jones Industrial Average. You can analyze this relationship simply by watching CNBC, looking at *Investor's Business Daily* or the *Wall Street Journal*, or going online to consult our Web site (www.MarketScoreboard.com). A 1-point movement in the S&P generally corresponds to 8 to 10 points of movement in the Dow. For example, if the Dow drops 16 to 20 points, but the S&P is still moving up a point, then S&P volatility is increasing. On the other side, if you see consistently where the Dow is moving and you are getting one-point movement in the S&P for more than 10 points movement in the Dow, then volatility on the S&P is decreasing. This is one way to determine volatility.

Another way to determine volatility is by checking out the range of the markets you wish to trade. The range is the difference between the high for the cycle and the low value for whatever cycle you wish to study (daily, weekly, etc.). If the Dow moves between a low of 7900 and a high of 7950, you have a range of 50 points. You can chart the daily range of any futures contract or stock and keep a running average of a market's range. If the range is greater than the average, then volatility is increasing and if the range is less than the average, then volatility is decreasing.

Determining the range or checking out the Dow/S&P relationship are two ways of determining volatility without a computer. You can use these techniques to your advantage to determine whether you should be buying, initiating a trade, or just waiting. Remember, option prices can change quite dramatically between high and low volatility.

CONCLUSION

Option pricing is based on a variety of factors. Each of these factors can be used to help determine the correct strategy to be used in a market. Volatility is a vital part of this process. Charting the volatility of your favorite markets will enable you to spot abnormalities that can translate into healthy profits. Since this is such a complicated subject, a great deal of time, money, and energy is spent to explore its daily fluctuations and profitable applications. We provide access to these insights as well as daily trading information on our Web site at www.MarketScoreboard.com.

9

Risk Profiles

Developing an understanding of the use of risk profiles can help you get the most out of delta neutral trading. A risk profile or curve is a graphical representation of what your overall risk looks like. When I find a likely trade, I begin by visualizing its risk. This simple process helps me to determine the potential profit opportunity. To become a successful trader using delta strategies, you must learn how to visualize a trade's risk curve.

Options have become increasingly popular because they offer limited risk and give traders the ability to participate in the market for a smaller investment. Every trade you place has a corresponding risk profile that graphically shows your potential risk and potential reward over a range of prices and time. Risk profiles view a certain strategy from a risk perspective. Determining the maximum risk of a trade is one of the keys to successful trading. Many people manage their risk by placing stops (stop orders). Unfortunately, if the market is moving quickly, it blows right through your stop order. Suddenly, you've lost $5000 instead of $500.

For example, I had a headset that connects my office to the floor of the S&P pit. On a particularly volatile day, I'm talking with my clerk in the pit using the headset. She is telling me the prices. "Offered at 50. Offered at even. Offered at 50. Offered at even." I keep trying to ask her what number "even" we are talking about. She has no clue. No one really knows. The numbers are so far off because the market is moving so fast. Even the floor traders have their hands in their pockets because they're not sure what's really going on. Meanwhile, the off-floor traders are panicking. They're losing money hand over fist if they're long the market and they simply can't get out. The market is blowing right through their stops and until the smoke clears there's no telling exactly how much they'll lose.

Many good trading firms have gone out of business because they just didn't manage their risk. If you had put on a delta neutral S&P trade the day the stock market crashed in 1987, you would have survived quite well. However, those who were long the market probably had to file for bankruptcy. Managing your risk just makes good sense, and risk profiles are the key to understanding the potentials.

Reading a risk profile is pretty easy. The horizontal numbers at the bottom of the chart show the market price of the underlying asset. The vertical numbers at the left show profit and loss. The black horizontal line at zero shows the trade's break-even. You can look at any given market price on a risk graph and determine its corresponding profit and loss (P/L). Let's take a look at a few basic risk profiles so that you can become familiar with them.

LONG FUTURES OR LONG STOCK

In a long futures or long stock trade, you are buying the underlying asset. This trade is placed when you expect the price of the market to rise. If you just wanted to go long a futures contract, your risk profile would look like the graph in Figure 9.1. As you can see, when the futures price rises, you make money; when it falls, you lose money. The same graph can be used to visualize a long stock position.

This example shows the trader long one September bond futures at a price of 109^26. A futures contract does not have premium or time decay. It has a one-to-one movement in price versus risk and reward. This means that the trade has virtually unlimited risk and reward depending on the movement of the market: for every point higher the September bond futures move, you will make $1000. Conversely, for every point the September bond futures fall below the purchase price, you will lose $1000.

All commodities have their own unique contract values. Bonds are especially tricky. Bond futures are traded in increments of 32nds. Each tick is worth $1/32$ of $1000 or $31.25. That's why the price of a bond uses a "^" instead of a decimal point. In addition, bond options are traded in increments of 64ths. Each tick is worth $1/64$ of $1000 or $15.625. This can be quite con-

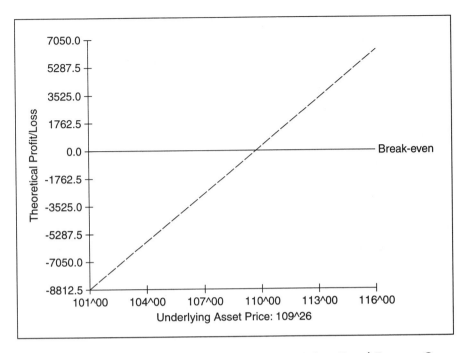

Figure 9.1   Risk Profile—Long Futures (Long 1 Sep Bond Futures @ 109^26)

fusing when you try to calculate values between futures and option prices. For example, break-evens are always expressed in 32nds, although the calculations combine options in 64ths and futures in 32nds. For purposes of clarity, we will try to use fractions in our calculations.

Although futures contracts do require margin, they are much less expensive than stock trades. Depending on your brokerage, stock trades usually require a 50 percent margin deposit from your account to place the trade. Margin requirements on futures markets vary from commodity to commodity. The actual cost of the previous long futures trade is $109,812.50 [(109 × 1000) + (26 × 31.25) = $109,812.50]. However, the margin on one T-bond futures contract is currently (as this book goes to press) only $2700. That means that for only $2700 you could have placed a trade controlling $109,812.50 worth of bonds. That kind of leverage is quite impressive. However, if the trade started to lose money, you would receive a margin call requiring more money from your account to stay in the trade.

In general, margin on futures markets tends to fluctuate and should be assessed each time you place a trade involving futures. A list of current margin requirements for commodities is available in the Appendix and through our Web site (www.MarketScoreboard.com).

SHORT FUTURES OR SHORT STOCK

In a short underlying trade, you are selling the underlying asset and receiving a credit to your account for the sales price. A short futures strategy is used when you expect the price of the futures or stock to fall. If you wanted to go short a futures contract, your risk curve would look like the graph in Figure 9.2. In a short trade, when the futures price falls, you make money; when it rises, you lose money. The curve of this graph would also apply to a short stock trade.

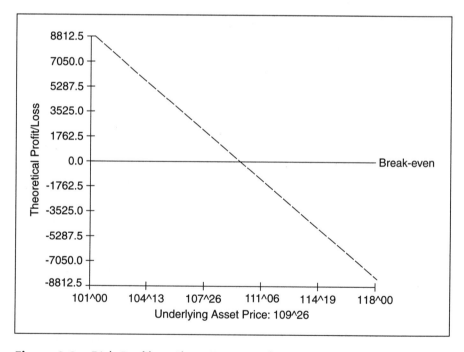

Figure 9.2 Risk Profile—Short Futures (Short 1 Sep Bond Futures @ 109^26)

This example shows that the trader is short one September bond futures contract at a price of 109^26. Since a futures contract does not have premium or time decay, it also has a one-to-one movement in price versus risk and reward, which translates into virtually unlimited risk and unlimited reward. In other words, for every point lower the September bond futures move, you will make $1000. The maximum reward occurs if the bond futures were to go to zero, a very unlikely event. If the bond was sold short at 109^26, the maximum reward would be $109,812.50 [(109 × 1000) + (26 × 31.25)] per contract. However, for every point the September bond futures rise above the purchase price, you lose $1000. There is no limit on how much you can lose. To break-even, bonds would have to close at 109^26. Once again, the contract value is different with each commodity. This trade requires margin in your account to execute. If the trade begins to lose money, you would be required to place additional funds in your margin account to cover the loss.

THE LONG CALL

In a long call trade, you are buying call options on futures contracts or stock shares. This strategy is placed when you expect the price of the underlying security to rise. If you want to go long a call, your risk curve would look like the graph in Figure 9.3. When the underlying security price rises, you make money; when it falls, you lose money. This strategy provides unlimited profit potential with limited risk. It is often used to get high leverage on an underlying security that you expect to increase in price. Zero margin borrowing is allowed. That means that you don't have to hold any margin in your account to place the trade. You pay a premium (cost of the calls), and this expenditure is your maximum risk. The risk graph in Figure 9.3 is an example of this strategy. The current price of bond futures is 109^26. The numbers that run from top to bottom indicate the profit and loss of this graph. The numbers that run left to right indicate the price of the underlying asset. The two lines that slope upward indicate the theoretical profit or loss of the call options at initiation and expiration of the trade according to the price of the underlying asset.

In this example, we placed the trade to buy 1 Bond Sep 110 Call @ 3^05. As previously discussed, bond options consist of 64 ticks per point, and each point is worth $1000 (each tick is worth $15.625). Bond futures, on the

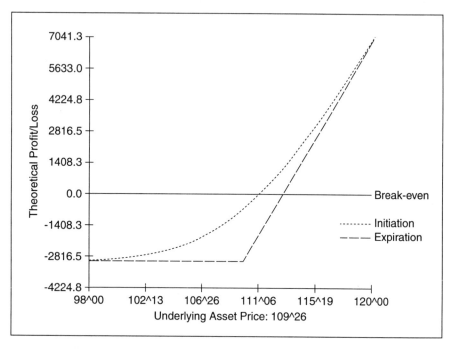

Figure 9.3   Risk Profile—Long Call (Long 1 Sep Bond Futures 110 Call @ 3^05)

other hand, are composed of 32 ticks per point, with each point worth $1000. This can be tricky when trying to calculate different values. This trade costs a total of $3078.12 plus commissions [(3 × $1000) + (5 × 15.625) = $3078.12]. The maximum risk is equal to the cost of the call option ($3078.12). The maximum reward is unlimited to the upside as bonds continue to rise.

In addition, the graph has two profit and loss lines. The top line is a curve sloping upward which represents the profit and loss at the trade's initiation based on the price of the underlying asset. The bottom line is the trade at expiration. It runs in a straight line until it crosses the price of 110, then heads upward, crossing the break-even point. Break-evens are always calculated at the price of the underlying and therefore, in the case of bonds, must be expressed in 32nds. The break-even of a long call option by expiration is derived by adding the cost of the option to its strike price. In this example, the

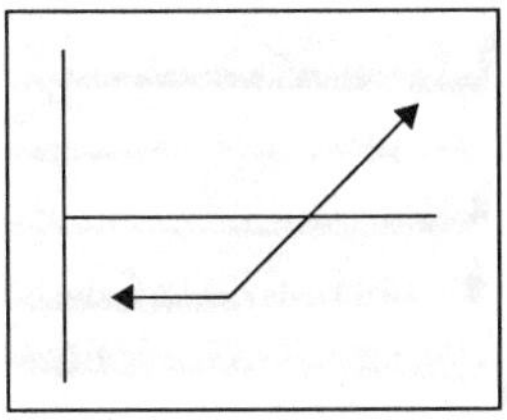

Strategy: Buy a call option.

Risk: Limited.

Profit: Unlimited.

Time Decay Effect: Detrimental.

Situation: Bullish on the market. Expect a move above break-even.

Profit: Unlimited with the increase of price in the underlying instrument.

Risk: Limited to the premium paid for the call option.

Break-even: Call strike price plus call premium.

Figure 9.4 Strategy Review—Long Call

break-even is equal to 113^025 or $113^{2.5}/_{32}$ ($110 + 3^5/_{64} = 113^5/_{64} = 113^{2.5}/_{32}$). (See Figure 9.4.)

THE SHORT CALL

In a short call trade, you are selling call options on futures or stock contracts. This strategy is placed when you expect the price of the underlying instrument to fall. If you want to go short a call, your risk curve would look like the graph in Figure 9.5. When the underlying instrument's price falls, you make money; when it rises, you lose money. This strategy provides limited profit potential with unlimited risk. It is often used to get high leverage on an underlying security that you expect to decrease in price.

In the case of selling options, be advised that you will initially receive money into your account in the from of a credit. This is the premium for which you sold the option. This strategy is used to generate income from the short sale of an option, since it provides immediate premium to the seller. The profit is limited to the premium received, and the position has an unlimited upside risk. If you sell a call, your risk curve slopes down to

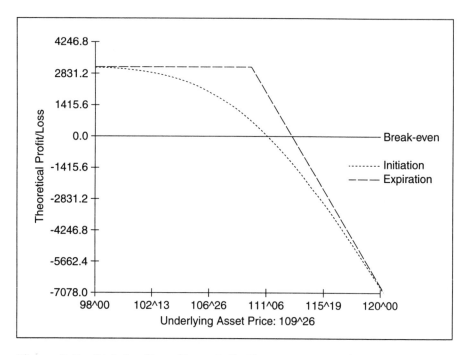

Figure 9.5 Risk Profile—Short Call (Short 1 Sep Bond Futures 110 Call @ 3^05)

the right into the loss zone as shown in the example of a short bond call in Figure 9.5. This is a very risky strategy, because it leaves you completely unprotected and requires a margin deposit to place the trade.

This example shows the trader short 1 Sep Bond 110 Call @ 3^05. The trader collected a $3078.12 [(3 × $1000) + (5 × 15.625) = $3078.12] credit minus commissions for this trade. The maximum reward is the credit the trader has received. However, the risk on this trade is unlimited if the price of the underlying asset rises, as the graph shows. The break-even of a short call equals the strike price of the call option plus the call premium. In this trade, the break-even at expiration is 113^025 (110 + $3^5/_{64}$ = $113^5/_{64}$ = $113^{2.5}/_{32}$). This is stated in 32nds ($^5/_{64}$ = $^{2.5}/_{32}$). If the market were to drop, the position would increase in value to the amount of premium taken in for the call. There is unlimited risk to the upside in the sale of a call above the break-even point. Notice on the risk graph that as the price of the asset rises, the loss of the short call position increases as well.

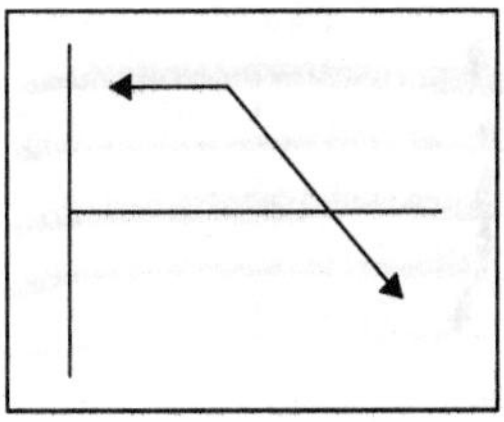

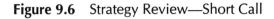

Strategy: Sell a call option.

Risk: Unlimited.

Profit: Limited.

Time Decay Effect: Helpful.

Situation: Bearish on the market. Expect falling or stable market.

Profit: Limited to the credit received for the call premium.

Risk: Unlimited as the price of the underlying instrument rises.

Break-even: Call option strike price plus call premium received.

Figure 9.6 Strategy Review—Short Call

Usually when you sell calls, you must have a bearish or neutral view of the market. (See Figure 9.6.) Remember that selling options gives you limited profits and *unlimited risk*. As mentioned earlier, you should not try selling calls until you have developed quite a bit of experience in options as a whole. It is very important that you learn how to create covered positions (i.e., sell an option and buy an option) to limit your risk and protect against unlimited loss.

THE LONG PUT

In a long put trade, you are buying put options on futures or stock contracts. This strategy is used when you expect the price of the underlying instrument to fall. If you want to go long a put, your risk curve would look like the graph in Figure 9.7. When the underlying instrument's price falls, you make money; when it rises, you lose money. This strategy provides unlimited profit potential with limited risk.

This position consists of going long 1 Sep Bond 110 Put @ 2^31. The cost of this position is $2484.38 [(2 × 1000) + (31 × 15.625) = 2484.38] plus

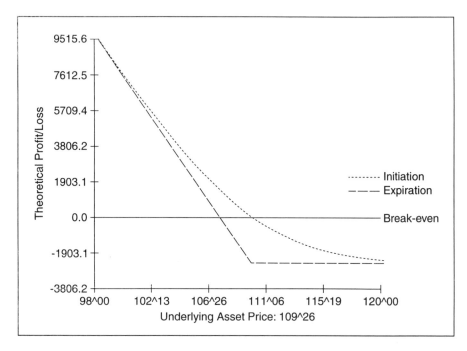

Figure 9.7   Risk Profile—Long Put (Long 1 Sep Bond Futures 110 Put @ 2^31)

commissions. The risk for this trade is limited to the premium of the put option while the reward is unlimited to the downside until the underlying asset reaches zero. Again with this graph, notice the profit and loss. Can you see the break-even point? The break-even is found by subtracting the premium from the put option's strike price. In this trade, bonds would have to move below the break-even of $107^{16.5}/_{32}$ ($110 - 2^{31}/_{64} = 107^{33}/_{64} = 107^{16.5}/_{32}$) to make a profit.

The long put strategy is often used to get high leverage on an underlying security that is expected to decrease in price. It requires a fairly small investment and consists of buying one or more puts with any strike and any expiration. (See Figure 9.8.) The buyer of put options has limited risk over the life of the option, regardless of the movement of the underlying asset. The put option buyer's maximum risk is limited to the amount paid for the put. The break-even of the put option by expiration is derived by subtracting the option premium paid from the strike price. Profits are realized in this

Strategy: Buy a put option.

Risk: Limited.

Profit: Unlimited.

Time Decay Effect: Detrimental.

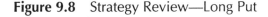

Situation: Bearish on the market. Look for a falling market.

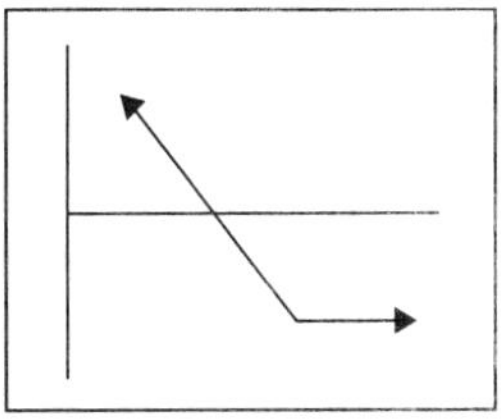

Profit: Unlimited with the decline of the underlying instrument until the asset reaches 0.

Risk: Premium paid for the put option.

Break-even: Put option strike price minus put premium.

Figure 9.8   Strategy Review—Long Put

case as the put increases in value as the underlying asset's value falls. There is no limit to the profit in buying put options. You are limited only by the fall in the price of the underlying asset.

THE SHORT PUT

In a short put trade, you are selling put options on futures or stock contracts. This strategy is used when you expect the price of the underlying instrument to rise. If you want to go short a put, your risk curve would look like the graph in Figure 9.9. When the underlying instrument's price rises, you make money; when it falls, you lose money. This strategy provides limited profit potential with unlimited risk. It is often used to get high leverage on an underlying security that you expect to increase in price. (See Figure 9.10.)

Once again, this position is similar to selling calls, only the risk graph shows a different profile. As explained earlier, when you sell options, you will initially receive a credit—the premium for which you sold the option—in the form of a credit into your account. The premium received is your maximum reward. The position has an unlimited downside risk until the underlying asset reaches zero.

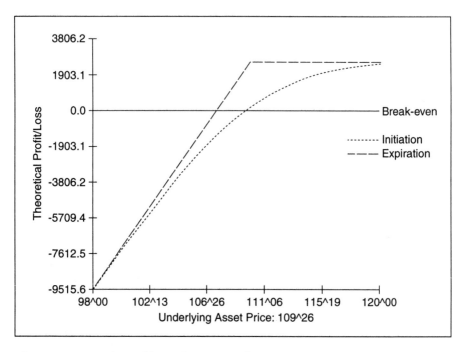

Figure 9.9   Risk Profile—Short Put (Short 1 Sep Bond Futures 110 Put @ 2^31)

This example shows a trader short 1 Sep Bond 110 Put @ 2^31. In this trade, the maximum reward is the credit received for selling the put option, or \$2484.38 [(2 × \$1000) + (31 × 15.625) = \$2484.38]. However, the risk on this trade is unlimited (until the bonds reach zero) if the bonds decline, as the graph shows. The maximum profit on this trade is the amount collected for the option (\$2484.38 minus commissions). The break-even on this position for the seller is derived by subtracting the premium received from the strike price of the put. In this case, the break-even is $107^{16.5}/_{32}$ ($110 - 2^{31}/_{64} = 107^{33}/_{64} = 107^{16.5}/_{32}$). If bonds rise above this price, the trade makes money. You earn the premium with the passage of time as the short option loses value.

What kind of a view of the market would you have to sell puts? You would have a bullish or neutral view. The break-even for initiating the trade is the strike price at which the puts are sold minus the premium received. If the market were to rise, the position would increase in value to the amount

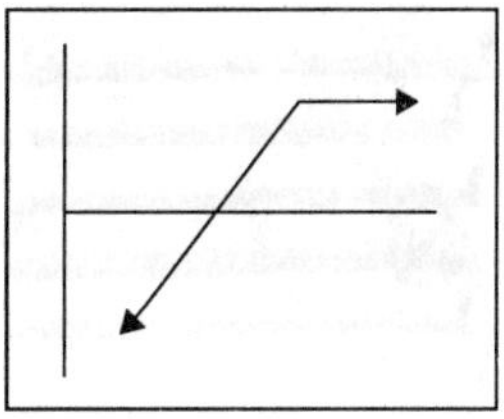

Strategy: Sell a put option.

Risk: Unlimited.

Profit: Limited.

Time Decay Effect: Helpful.

Situation: Bullish on the market. Expect rising or stable market.

Profit: Limited to the credit received for the put premium.

Risk: Unlimited as the price of the underlying instrument falls, until asset reaches 0.

Break-even: Put option strike price minus put premium received.

Figure 9.10   Strategy Review—Short Put

of premium taken in for the puts. By looking at the graph, notice that as the price of the asset falls, the loss of your short put position increases. This strategy requires a margin deposit to place.

CONCLUSION

You have now been introduced to the six basic risk profiles. Risk curves of more advanced strategies are just combinations of these six basic risk graphs. To be a successful trader, you must learn how to combine trading instruments to create an optimal risk curve. For example, selling options alone (naked options) gives you limited profit and unlimited risk. I never recommend selling naked options. Instead, I prefer to sell options by hedging the position to limit my risk. This makes my profit potential much less dependent on market direction. Typically, an optimal risk curve is a combination of these simpler strategies to create a U-shaped curve, as will be discussed later in this book.

10

Risk and Margin

When you put on a trade, you need to look at the worst-case scenario to determine just how much your investment could possibly lose. Then you have to decide just how much you are willing to risk—$100, $1000, or $100,000? When professional traders put on a trade, the first thing they look at (if they know what they're doing) is their risk.

For example, if you're a trader with a large bank trading in currencies, you're not trading just $100. You're trading $10 million per contract. To be able to profitably handle such sums, these traders have to be able to manage their risk. The most profitable trades have two key elements: limited risk and unlimited reward. After all, you can create trades with limited risk all day long, but most of them will also have a limited reward. A $100 risk for a $100 reward is simply not acceptable. No one wants to risk $100 to get $100, even if you win 50 percent of the time. Only if you increase your winning percentage will it be an acceptable risk to reward ratio. Would you take a $100 risk for a $500 reward? I would. But how many times are you going to be right? That's why it's imperative to find trades with limited risk and strong rewards with a high probability of being correct.

I am frequently asked, "What will it cost me to invest?" This is a difficult question to answer. The necessary amount depends on a number of factors. The most important factors are the size of the transaction (number of shares/futures or options) and the risk calculated on the trade.

There are two types of transactions—cash and margin. Cash trades require you to put up 100 percent of the money. Margin trades allow you to put up a percentage of the calculated amount in cash, and the rest is on account. Both types of accounts are set up to settle trades and payments for trades; yet, they are quite different. With a cash account, all transactions are paid in full by settlement day. Most of the time, the cash is already in the account before the trade is placed. If you bought 100 shares of IBM at 100, this trade would cost $10,000 plus commissions paid out of your cash account. If IBM were to rise to 110, your account would then show an open position profit of $1000, or a 10 percent rise in the account.

WHAT IS MARGIN?

Margin is defined as the amount of cash required to be on deposit with your clearing firm to secure the integrity of the trade. Most traders and investors prefer margin accounts in order to leverage their assets to produce a higher return. The amount of margin required on every trade is the calculated figure required by securities and commodities regulators, exchanges, and brokers to protect them from default. Margin is the amount required to protect these various parties against your "falling off the face of the earth."

A margin account allows the trader to borrow against the securities owned. In order to set up a margin account, you have to fill out additional applications with your broker. You can use the money for anything you want; however, many traders use it as a type of leveraging vehicle with which to buy more stock. Margin accounts allow a trader to extract up to 50 percent of the cash value of securities, or to have two-to-one leverage in buying stocks. This means that for every share of stock you own, the brokerage firm will lend you money to buy another share. This doubles your reward, but also *doubles your risk.*

If you buy 200 shares of IBM at 100 using a margin account, this trade will cost $10,000 plus commissions ($20,000 ÷ 2), since the brokerage firm loans you the money to purchase half of this position. If IBM were to rise to 110, the margin account would show an open position profit of $2000, or a 20 percent rise in the account, while you still only have $10,000 invested in this position.

The margins on futures are significantly lower than the margins on stocks. The increased leverage that futures markets offer has contributed to their rise in popularity. As previously discussed, the margin requirements for futures vary from market to market. These requirements change frequently as the price of the commodity fluctuates. A margin requirement chart is included in the Appendix; however, you should check with your broker to determine the current margin requirement for any futures you are considering trading. In most cases, if your trade starts to lose money, you will receive a margin call from your broker which requires you to increase your margin deposit to maintain your position.

When trading a margin account, brokerage firms charge interest against the cash loaned to the trader. The interest rate is usually broker call rate plus the firm's add-on points. The rate is lower than for most loans due to the fact that it is a secure loan. The broker has your stock, and in most cases will get cash back before you get your stock back.

Keeping your margin requirement low is essential to lowering stress. Many people find it difficult to stay in a high-stress trade. They think about it too much, fretting about how they might lose $5000. After all, it took them two months to earn that $5000. Suddenly, they're out of the game. Lowering your stress gives you a clear mind with which to make good decisions. When you put on a trade, try to keep the cost of capital as low as possible and the return on your investment as high as possible. Maintaining a low margin is the natural extension of limiting your risk.

If you are buying options as part of your delta neutral strategy, or doing futures with options, your margins should be pretty close to zero. You will, however, have to pay for the options in full. Now, as the trade starts working, if your futures side makes money, you shouldn't really have to add any more money to your margin account. However, if your futures side is losing money, you may have to. There's nothing like receiving a margin call in the early hours of the morning to ruin your whole day.

If you have a $100,000 account and you spend $50,000 on your options, there is still $50,000 in your account to support a losing futures position. The problem is that in the options market you cannot touch your long option value, although it is probably keeping pace with the futures loss. It is almost like it's in escrow. It's there, but you cannot touch it. The only way you can get to it is to exit your position. You may have to add more money temporarily to your account to stay in the trade.

If money was absolutely no object whatsoever—go ahead and dream big—then you wouldn't care if you had to feed your account. You'd probably be better off if your option side was the one working because of the long gamma. For example, let's say you initiate a delta neutral trade with ATM options. As the market goes up, your options are getting longer and longer. That is definitely the preferable position to be in. Unfortunately, for most of us, money is not only an object, but the driving force behind most of our decisions each and every day.

When you are choosing which side you should concentrate on—the long side or the short side for your futures—keep in mind that you may have to add more money. This is why it is sometimes beneficial to try to forecast market direction. Loans against your securities do not have any scheduled payments. Therefore, you can pay back your loan on your terms. Borrowing from your margin account also has tax considerations if you have stock that you do not want to sell.

If the perceived risk of your trade increases, then the margin requirement will also increase. If you have enough money in your account to cover the increased perceived risk, then you won't be required to put up any more money. However, if you do not have the cash required to cover this additional perceived risk, then you will get a margin call. A margin call is a call from your broker requiring you to place additional funds in your account. If you do not place these additional funds in your account, your positions will be liquidated. (If you bought something it will be sold, and if you sold something it will be repurchased. This will close out your position.)

Why should you be concerned about margin? Most new investors and traders rarely consider the margin other than from the standpoint of how much money they have to put up initially. However, an investor or trader should look at margin as a cost of doing business. There may also be opportunity costs incurred by placing a trade. In other words, the best way to make money over the long term is to use limited resources (capital) to achieve the highest return with the lowest risk over the shortest period of time. You may have a chance to put on 10 different trades, each with different risk/reward and timing profiles. Each potential trade should be placed in order of the highest return on capital with the least risk.

New investors or traders need time to figure this out. However, once you reach a level of proficiency sufficient to understand and numerically calculate these levels and categorize them, you will achieve your goal of generating the highest return while minimizing your risk.

Let's take a look at the established general margin requirements. Then we will explore some examples of capital analysis.

MARGIN REQUIREMENTS

Stocks

Based on the rules of the Securities and Exchange Commission and the clearing firms, margin equals 50 percent of the amount of the trade. For example, if 100 shares of IBM at $100 cost $10,000, then you are required to have a minimum of $5000 on deposit in your margin account. There are other levels, but the general public rule of thumb is leverage equals two to one. If the price of the stock rises, then everyone wins. If the price of the stock falls below 75 percent of the total value of the investment, the trader receives a margin call from the broker requesting additional funds to be placed in the margin account. Brokerages may set their own margin requirements, but it is never less than 75 percent, which is the amount required by the Fed.

Margin on short selling stocks is extremely expensive. You have to be able to cover the entire cost of the stock plus 50 percent more. This value will change as the market price fluctuates. For example, if you wanted to short sell 100 shares of IBM at $100 each, you would need to have $15,000 as margin in your account—that's $10,000 plus 50 percent more. If the market price falls, you can buy back the shares at the lower price to repay the loan from your broker and pocket the difference. If the stock price rises, you will be required to post additional margin. Exactly how much is up to the discretion of your broker.

Futures

Margin requirements for futures vary significantly from market to market due to the volatility of the markets as well as the current price. A comprehensive Margin Commodity Table detailing a variety of futures margins can be found in the Appendixes. However, you should consult your broker for current margin requirements or check our Web site at www.MarketScoreboard.com.

Options

Long options do not require margins. They must be paid for up front, but at a fraction of the cost of buying the underlying futures contract or stock. For example, since each point in stocks costs $100, a stock option at $3\frac{1}{2}$ will cost you $350 regardless of the underlying asset's current market price.

However, if you chose to short sell the same option, you would have to have a certain amount of margin in your account. If you were short selling the option without a corresponding hedge, many brokers would require at least $50,000 in your account to place a short option trade. If you are hedging the short option, then the margin amount is up to your broker's discretion.

Selling naked options—placing a trade with unlimited risk—has the highest margin requirements. (You should never sell naked options. All short options should have a corresponding long option to cover you against unlimited risk.)

Combination Trades

Combining the buying and selling of options, stocks, and/or futures creates a more complex calculation; however, this can reduce your margin requirements dramatically. An important rule of thumb: If you're worried about the margin at the onset of the trade, you should not be doing the trade. This rule keeps me away from putting on positions that are much larger than I can really handle. Obviously, the larger your capital base becomes, the less you worry about margin. However, it's always in your best interest to look for the best trade—one with the highest return and the lowest risk—no matter how much money you have available in your account. Individuals with large investment accounts may be tempted to make trades that are too big for their knowledge level. Start small. Build your account intelligently as you build your knowledge base.

CAPITAL ANALYSES

Let's explore a few examples to get a better feel for risk, margin, and leverage.

Gold Futures

Margin:	$1350
Price:	$290
Contract value:	$290 × 100 = $29,000
Leverage:	approximately 21 to 1
1 percent move:	+/–$290
Percent return on margin on 1 percent move:	$290 ÷ $1350 = 21 percent

S&P 500 Stock Index Futures

Margin:	$12,562
Price:	$975
Contract value:	$975 × 250 = $243,750
Leverage:	approximately 19 to 1
1 percent move:	+/–$2437
Percent return on margin on 1 percent move:	$2437 ÷ $12,562 = 19 percent

Crude Oil Futures

Margin:	$2025
Price:	$20
Contract value:	$20 × 1000 = $20,000
Leverage:	approximately 10 to 1
1 percent move:	+/–$200
Percent return on margin on 1 percent move:	$200 ÷ $2025 = 10 percent

IBM Stock

Margin:	$500
Price:	$100
Value of 10 shares:	$100 × 10 = $1000
Leverage:	2 to 1
1 percent move:	+/–$10
Percent return on margin on 1 percent move:	$10 ÷ $500 = 2 percent

Example Summary

Gold futures:	21 percent return on a 1 percent move
S&P 500 Stock Index futures:	19 percent return on a 1 percent move
Crude oil futures:	10 percent return on a 1 percent move
IBM stock:	2 percent return on a 1 percent move

The first three examples are futures contracts. The last example (IBM) is a stock. As you can see, you get a great deal more leverage (ability to use less capital for a larger potential return) by trading in the futures markets than you do in the stock market. This is what attracts the majority of individuals to the futures market—dreams of big profits using small sums of money.

However, with leverage also comes risk. On a 1 percent move against you in the first three examples (futures transactions), you can lose a great deal more than in the last example, which is a stock transaction. This is why individuals who are seriously risk-conscious typically stay away from futures speculation; they are looking at the negative consequences of a move against them.

CONCLUSION

You must be aware of all the risks—as well as potential rewards—regardless of whether you're looking to make investments in stocks or trade in futures. It is essential to understand the risks, and most importantly, learn how to protect yourself intelligently when investing and trading. To achieve success, you must become a risk manager. In the beginning, this will not be easy. That's why it's so important to start small. Mistakes will be made and you don't want your account to be wiped out before you get the chance to spread your wings. Practice the art of risk management by setting up paper trades. Learning to protect yourself by managing your risk is the most vital part of successful trading.

11

Basic Trading Strategies

There are three fundamental approaches on which all trading strategies are based: strategic trades, long-term trades, and delta neutral trades. Each has its own set of conditions and rules that foster a unique trading style.

Strategic trades are typically short-term trading opportunities geared especially for day traders and short-term traders who have the opportunity to monitor the markets very closely each day. Strategic trades are specific to certain markets and may be driven by economic data or events. Many strategic traders use the S&P 500 as the key index on which they focus their attention when trading stock market–related instruments. The Dow is also watched closely to tip off certain bond and currency trades. Traders who consistently use a strategic trading approach will develop their own personal trading style based on the patterns they have encountered in the markets.

Long-term trading methodologies differ greatly from strategic trades. Long-term traders do not look at trades from a second-to-second perspective. Instead, they approach trades from the perspective of a couple of days to a few months, or even into the next year. These trades are based more on market trends and seasonal factors. They take a while to blossom and bear fruit, which gives the long-term trader more time to develop the art of patience.

Delta neutral trades make up the third kind of trades, and probably the most complex. These strategies create hedged trades in which the overall position delta equals zero. As the market rises and falls, the overall position delta moves away from zero. Adjustments can then be made by buying or selling instruments in such a way to bring the overall position delta back to zero. Each adjustment has profit-making potential. Most delta neutral trades can be structured in such a way that your total cost and risk are minimized.

Delta neutral trading strategies and longer-term trading opportunities are better suited for traders who are not able to sit in front of their computers all day watching the markets move. Successful delta neutral traders create a trading system with a time frame they feel comfortable working in. You can create trades that are three months out, some that are two months out, some that are one month out, some that are one day out. If you are the type of person who does not want to think about your trading every single day, simply take a longer-term approach.

Delta neutral strategies can be applied to any market. It can be advantageous to learn to trade both futures and stocks. Even if you think you want to just trade futures, you can make just as much money trading stocks if you use delta neutral strategies. The Options Strategy Quick Reference Guide in the Appendixes summarizes the wide variety of option strategies that can be applied to futures and stock markets, including delta neutral strategies. The chart details profit potential, risk potential, time decay effect, and the market outlook you should probably have to implement a particular strategy.

COVERED WRITE

Covered Call

The strategy that seems to be promoted most by the investment community is covered call writing (selling). Many stockbrokers use this technique as their primary options strategy, perhaps because it is the one technique they are trained to share with their clients. It is also widely used by many so-called professional managers. Nevertheless, it can be a dangerous strategy for those who do not understand the risks involved. A few publications describe this technique as a "get rich quick" method for investing in the stock market, but it can become a "get poor quick" strategy if done incorrectly.

What is this technique all about? The purpose of the covered write is to increase cash income from a stock or futures position. It provides some protection against decreases in the price of a long underlying position or increases in the price of a short underlying position. A covered write has limited profit potential and can result in substantial losses; but these potential losses are less than those for an unprotected long stock or futures position.

The basis of a covered call write is the purchase of a stock (or futures contract) and the sale of a call option against the purchased underlying asset. Remember, the buyer of a call option has the right to "call" the option seller (writer) to deliver the stock at the price at which the option was purchased. Therefore, if you write an option you are the seller, and you are responsible for delivering the stock at the strike price at which the option was sold to the purchaser if the option is exercised. At the inception of the transaction, you receive a premium, which pays you for the time value of the option as well as any intrinsic value the option may have at that time.

You may be wondering what is wrong with the whole concept of covered call writing. Why are so many people incorrect when they use this strategy? Many traders simply do not know the risks they are assuming when they implement this overused technique. If you placed covered calls in stocks that only go up, you could make out very well. However, how many people pick stocks that only go up?

Let's look at an example using a technology stock. Dell Computer (Corporation), one of the world's leading computer sellers, made more than 400 percent in a one-year period. (With profits like this, it's no wonder that high-technology stocks have become so popular in the investment community in the last decade.) Let's say Dell Computer is trading at $89 per share after numerous stock splits, and we decide to place a covered call trade.

Step 1: Buy the Stock.   Let's buy 100 shares of Dell Computer at $89 each. This part of the trade costs $8900 ($89 × 100). The amount of margin (the capital required) would be half this amount, or $4450.

Step 2: Sell an Option.   In a covered call strategy, a trader can offset the purchase cost of stock shares with the sale of an option. The covered call consists of selling one call for each 100 shares of stock owned. The call can have any strike and any expiration. This step can be difficult. You have to choose which option to sell. You have a multitude of choices: near-term, long-term, in-the-money, out-of-the-money, at-the-money, and so on. Many covered call writers sell options one or two strikes out-of-the-money (OTM) because they want the stock to have a little room to run up before reaching the strike price at which the option was sold.

On September 9, with Dell Computer's stock trading at $89, the October 90 and 95 call options (which have 40 days to expiration) have the following option premiums: October 90 Call @ Bid $5^1/_2$, Offer $5^3/_4$; October 95 Call @ Bid $3^1/_2$, Offer $3^3/_4$.

I prefer to sell options with around 30 days left to expiration because as an options seller, I receive a credit that I hope to keep by having the stock expire out-of-the-money. I want as little time as possible on the life of the option because options lose the most value in their last 30 days. In this example I am selling an option with 40 days until expiration. I chose the October options over the September options because the September options had only 10 days remaining to expiration and therefore had very little time premium left. They were not worth selling. For example, the September 90 call could only be sold for a premium of 2, versus $5^3/_4$ for the October 90 call. The September 95 call could only be sold for $^7/_{16}$ versus $3^3/_4$ for the October 95 call.

Let's explore two covered call scenarios, one using October 90 call options, and the other using October 95 call options.

Scenario #1: Long 100 Shares of Dell Computer Stock @ 89, Short 1 Dell Computer (DLQ) Oct 90 Call @ $5^3/_4$. This transaction has two sides, the debit (purchase of stock) and the credit (sale of option). The debit equals $8900 ($89 × 100); however, the amount of margin (the capital required to place the trade) would be half this amount, or $4450. In addition, you would receive a $575 credit ($5^3/_4$ × $100 = $575) for the short option on 100 shares of stock. The risk profile for this trade is shown in Figure 11.1.

If the stock rises from $89 to $90, the strike price of the option, you make an additional $100. You also get to keep the $5^3/_4$ ($575) credit you received. In total, your profit will be $6^3/_4$ or $675. If the stock goes to $95 you still get $675. If the stock goes to $100 you still get only $675. In both these instances, you have to deliver the stock to the purchaser of the option as it will be exercised at expiration since the option is in-the-money (i.e., the stock price is greater than the strike price of the option). That means that for an investment of $3875 ($4450 – $575 = $3875), you can make $675 if the stock rises to at least 90 by expiration. That's a 17 percent return in only 40 days. The break-even of a covered call is calculated by subtracting the credit received on the short call from the price of the underlying security. In this trade, the break-even is $83^1/_4$ ($89 – $5^3/_4$ = $83^1/_4$).

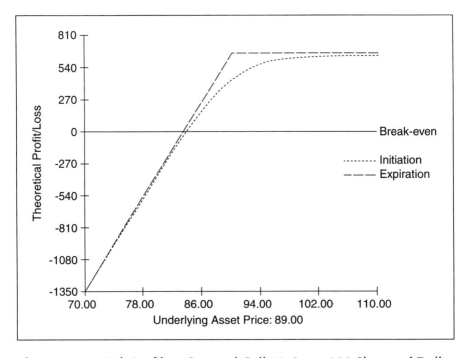

Figure 11.1 Risk Profile—Covered Call #1 (Long 100 Shares of Dell Computer Stock @ 89, Short 1 Dell Computer Oct 90 Call @ 5³/₄)

Scenario #2: Long 100 Shares of Dell Computer Stock @ 89, Short 1 Oct 95 Dell Computer Call @ 3³/₄. The debit equals $8900 ($89 × 100), and once again the margin is only half that much, or $4450. The credit equals $375 (3³/₄ = 3.75 × 100 = $375) for the short option on 100 shares of stock. The initial risk profile for this trade is shown in Figure 11.2.

For every point the stock rises, you can make $100 profit and you get to keep $375 from the option premium. The maximum profit on this trade is $975—if the stock goes up to the strike price of the option, you make the $600 on the stock rising, and you get to keep the 3³/₄ ($375) premium you received. If the stock goes to 100 you still get $975. In both of these instances, you will have to deliver the stock to the purchaser of the option as it will be exercised at expiration as the option is at- or in-the-money. For an investment of $4075 ($4450 − $375 = $4075), you can make $975 if the

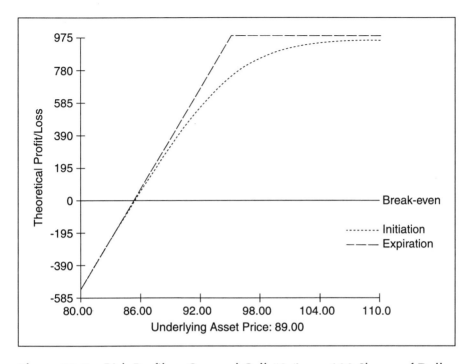

Figure 11.2 Risk Profile—Covered Call #2 (Long 100 Shares of Dell Computer Stock @ 89, Short 1 Dell Computer Oct 95 Call @ 3¾)

stock rises to at least 95 by expiration. That's a 24 percent return in only 40 days. The break-even on this trade is 85¼ (89 – 3¾ = 85¼).

There are still risks involved with this strategy. What would happen if the stock goes down? If you sell the aforementioned October 90 calls for 5¾ and buy the stock for $89, the break-even is $83¼ ($89 – 5¾ = $83¼). Overall, you are better off than if you simply purchase the stock at $89 and watch it drop, because you have reduced your break-even price by 5¾ points. Dell must drop below this new break-even price to start losing money at expiration. If you sell the October 95 calls, then your break-even price is higher at $85¼ ($89 less the 3¾ received for selling the 95 call). By selecting the higher-strike call option to sell, you will receive less of a credit, and raise your break-even price for the stock. However, then you have a greater potential return on the investment if and when the stock goes up. Obviously, you lose money when the stock goes below the break-even price. Each option has a certain trade-off for the option writer. You have to decide which one best fits the market you are trading.

As mentioned previously, the price of Dell Computer stock has been going up significantly over the past year. Covered call writing would not have hurt you. You may not have received the 400 percent gain stock purchasers received, but perhaps you could have slept better at night, as you would have reduced your break-even point. Unfortunately, traders may select stocks that have just begun a tailspin and lose 50 percent of their value overnight. In these cases, a covered call strategy will not help. These traders may get to keep the short option's credit, but that will not go very far in the light of losing 50 percent or more on the total price of the stock. There are numerous examples of companies losing 30 percent, 40 percent, 75 percent, or all their value in one day. Do not count on this strategy to save you from losing large sums of money if the stock makes a big drop. Writing covered calls can work. However, you must find stocks that meet one of two criteria: trending upwards or maintaining a trading range. Let's take a look at both scenarios.

As exhibited with Dell Computer, covered calls work well with stocks on the rise. Unfortunately, even stocks with upward trends have moments in which they make sharp corrections. These periods are difficult for covered call writers as they watch their accounts shrink, because the covered call does not offer comprehensive protection to the downside. However, in many cases good stocks will rebound. If you do choose to write covered calls, do so only in high-grade stocks that have been in a consistent uptrend and have exhibited strong growth in earnings per share.

As previously mentioned, a range-bound stock exhibits price action between two specified points: resistance and support. Resistance is the point at which prices stop rising and tend to start to drop. Support is the point at which prices stop dropping and tend to start to rise. When a stock rises it hits a certain price where the sellers rush in, outnumbering the buyers and thereby causing the prices to start to fall off. The place where the price has become low enough for buyers to start to outnumber the sellers and the price begins to rise again is the support level. If this recurs over a specified period of time (e.g., six months), strong support and resistance levels have probably been established.

Stocks that exhibit these tendencies can be excellent candidates for covered call writing. However, you must be aware that nontrending stocks also can begin trends, and many may begin trending to the downside.

Let's look at another example using a fictitious stock, XYZ. If XYZ has been in a trading range between $10 and $15 per share for six months, what is the best tactic to take? The best strategy is to buy the stock at the low end of the range ($10) and write a call one month out at least one strike out of the money. In this case, you would write a 12½ call or a 15 call, depending on the time premium you could sell. As the stock moves up, you make money on the stock and make the time premium sold. When the option expires, you write another, and you can continue to place this trade month after month. This is an optimal situation, and trading rarely goes this smoothly. However, it is the way a range-bound stock can be used profitably for covered call writing.

Another example: The risk profile in Figure 11.3 is of the following covered call trade: long 100 Shares of IBM Stock @ 106 and short 1 Jun IBM 110 Call @ 1.

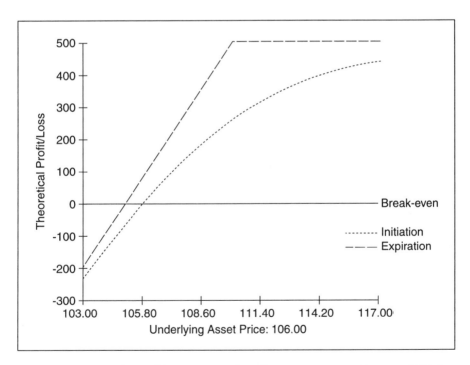

Figure 11.3 Risk Profile—Covered Call #3 (Long 100 Shares of IBM Stock @ 106, Short 1 IBM Jun 110 Call @ 1)

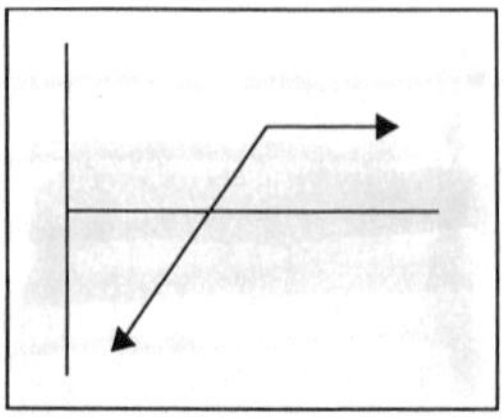

Strategy: Buy the underlying security. Sell an OTM call option.

Risk: Unlimited.

Profit: Limited.

Time Decay Effect: Helpful.

Situation: Slightly bullish to neutral. Look for a market where you expect a slow rise or stability in price with little risk of decline.

Profit: Limited to the credit received on the short call option plus (strike price of option sold less price of asset purchased) times value per point.

Risk: Unlimited as the underlying instrument falls to zero.

Break-even: Price of underlying security minus call premium received.

Figure 11.4   Strategy Review—Covered Call

In this example, the trader is bullish (believes the market will rise) on the stock and hopes to collect $100 of premium for the short call. The trader's risk is unlimited, but the combination is safer than just owning the stock because the break-even is slightly lower. Reward is limited, but additional income is received by the short sale of the option. The break-even price is calculated by subtracting the premium from the price at which the stock was sold (106 – 1 = 105). (See Figure 11.4.)

To protect yourself from severe down moves, you can combine covered calls with buying puts for protection. If you purchase long-term puts (over six months), you can continue to write calls month after month, but you will have the added protection of the long puts.

Covered Put

You can also use a covered put in a bearish market to cover the possible increase in a short stock or futures position. A covered put consists of selling

the underlying futures or stock position and selling a put to cover the underlying asset's position. This trade can be very risky, because it involves short
selling a stock that requires a high margin. The reward on a covered put is
limited to the difference in the price of the short underlying asset minus the
strike price of the short put plus the credit received for the option premium.
For example, let's create a covered put by going short 100 Shares of IBM
Stock @ 100 and short 1 Jun IBM 95 Put @ 3. The risk profile in Figure
11.5 shows a covered put trade.

The risk graph shows a covered put position at initiation and expiration.
If the market moves to the upside, there is unlimited risk. Your margin is
$15,000 (stock price plus 50 percent more); however, the credit on the short
stock is $10,000. In addition, the credit on the short put is $300. Total credit
is $10,300. The maximum reward on this trade is $800 [(100 − 95) + 3 × 100
= 800] if the trade closes at or below 95 at expiration.

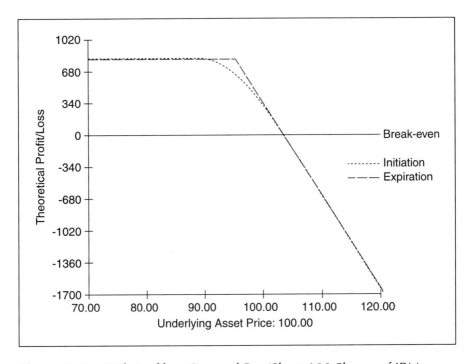

Figure 11.5 Risk Profile—Covered Put (Short 100 Shares of IBM
Stock @ 100, Short 1 IBM Jun 95 Put @ 3)

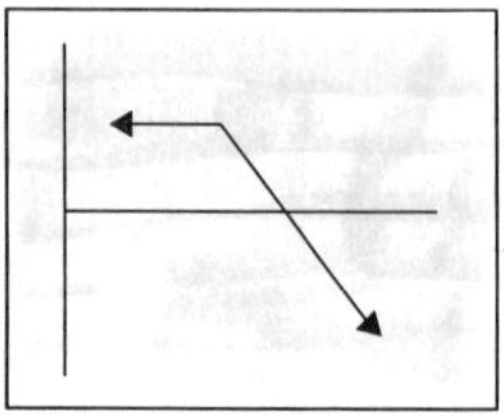

Strategy: Sell the underlying security. Sell an OTM put option.

Risk: Unlimited.

Profit: Limited.

Time Decay Effect: Helpful.

Situation: Slightly bearish to neutral. Look for a market where you expect a decline or stability in price with little risk of the market rising.

Profit: Limited to the credit received on the short put option plus (price of security sold less put option strike price) times value per point.

Risk: Unlimited as the price of the underlying increases above break-even.

Break-even: Price of underlying security plus put premium received.

Figure 11.6   Strategy Review—Covered Put

As with most short strategies, this trade is hazardous because it has unlimited risk. The break-even of a covered put strategy equals the price of the underlying asset plus the option premium. In this trade, the break-even is 103 (100 + 3 = 103). That means that if IBM moves above 103, the trade will lose $100 for each point it rises. In fact, the higher the underlying asset climbs, the more money will be lost. (See Figure 11.6.)

Both covered calls and covered puts are high-risk strategies, although they can be used to try to increase the profit on a trade. It is essential to be aware of the risks involved and to be extremely careful in selecting the underlying markets for your covered call or put writing strategies.

BULL CALL SPREAD

The bull call spread is a high-leverage strategy consisting of going long one call at a lower strike price and short one call at a higher strike price. The calls must have the same expiration date. The shortest time left to expiration usually provides the most leverage, but also provides less time to be right.

Over a limited range of stock prices, your profit on this strategy can increase by as much as 1 point for each 1-point increase in the price of the underlying asset. However, the total investment is usually far less than the amount required to buy the stock (or futures). The bull call strategy has both limited profit potential and limited downside risk.

Figure 11.7 shows an example using the following spread: long 1 Jun IBM 105 Call @ $3\frac{1}{2}$ and short 1 Jun IBM 110 Call @ $1\frac{1}{2}$ where IBM is currently trading at 106.

In this example, the difference between the premium for the long 105 call and the credit received from the short 110 call leaves a net debit of $200. The maximum risk for this trade is the debit paid for the spread ($200). The reward for the trade is calculated by subtracting the debit paid from the differences in the strike ($500 − $200 = $300). The break-even on this strategy occurs when the underlying asset's price equals the lower strike plus the net debit. In this case, the net debit is 2 points ($3\frac{1}{2} − 1\frac{1}{2} = 2$). If we add 2 points

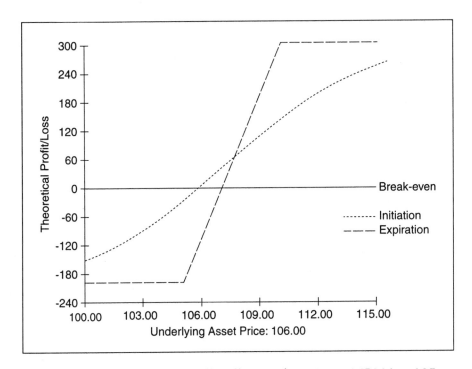

Figure 11.7 Risk Profile—Bull Call Spread #1 (Long 1 IBM Jun 105 Call @ $3\frac{1}{2}$, Short 1 IBM Jun 110 Call @ $1\frac{1}{2}$)

to 105 (the lower strike price), we get a break-even of 107. This means that the trade makes money as long as the underlying asset closes above 107.

Let's try another more detailed example in which we go long 1 Dec Gold 300 Call @ 8.50 and short 1 Dec Gold 320 Call @ 3.60 for a net debit of 4.90. The risk profile for this trade is shown in Figure 11.8.

With gold futures trading at 290, we are buying 1 Dec Gold 300 Call @ 8.50 (the call with the lower strike price) and selling 1 Dec Gold 320 Call @ 3.60 (the call with the higher strike price). However, what if we were really bullish on the gold market? If we thought the market could move up to 500, we would be implementing the wrong strategy. When you place a trade using this kind of spread, your maximum profit potential is the difference between the two strike prices (in this case between 300 and 320) minus the debit paid (8.50 – 3.60 = 4.90). This trade has a maximum profit potential of $1510 [(320 – 300) × 100] – 490 = $1510]. The maximum risk is the net

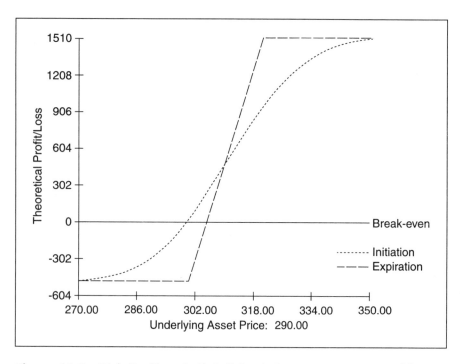

Figure 11.8   Risk Profile—Bull Call Spread #2 (Long 1 Dec Gold 300 Call @ 8.50, Short 1 Dec Gold 320 Call @ 3.60)

debit paid or $490 [(8.50 − 3.60) × 100 = $490]. The break-even on this trade is 304.90 (300 + 4.90 = 304.90). This means the trade makes a profit as long as the price of gold closes above 304.90.

A bull call spread is best used when you are moderately bullish rather than extremely optimistic about a major move in the market. (See Figure 11.9.) If you choose to simply buy the 300 call for a premium of $850, you would be trading naked with increased risk. By placing a bull call spread, you are mitigating your risk by selling the 320 call, which brings in a credit of $360. This helps to offset the overall cost of the trade, reducing your risk to only $490 out-of-pocket cost, a savings of approximately 42 percent. Even though this trade involves the sale of an option, the risk is totally covered as long as the ratio is one for one.

If gold goes to 350, the 300 call would be worth 50 (350 − 300 = 50), or $5000 (50 × $100). What happens if you're short and you sell a call? If you are assigned, you have a short position. Therefore, you are long at 300 and short at 320. If gold goes to 350, the short 320 call suffers a loss of 30. However,

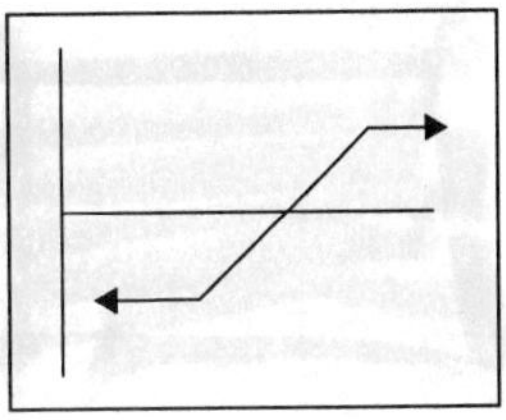

Strategy: Buy a call at a lower strike price. Sell a call at a higher strike price. Both options must have identical expiration dates.

Risk: Limited.

Profit: Limited.

Time Decay Effect: Mixed.

Situation: Look for a moderately bullish to bullish market where you expect an increase in the price of the underlying asset above the price of the call option sold.

Profit: Limited (difference in strike prices times value per point, minus net debit paid). Profit results when the market closes above the strike price of the long call plus the net debit.

Risk: Limited to the net debit paid for the spread. Maximum risk results when the market closes at or below the strike price of the long call.

Break-even: Strike price of lower call plus net debit paid.

Figure 11.9   Strategy Review—Bull Call Spread

since you made 50 on the long call, your loss has been canceled out for a profit of $1510 ($2000 – 490 debit). As long as you sell a higher strike price than the one you bought, your position is totally covered just as if you'd bought the futures and sold the call at a decreased out-of-pocket cost. Although the profit potential is capped between the two strike prices, the overall risk of the trade has been reduced. The savings could be applied to a second contract or another trade entirely. In trading, grand slams are much more rare than base hits.

BULL PUT SPREAD

In a bull put spread, you buy a lower-strike put and sell a higher-strike put using the same number of options and identical expirations. (See Figures 11.10 and 11.11.) The maximum reward of this strategy is when the market closes

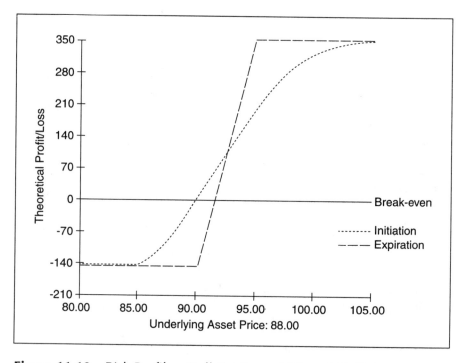

Figure 11.10 Risk Profile—Bull Put Spread (Short 1 Dell Computer Oct 95 Put @ 10, Long 1 Dell Computer Oct 90 Put @ 6½)

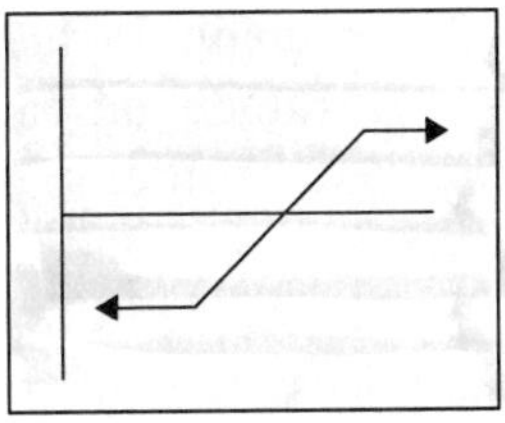

Strategy: Buy a put at a lower strike price. Sell a put at a higher strike price. Both options must have identical expiration dates.

Risk: Limited.

Profit: Limited.

Time Decay Effect: Mixed.

Situation: Look for a moderately bullish to bullish market where you expect an increase in the price of the underlying asset above the strike price of the put option sold.

Profit: Limited to the net credit received. Profit is made when the market closes above the strike price of the short put option. This is a credit trade when initiated.

Risk: Limited (difference in strikes times the value per point, minus net credit).

Break-even: Strike price of higher put minus net credit received.

Figure 11.11   Strategy Review—Bull Put Spread

above the strike price of the short put option. Therefore, this strategy is implemented when you are bullish and expect the market to close above the strike price of the put option sold. The maximum risk is equal to the difference between strike prices minus the net credit. A bull put spread receives a credit when initiated.

Basically a bull put spread combines the following positions: long one lower-strike put, short one higher-strike put. The risk profile for the following example of a bull put spread is shown in Figure 11.10: short 1 Oct 95 Dell Computer Put @ 10, long 1 Oct 90 Dell Computer Put @ 6½.

In this trade, you are bullish on Dell Computers with the stock currently trading at 88. You expect a move upward for a close above 95 by next month. To initiate a bull put spread, you sell a higher-strike put (95) and purchase a lower-strike put (90). Both strikes are close enough to allow Dell to reach the projected strike price of 95. The object of this strategy is to have both options expire worthless and be able to keep the net credit. In this example, the maximum reward is the net credit of 3½ or $350. The break-even occurs when the underlying asset's price equals the higher strike price minus the net credit. In this case, the break-even equals $91\frac{1}{2}$ [95 – (10 – $6\frac{1}{2}$) = $91\frac{1}{2}$]. This trade makes the maximum profit if Dell Computer closes at or above 95 at expiration. You get to keep a lesser portion if the trade closes between $91\frac{1}{2}$ and 95. As long as Dell closes above the break-even point of $91\frac{1}{2}$, you won't lose money. The maximum risk equals the difference in strike prices minus the net credit. In this trade the maximum risk is $150 [(95 – 90) × 100] – 350 = $150]. If Dell closes below 90, you lose $150.

BEAR CALL SPREAD

In a bear call spread, you sell the lower strike call and buy the higher strike call using the same number of options and identical expiration dates. (See Figures

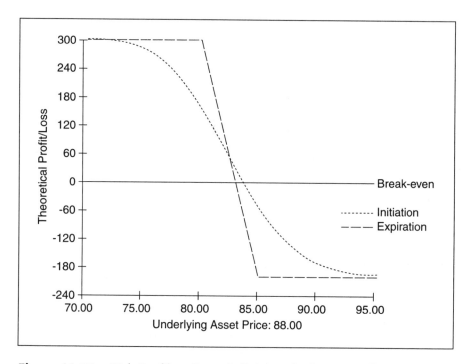

Figure 11.12   Risk Profile—Bear Call Spread (Short 1 Dell Computer Nov 80 Call @ $9\frac{5}{8}$, Long 1 Dell Computer Nov 85 Call @ $6\frac{5}{8}$)

Strategy: Buy a call at a higher strike price. Sell a call at a lower strike price. Both options must have identical expiration dates.

Risk: Limited.

Profit: Limited.

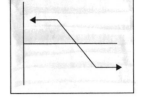

Time Decay Effect: Mixed.

Situation: Look for a moderately bearish to bearish market where you expect a decrease in the price of the underlying asset below the strike price of the call option sold.

Profit: Limited to the net credit received. Maximum profit is made when the market closes below the strike price of the short call. This is a credit trade when initiated.

Risk: Limited (difference in strike prices times value per point, minus net credit). Maximum risk results when the market closes at or above the strike price of the long option.

Break-even: Strike price of lower call plus net credit received.

Figure 11.13   Strategy Review—Bear Call Spread

11.12 and 11.13.) This is a credit trade when initiated and makes money when the market closes below the strike of the option sold. This strategy is used when you have a bearish view of a stock or future. It offers a limited profit potential with limited risk. The maximum reward is achieved when the closing price of the underlying security is below the lower strike call yielding the net credit received for the trade. Therefore, you want to implement this trade by selling options that have a high probability of expiring worthless so you can keep the net credit.

The maximum risk is equal to the difference between strike prices minus the net credit. Your maximum risk occurs when the stock or futures contract closes at or above the strike price of the option you purchased. This means that the short option will have increased in value while the one you purchased has not increased in value as much.

A bear call spread combines the following positions: short one lower strike call and long one higher strike call with the same expiration month.

For example, Dell Computer is trading at $88 and you think it's ready for a correction. You decide to initiate a bear call spread by going short 1 Dell Computer Nov 80 Call @ $9^5/_8$ and long 1 Dell Computer Nov 85 Call @ $6^5/_8$. Dell Computer is trading at 88 when the trade is placed. When you initiate this trade, you receive a credit of 3, or $300 [$(9^5/_8 - 6^5/_8) \times 100 = \$300$]. This is the maximum reward that would be earned at expiration if Dell Computer closes at or below $80 per share.

The maximum risk of $200 [$(85 - 80) \times 100] - 300 = \$200$] is reached if Dell closes at or above 85. The short option would have a value of 5 (85 less the 80 strike sold). The 85 call you purchased would expire worthless; therefore, your position would lose 5 points, or $500. However, you received a credit of $300; therefore, your risk is a net $200 ($500 – $300 = $200). The break-even on this trade occurs when the underlying stock price equals the lower strike price plus the net credit. In this trade, the break-even is 83 [$80 + (9^5/_8 - 6^5/_8) = 83$]. The trade makes money as long as Dell does not go above 83 at expiration.

BEAR PUT SPREAD

In a bear put spread, you buy a put at higher strike price and sell a put at a lower strike price (Figures 11.14 and 11.15). Both options must expire in the same month. This is a bearish strategy and should be implemented when you expect the market to close below the strike price of the short put option. This is the point of maximum reward at expiration.

A bear put spread combines going long one higher-strike put and short one lower-strike put with the same expiration month. The risk profile for the following bear put spread example is shown in Figure 11.14: long 1 Jun IBM 105 Put @ 2 and short 1 Jun IBM 100 Put @ $^1/_2$ with IBM trading at 106.

The difference between the long 105 put premium of 2 ($200) and the credit received for the short 100 put ($^1/_2$, or $50) is a net debit of $150. The net debit is the maximum risk for a bear put spread. The maximum reward for the trade is calculated by subtracting the net debit paid from the difference in the strike prices [$(105 - 100) \times 100] - 150 = \$350$]. Even though the reward is limited to $350, the break-even on this position has been lowered by selling the 100 put. The break-even occurs when the underlying asset's price equals the higher strike price minus the net debit. In this case, the break-even would be $103^1/_2$ [$105 - (2 - ^1/_2) = 103^1/_2$].

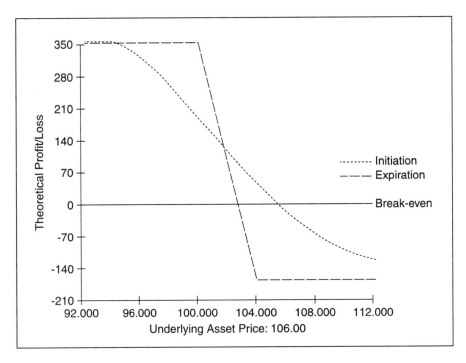

Figure 11.14 Risk Profile—Bear Put Spread (Long 1 IBM Jun 105 Put @ 2, Short 1 IBM Jun 100 Put @ ½)

This high-leverage strategy works over a limited range of stock and futures prices. Your profit on this strategy can increase by as much as 1 point for each 1-point decrease in the price of the underlying asset. Once again, the total investment is usually far less than that required to sell the stock. The bear put spread has both limited profit potential and limited upside risk. Puts with the shortest time left to expiration usually provide the most leverage, but also reduce the time frame you have for the market to move to the maximum reward strike price.

CONCLUSION

These strategies (covered call, covered put, bull call spread, bull put spread, bear call spread, and bear put spread) are six of the most basic op-

---

Strategy: Buy a put at a higher strike price. Sell a put at a lower strike price. Both options must have identical expiration dates.

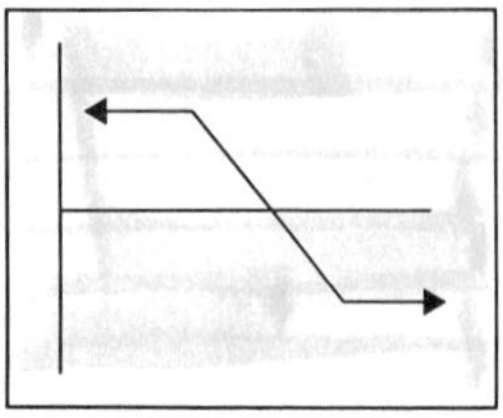

Risk: Limited.

Profit: Limited.

Time Decay Effect: Mixed.

Situation: Look for a moderately bearish to bearish market where you expect a decrease in the price of the underlying asset below the strike price of the put option sold.

Profit: Limited (difference in strike prices times value per point, minus net debit paid). Maximum profit results when the market closes at or below the strike price of the short put option.

Risk: Limited to the net debit paid for the spread. Maximum risk results when the market closes at or above the strike price of the long put.

Break-even: Strike price of higher put minus net debit paid.

Figure 11.15   Strategy Review—Bear Put Spread

tion strategies available. Since the latter four offer limited risk and limited profit, close attention needs to be paid to the risk-to-reward ratio. Never take the risk unless you know it's worth it. Each of these strategies can be implemented in any market for a fraction of the cost of buying or selling the underlying instruments straight out. Mastering these strategies gives you a strong foundation, since they are the building blocks of more advanced strategies.

12

The Nuts and Bolts
of Delta Neutral Trading

A delta neutral trader has to get in the habit of looking at various market scenarios until the optimal mathematical relationship is determined. The final strategy creates the highest probability of profitability and enables the trader to enjoy consistent returns on investments. For example, if I'm going to buy S&P futures, I'm also going to buy or sell something in the S&P options pit. When I put on one trade, I simultaneously put on another. These kinds of multiple trade strategies require a trader to consider the market from three directions. What if the market goes up? What if it goes down? What if it doesn't go anywhere at all? Do not confuse assessing the possibilities with trying to forecast market direction. Delta neutral traders do not need to guess which way the market will move because they have assessed in advance their reactions to market direction. They have set the trade up to maximize their potential profits and minimize their risk regardless of market direction.

I must admit that once in a while I still try to guess market direction. Unfortunately, I'm usually wrong. I just start guessing because I'm bored with the safety inherent in delta neutral trading. Sooner or later, I lose money and then go back to looking for the delta neutral trades, because that's where my bread and butter is.

Setting up a delta neutral trade requires selecting a calculated ratio of short and long positions to create an overall position delta of zero. As previously mentioned in Chapter 8, the delta of one futures or stock contract equals plus or minus 100. Stocks are traded in 100-share lots. That means that 100 shares of stock (or one futures contract) equals 100 deltas. If you are buying one futures contract or 100 shares of stock, you are +100 deltas; if you are selling one contract, you are −100 deltas. That's a pretty simple number to work with. It is not an abstract number. It's +100 or −100 and that's it. You can do that much in your head once you get good at it. No matter what futures contract or stock market it is— S&Ps, bonds, currencies, soybeans, IBM, Dell, or Intel—it has a delta of plus or minus 100.

Options deltas are a little more complex. They depend on what kind of option you are trading—at-the-money (ATM), in-the-money (ITM), or out-of-the-money (OTM)—which is determined by the option's strike price and its relationship to the price of the underlying asset. Let's develop an example using the gold market. If the gold market has a price of 290, and gold has options at 280, 285, 290, 295, and 300 (each $5 increment), the 290s are the ATM options. ATM options have strikes of about +50 or −50. Once again, this is a pretty easy calculation. It could be off a little bit, but plus or minus 50 is the general rule for an ATM option. This also means that there is a 50–50 chance of an ATM option closing in-the-money. It's similar to a coin flip; it can go either way.

Using these values, let's create a delta neutral trade. If we buy one futures contract, we have +100 deltas. To get to delta neutral, we have to balance out the futures contract by finding −100 deltas. This would bring our overall position delta to zero. Two ATM options can produce the required −100 deltas.

However, how do you determine which options equal −50? If you buy an ATM call, do you think you're +50 or −50? Is that a bullish or bearish sign? If you buy a call, you expect the market to go up. Therefore, you want to buy a call in a bullish market. Subsequently, if you buy an ATM call option, you have +50 deltas. Likewise, if you buy a put, it's in a bearish market and will have a delta of −50. The plus and minus just mean that you expect the market to move up or down. In the easiest of terms, buying calls creates a positive delta. Selling calls creates a negative delta. Buying puts creates a negative delta. Selling puts creates a positive delta. These rules govern all delta neutral trading opportunities.

Positive Deltas—	*Negative Deltas—*
Market Expectation Up	*Market Expectation Down*
Buy calls.	Sell calls.
Sell puts.	Buy puts.
Buy futures.	Sell futures.
Buy stocks.	Sell stocks.

Let's return to our quest for a delta neutral trade. We've entered the market with +100 deltas by buying a futures contract. To make the overall trade delta neutral, we have two choices using ATM options. We can either buy two ATM puts or sell two ATM calls. The question becomes whether it is better to sell ATM calls or buy ATM puts to get the necessary –100 deltas. When you sell an option, what happens to your account? You receive a credit for the total premiums of the options you sold. In other words, you have put money in your pocket. (However, you can't go out and spend the credit; you may have to pay it back if you are wrong. It represents a potential credit.) However, you have also assumed more risk. As usual, there's no such thing as a free lunch. Although putting money in your pocket sounds like a good thing, the unlimited risk you have to assume can be a harrowing experience.

So far, setting up a delta neutral trade has been quite simple. However, it takes experience and skill to know which strategy—sell ATM calls or buy ATM puts—has the greater chance of making money. Since delta neutral trades do not rely on market direction, a profit is possible in most cases regardless of whether the market goes up, down, or sideways. For example, we can create a delta neutral trade by purchasing one S&P futures contract and two ATM put options. If the market swings up, the futures contract makes money. However, we lose the premium paid on the two long puts. If the market takes a dive, our futures contract may lose money, but we'll make a profit on the two puts by using one as protection and making money on the other one. In other words, the deltas of my two puts will increase faster than the delta of the futures. Obviously, a major ingredient to profit-making is setting up trades in such a way that your profits outweigh your losses.

Let's try another approach to setting up a delta neutral trade. If we are intent upon buying an S&P futures contract at +100, we can offset it by selling two ATM calls. We could also sell one S&P futures contract and buy two

ATM calls or sell two ATM puts. We have now determined four ways of creating perfect delta neutral trades using ATM options.

However, options aren't always at-the-money. You can trade a wide variety of options with many different expiration dates. Many people have a problem deciding which options to work with. In general, ATM options are the easiest to work with, but not necessarily the most profitable. How do we determine which options to use? Once again, we need to visually see the profit and loss potentials of each trade by setting up its respective risk profile.

In the trade shown in Figure 12.1, the risk graph looks like a "U," which is an optimal risk curve. By purchasing futures and buying puts, a risk curve is created with unlimited potential profit and limited risk. The risk is limited to the premium paid for the ATM puts. In this case the risk is ($30 × 2) × $250 (value per point), which equals $15,000. This is the risk if you made no trade adjustments and the options expire worthless.

In the trade shown in Figure 12.2, the risk curve resembles an upside-

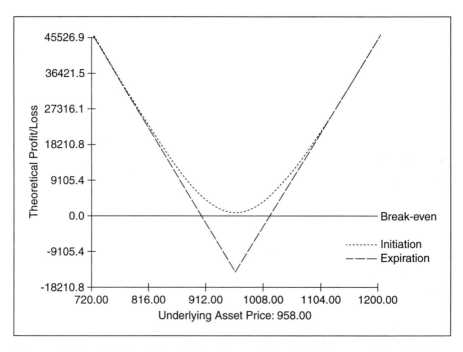

Figure 12.1   Risk Profile—Delta Neutral Trade #1 (Long 1 Dec S&P Futures @ 958.00, Long 2 Dec S&P Futures 960 Puts @ 30.00)

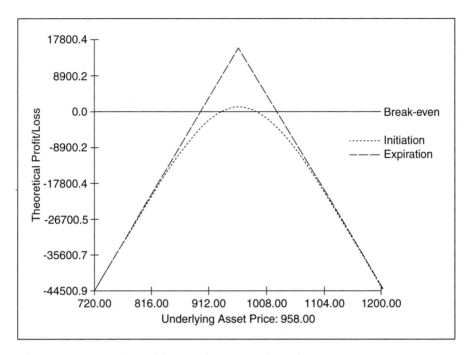

Figure 12.2   Risk Profile—Delta Neutral Trade #2 (Long 1 Dec S&P Futures @ 958.00, Short 2 Dec S&P Futures 960 Calls @ 30.00)

down "U." By purchasing futures and selling calls, we have created a risk curve with limited profit and unlimited risk. This would be the same risk curve if you purchased 100 shares of stock and sold 2 ATM calls. The maximum profit is the total credit received for the short calls, or $15,000 (2 × 30 × $250). This strategy can be quite dangerous because we're responsible for the potentially unlimited risk of the short calls. I prefer to teach traders to create trades with U-shaped curves, not upside-down U-shaped curves. Although the latter can be quite profitable, they can require traders to move quickly when things are not working out right. Typically, I favor buying futures or stock and buying puts.

You can also sell a futures contract and buy two ATM calls to make another delta neutral trade. This trade has a low margin requirement, which means that you can walk away until expiration if you want. In most cases, you would just wait to see what happens next. The risk graph for this strategy is shown in Figure 12.3. This trade has a U-shaped curve, which reflects

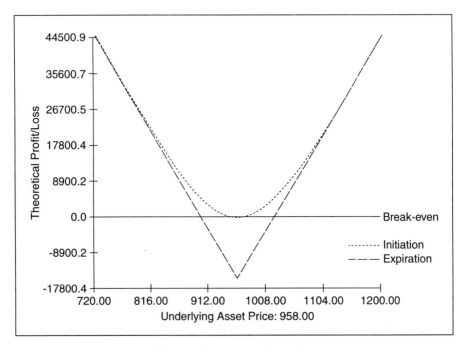

Figure 12.3   Risk Profile—Delta Neutral Trade #3 (Short 1 Dec S&P Futures @ 958.00, Long 2 Dec S&P Futures 960 Calls @ 30.00)

unlimited profit potential and risk is limited to the total premium paid or $15,000 (2 × 30 × $250).

The final possibility is to sell one futures contract and sell two ATM puts. Figure 12.4 is the risk graph that corresponds to this trade. This trade creates an upside-down U-shaped curve, which reveals limited profit potential (total credit received of $15,000) and unlimited risk. Once again, this trade involves shorting options, which can be extremely risky. If the market crashes you will lose a great deal of money. Conversely, if it moves up quickly you will also lose money.

Although all four of these examples are delta neutral trades, I urge you to avoid unlimited risk until you are have developed a strong track record. There are a variety of factors that you need to be familiar with to help you to determine which strategy has the best profit-making potential for a particular market. Once the underlying instrument moves far enough away from its initial position, you should be able to make money

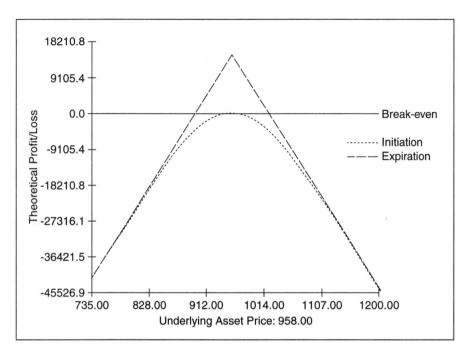

Figure 12.4 Risk Profile—Delta Neutral Trade #4 (Short 1 Dec S&P Futures @ 958.00, Short 2 Dec S&P Futures 960 Puts @ 30.00)

on one of the legs in your trade. In many cases, you can actually make a positive or negative adjustment to your original position depending on how many deltas your overall position has moved and how many contracts make up the trade.

Which strategy do I prefer? In general, I prefer lower-risk trades. They are much less stressful. However, before I would place a trade either way, I would set up a risk profile of each possible strategy and calculate my risk-to-reward ratio. This is by far the best way to find an answer to our question of buying versus selling options. In general, whenever you are buying options as part of a delta neutral trade, you are creating a risk graph with a U-shaped curve; and whenever you are selling options as part of a delta neutral trade, you are creating an upside-down U-shaped curve. I prefer to work with trades with upward U-shaped curves because they feature limited risk. This is a much safer strategy, especially for beginners. However, as you progress up your own trader's learning curve, opportunities will present themselves where you will want to take a higher risk in order to receive a potentially higher reward.

Let's take a closer look at some of the most basic delta neutral strategies before moving on to the more complex ones.

LONG STRADDLES

Buying a straddle involves buying both an ATM call and an ATM put with identical strike prices and expiration months. If you calculate the deltas, you will note that they add up to zero (long ATM call = +50; long ATM put = –50). Buying a straddle can be fairly expensive, because you have to pay both premiums and your total risk is the cost of the double premiums. For you to gain a profit, the market has to move sufficiently to make up the cost of that double premium. But, at least there are no margin requirements to worry about.

To place a long straddle, you need to locate a market with impending high volatility, such as currencies or bonds. For example, you might want to buy a straddle in the Treasury bonds during a period of low volatility in anticipation of a period of high volatility. The most volatile day of the month for the bond market is the first Friday of each month when the employment report is released. This is the mother of all reports and has the ability to move the market in an absolutely psychotic fashion, typically guaranteeing a highly volatile day. The volatility might even pick up starting on Thursday, so I often place a straddle on the previous Wednesday. One important thing to remember about straddles is that you don't have to predict market direction. Regardless of whether it moves up or down, you can make some money. The essential factor is volatility.

Two other reports have an effect on market volatility, especially the financial markets: the consumer price index (CPI) and the producer price index (PPI). Unfortunately, these do not have a fixed date of release, although they usually come out the week after the employment report (i.e., the second week of the month). You should mark these dates on your calendar as a reminder. Actually, any report can move the market if the information is unexpected regarding housing starts, durable goods, or leading economic indicators. However, the ones to pay particular attention to are the previously mentioned big three. You may have an opportunity to buy a straddle a couple of days before they appear and make some money.

For example, let's create a long straddle by going long 1 Bond Sep 102 Call @ 2^16 and long 1 Bond Sep 102 Put @ 2^16. The maximum profit of this trade is unlimited. Bond options trade in 64ths (worth $15.625) with each full point worth $1000. Therefore, each 102 option in this trade would cost $2250 [(2 × $1000) + (16 × $15.625) = $2250)] for a maximum risk of $4500. Both options have the same expiration month and the same strike price. Let's take a look at a long straddle's risk profile. As previously defined, buying a straddle requires the purchase of a call and a put at the same strike price and the same expiration period. To visualize the risk profile of a straddle, it can be helpful to imagine what each leg of the trade looks like. Risk curves of complex strategies are only combinations of more basic trades. Therefore, the risk profile of a long straddle is a combination of a long call risk curve and a long put risk curve, which creates a U-shaped curve. (See Figure 12.5.) This important factor tells us that

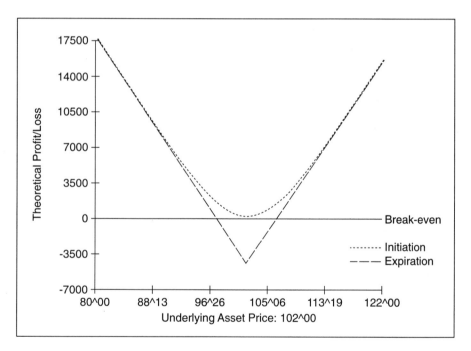

Figure 12.5   Risk Profile—Long Straddle (Long 1 Sep Bond Futures 102 Call @ 2^16, Long 1 Sep Bond Futures 102 Put @ 2^16)

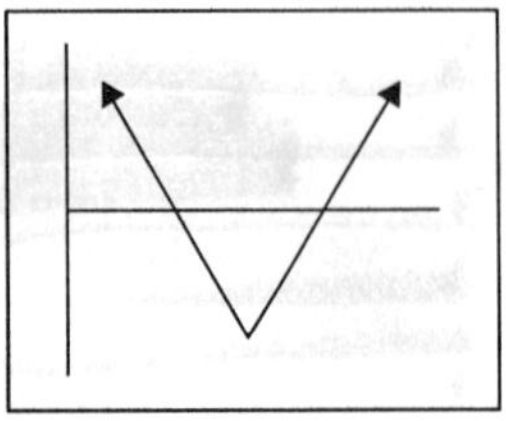

Strategy: Buy an ATM call and an ATM put with the same strike price and expiration date.

Risk: Limited.

Profit: Unlimited.

Time Decay Effect: Detrimental.

Situation: Look for a market with low volatility about to experience a sharp increase in volatility.

Profit: Unlimited. Profit requires sufficient market movement but does not depend on market direction.

Risk: Limited to the net debit paid. Margin is not required.

Upside Break-even: Strike price plus net debit paid.

Downside Break-even: Strike price minus net debit paid.

Figure 12.6   Strategy Review—Long Straddle

long straddles have unlimited profit potential and limited risk (the price of the two premiums).

When you create a long straddle, it is very important to determine the trade's range of profitability. To accomplish this, you need to calculate the upside break-even and the downside break-even. The upside break-even occurs when underlying asset's price equals the strike price plus the total premium. In the example above, the upside break-even is $106^{16}/_{32}$ ($102 + 2^{16}/_{64} + 2^{16}/_{64} = 106^{32}/_{64} = 106^{16}/_{32}$). The downside break-even occurs when the underlying asset's price equals the strike price minus the total premium. In this case, the downside break-even equals $97^{16}/_{32}$ ($102 - 4^{32}/_{64} = 97^{16}/_{32}$). The bond futures have to move below $97^{16}/_{32}$ to make money by expiration. See Figure 12.6.

SHORT STRADDLES

A short straddle involves selling both a put and a call with identical strike prices and expiration months. This strategy is useful should the underlying futures remain fairly stable. It is attractive to the aggressive strategist who is interested in selling large amounts of time premium in hopes of collecting all or most of this premium as profit. In general, this is a neutral strategy with limited profit potential (the total credit from the short options) and unlimited risk. There is a significant probability of profit-making but the risk can be very large.

For example, imagine you are selling a straddle in Japanese yen where December yen futures are trading at 74.66. (See Figures 12.7 and 12.8). The short March 75 call option is trading at 2.10 and the short March 75 put option is trading at 2.43. You forecast that the underlying yen futures contract is going to continue trading in a narrow range, which results in a decrease in volatility. Again, if you are expecting a decrease in volatility, you want to sell options. You want to sell high volatility and buy low volatility.

Remember, Japanese yen futures are at 74.66 in this example. You have

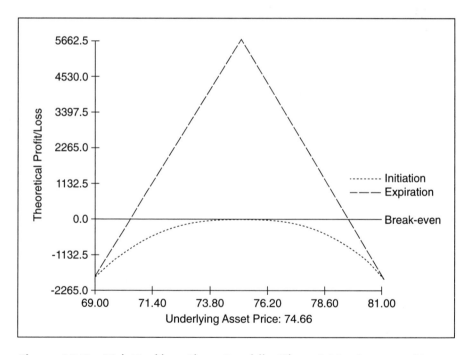

Figure 12.7   Risk Profile—Short Straddle (Short 1 Mar Japanese Yen Futures 75 Call @ 2.10, Short 1 Mar Japanese Yen Futures 75 Put @ 2.43)

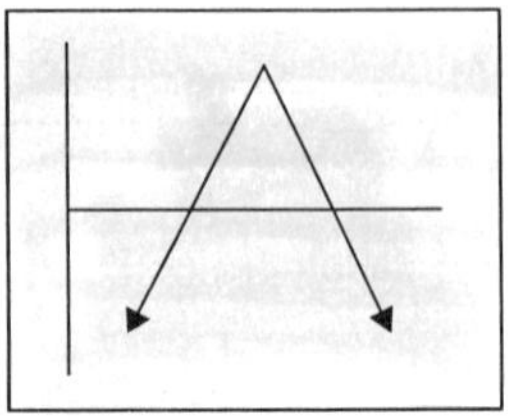

Strategy: Sell an ATM call and an ATM put with the same strike price and expiration date.

Risk: Unlimited.

Profit: Limited.

Time Decay Effect: Helpful.

Situation: Look for a highly volatile market that seems to be entering a period of low volatility.

Profit: Limited to the net credit received. The less the market moves, the better chance you have of keeping the premiums.

Risk: Unlimited on both sides. Margin is required.

Upside Break-even: Strike price plus net credit received.

Downside Break-even: Strike price minus net credit received.

Figure 12.8 Strategy Review—Short Straddle

collected 4.53 points of net premium from the short options. In the currencies, at least in yen, Swiss francs, and deutsche marks, a point in the options is worth $1250. If you multiply $1250 times 2.10 the result is $2625 that you have collected for selling the 75 call. For selling the 75 put, you receive 2.43 points, which equals $3037.50. Your net premium of 4.53 for selling the straddle translates into a maximum profit of $5662.50. The danger in this trade is that your maximum risk is unlimited on both sides. Remember, the safest trades have limited risk and unlimited reward potential or limited reward with a high probability of being correct. Although it's unlikely, the Japanese yen could go to zero. The call side is also unlimited. Luckily, at expiration, only one side could be wrong. They cannot both be wrong.

Any time you sell an option, the net credit you receive is the maximum profit. Remember, when you sell options, you do not want market movement. You want the market to stabilize and go in a straight line. In this trade, you have collected $5662.50. If the yen stays between 79.53 and 70.47, you will make a profit. This is referred to as the profit range. When you sell straddles, it is vital to calculate this range by calculating the upside and downside break-evens. This will enable you to determine the point at which the trouble starts. The upside break-even occurs when the underlying asset's price equals the option strike price plus the net premium. The downside break-even occurs when the underlying asset's price equals the option strike price minus the net premium. For example, the net premium for this trade is 4.53. Therefore, the upside break-even is calculated by adding 4.53 to 75 to get 79.53. The downside break-even is calculated by subtracting 4.53 from 75, which equals 70.47. Thus, your profit range exists between 79.53 and 70.47.

If futures rise to 81 (remember they were at 74.66 when we sold the 75 straddle), then the put that you have sold is worthless now, which is great. You get to keep the money on the put side. But the call that you sold has gone against you. It is now in-the-money by 6 points, so you have a loss there. You have received 4.53 points for selling this straddle. You have to buy the call back at 6 for a loss of 1.47 or $1837.50. You have lost money on the trade, but it could have been worse.

What happens if the futures rise to 78? Remember, they were at 74.66. Since the put is still worthless, you get to keep the money you received on the put side (2.43 points = $3037.50). The call is in-the-money by 3 points, so you have to buy it back for 3 points or $3750. That leaves a balance of 1.53 (4.53 – 3) points, which translates to $1912.50—a tidy little profit. You did not get to keep all the money you originally collected, but you still made a profit.

If futures fall to the downside break-even of 70.47, you are going to lose 4.53 on the put. But, you are going to keep all the money on the call side. You took in 4.53 points; now you have to buy it back for 4.53 points. This makes the trade a washout except for commissions.

The risk profile for a short straddle looks like the opposite of a long straddle's risk graph. Since a long straddle has a U-shaped curve, a short straddle has an upside-down U-shaped curve because it is the combination of a short call and a short put. This shape clues us into the fact that short straddles have limited profit potential and unlimited risk.

If a market moves significantly from the center line, you have unlimited potential to make profits when buying a straddle and unlimited risk when selling the straddle. Maximum profit is achieved if the market closes exactly at 75 on the expiration date. Selling straddles is a risky trade unless you find markets that are not likely to move away from a center line. There are methods that can be utilized to substantially reduce the risks associated with this strategy. One strategy to help reduce risk is to buy a strangle against it, thereby creating a condor.

LONG STRANGLES

Strangles are quite similar to straddles, except they use OTM options. This changes the dynamics of the trade entirely. To construct a long strangle, you buy both an OTM call and an OTM put with the same expiration month but different strike prices. For example, if September bonds are currently priced at 102, you could buy a September bond 106 call and a September bond 98 put. (See Figures 12.9 and 12.10.) Once again, although you have no margin requirement, you are still going to have to pay both premiums. However, you are going to pay less than if you bought a straddle, because a strangle uses OTM options. Unfortunately, even though they cost less, you will need the market to make even greater moves to ever get your money out. Let's use an example where bonds are trading at 102^00 when the trade is placed. The risk profile for this trade is shown in Figure 12.9.

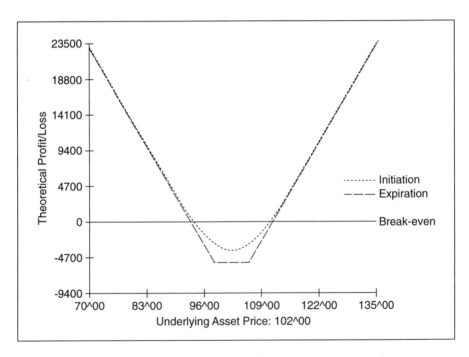

Figure 12.9 Risk Profile—Long Strangle (Long 1 Sep Bond Futures 106 Call @ 3^16, Long 1 Sep Bond Futures 98 Put @ 2^16)

Strategy: Buy an OTM call and an OTM put with the same expiration date.

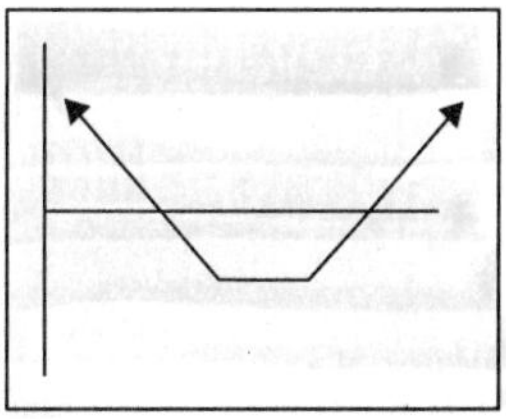

Risk: Limited.

Profit: Unlimited.

Time Decay Effect: Detrimental.

Situation: Look for a relatively stagnant market where you anticipate an explosion of volatility.

Profit: Unlimited. Profit requires expansive market movement but does not depend on market direction.

Risk: Limited to net debit paid. Loss is less than that of a straddle. Margin is not required.

Upside Break-even: Call strike price plus net debit paid.

Downside Break-even: Put strike price minus net debit paid.

Figure 12.10   Strategy Review—Long Strangle

This trade is delta neutral because both OTM options combine to create an overall position delta of zero (OTM call = +30; OTM put = −30). The maximum risk on this trade is the cost of the double premiums, which equals \$5500 [($3^{16}/_{64} + 2^{16}/_{64} = 5^{32}/_{64}$) = (5 × \$1000) + (32 × \$15.625) = \$5500]. Your maximum profit is unlimited. As shown by the long strangle's U-shaped risk curve, this strategy has unlimited profit potential and limited risk. The upside break-even occurs when the underlying asset equals the call strike price plus the net debit paid. In this case, the upside break-even equals $111^{16}/_{32}$ ($106 + 5^{32}/_{64} = 111^{32}/_{64} = 111^{16}/_{32}$). The downside break-even occurs when the underlying asset equals the put strike price minus the net debit. The downside break-even equals $92^{16}/_{32}$ ($98 − 5^{32}/_{64} = 92^{32}/_{64} = 92^{16}/_{32}$). The profit range is therefore above 111^16 and below 92^16. Unfortunately, profit depends on a large move in the underlying instruments. A market with extremely high volatility might give you the kick necessary to harvest a profit from a long strangle.

SHORT STRANGLES

A short strangle is simply the opposite of a long strangle—you sell an OTM call and an OTM put with different strike prices and the identical expiration month. For example, using September bonds at 102, you sell a September bond futures 106 call at 3^00 and sell a September bond futures 100 put at 2^16. This is a classic example of selling a strangle. Figure 12.11 shows a risk profile for this short strangle example.

Your maximum reward is the net credit of the option premiums or 5^16, which equals \$5250 [$(3 + 2^{16}/_{64}) = 5^{16}/_{64} = (5 \times \$1000) + (16 \times \$15.625) = \$5250$]. The maximum risk is unlimited. The upside break-even occurs when the underlying asset equals the call strike price plus the net credit. The upside break-even for this trade is $111^8/_{32}$ [$(106 + 5^{16}/_{64}) = 111^{16}/_{64} = 111^8/_{32}$]. The downside break-even occurs when the underlying asset equals

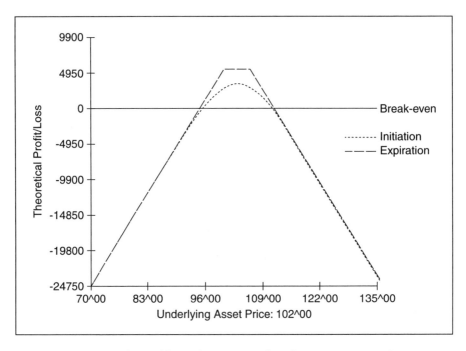

Figure 12.11 Risk Profile—Short Strangle (Short 1 Sep Bond Futures 106 Call @ 3^00, Short 1 Sep Bond Futures 100 Put @ 2^16)

the put strike price minus the net credit, which is $94^{24}/_{32}$ [$(100 - 5^{16}/_{64})$ = $94^{48}/_{64} = 94^{24}/_{32}$] in this trade. Therefore the profit range is between 94^24 and 111^08.

A short strangle has an upside-down U-shaped risk curve, which tells us that it has limited profit potential and unlimited risk. (See Figure 12.12.) In fact, your potential profits are less than when you place a short straddle because OTM premiums cost less than ATM premiums and deliver a reduced overall credit to the seller. However, your risk is also a little less than the straddle because the market has to make a bigger move against you to reach the limits of your profit range. In most cases, you will have a margin requirement on this kind of trade. Short strangles are market neutral strategies just like short straddles. If the market doesn't move, you get to keep the premium. If you were expecting a huge move, with lots of volatility, would you sell a straddle or a strangle? Neither, not unless you have a death wish. Increasing volatility is a signal for long straddles and strangles.

Short strangles are best used in combinations of spreads and butterflies

---

Strategy: Sell an OTM call and an OTM put with the same expiration date.

Risk: Unlimited.

Profit: Limited.

Time Decay Effect: Helpful.

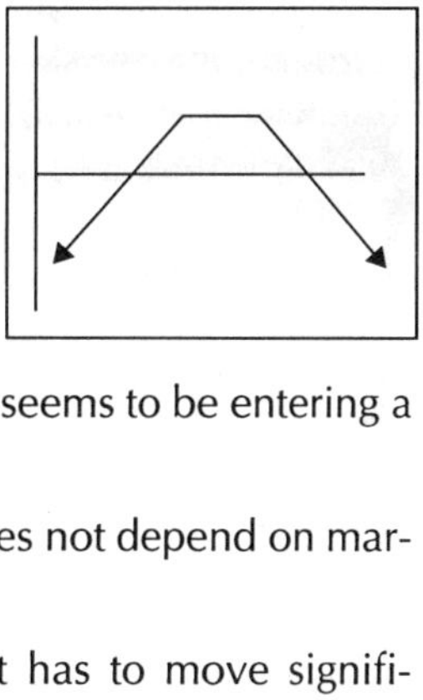

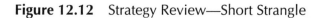

Situation: Look for a highly volatile market which seems to be entering a period of low volatility or stagnation.

Profit: Limited to the net credit received. Profit does not depend on market direction.

Risk: Unlimited on both sides. However, market has to move significantly for loss to occur. Margin is required.

Upside Break-even: Call strike price plus net credit received.

Downside Break-even: Put strike price minus net credit received.

Figure 12.12   Strategy Review—Short Strangle

and other option strategies. They can be added to these types of trades for extra protection. You will rarely place a short strangle all by itself, but it is essential to understand how they work so that you can integrate them into other trades.

FIXED STRADDLES

A straddle is a strategy that covers both sides of the market. This is the beginning of delta neutral trading. We are looking for trades that do not depend on market direction, but still make a profit on a fair amount of market movement. Another type of straddle is the fixed straddle.

If I choose to buy and sell the S&P 500 futures at 950, what did I just do? I gave my broker a good commission. What did I do for myself? I did absolutely nothing. Let us assume for a minute that you could actually do that. If I bought and sold a September S&P 500 futures at 950 and the market moved to 960, then any profits I made on the upside I lost on the downside. This is not the type of straddle you want to use, because you don't have much chance of making any money on it.

Long and short straddles rarely work for a delta neutral trader. Don't get me wrong; putting straddles on during low volatility and taking them off during high volatility is a great concept, and it does work. However, I prefer to place straddles and then adjust them throughout the course of the trade as the market moves.

For example, let's buy a 950 S&P put and a 950 S&P call for September. If each of them costs 10 points of premium, we have just paid 20 points or $5000 [20 points × $250 (value per point)] for this straddle. If the market moves from 950 to 955, did we make any money out of this straddle? We may have made a little bit, but the situation hinges on whatever we gained on the upside with the call. Unfortunately, we lost most of it on the long put.

Now, it's time to apply our knowledge of an option's time value and intrinsic value. Remember, options work on a curve. You are going to make a little more money as you go in-the-money and you are going to lose a little less coming out-of-the-money. Can you adjust this position? No, you cannot, unless you use options other than those that are part of the initial position. The reason we put straddles on is for one reason only—to make money from some sort of market movement outside of the initial investment. An adjustment to a trade brings it back to delta neutral after the market makes a move.

Where is our break-even point in this trade? If we bought a 950 put and a 950 call in the S&P futures for September and paid 20 points for this position, our break-even point at the end of expiration is at 970 on the upside and 930 on the downside. We have to get to 970 or 930 (950 + 20 = 970 or 950 – 20 = 930) to break even by the end of expiration. That's a position we may or may not want to look at every day. Can we adjust this position as the market moves back and forth? No, we cannot. We simply put on this kind of trade and take it off, which is why it is referred to as a fixed straddle.

What happens if we try to make an adjustment to a fixed straddle? The market might move up to 960 and we then decide to sell the long side. We sell the calls because we can make a couple of points on them. But what did we just do? We took off half our straddle and now we are no longer delta neutral. We are only playing one side of the market, which means our profits now depend on picking the right market direction. In this case, we took a bearish view by selling the long calls.

LONG SYNTHETIC STRADDLES

One of my favorite delta neutral strategies is the long synthetic straddle. It can be especially profitable because you can make adjustments to increase your return as the market moves. In this kind of straddle, you are combining options and futures or options and stocks; and as the market moves up or down, you can make money both ways. Perhaps this seems like a magic trick, especially if you are short futures and long calls. Obviously one leg of the trade will lose money as the other makes a profit. The difference is what you are going to be able to pocket with certain types of positions. Many factors govern the amount of profit, including the size of your account, the size of the trade, and whether you can adjust the trade to put yourself back to delta neutral after the market makes a move. Bottom line: You can make money on the adjustments.

For example, let's say you put on a long synthetic straddle and the market moves 10 points. How many times have you seen the S&P 500 futures move at least 10 points in a range over a month? This has been happening every week, as far as I can remember. You can also take advantage of this in the bonds, currencies, and other highly volatile markets. This type of trading can be done in any market where you have some liquidity and market movement.

A long synthetic straddle's risk curve resembles a long straddle. Let's set up a long synthetic straddle by going long 1 Aug Bond Futures @ 109^23 and long 2 Aug Bond Futures 110 Puts @ 2. The risk profile for this trade is shown in Figure 12.13.

In this trade, when the market goes up, you have a profit on the future and a smaller loss on the options (because their delta decreased). This leaves a net profit. When the market goes down, you have a loss on the underlying asset but you have a bigger profit on the options (because their delta increased), so again you have a net profit. Either way, when the market moves, you can make additional profits by adjusting the trade back to delta neutral. The risk is due to the time decay of the options. Risk on this example is the cost of the

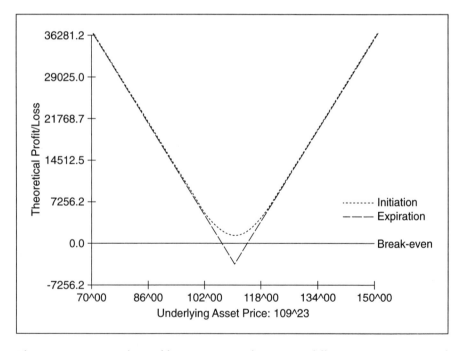

Figure 12.13 Risk Profile—Long Synthetic Straddle (Long 1 Aug Bond Futures @ 109^23, Long 2 Aug Bond Futures 110 Puts @ 2^00)

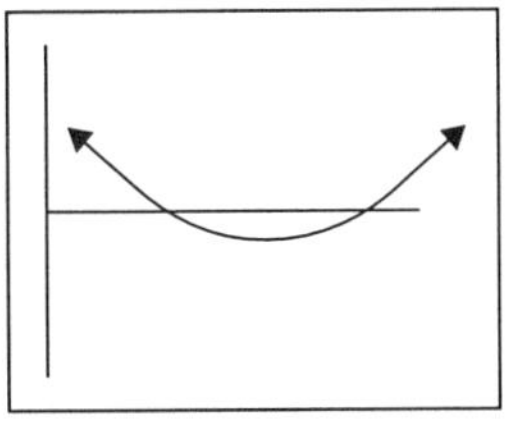

Strategy: Buy 1 underlying asset and buy 2 ATM puts. OR Sell 1 underlying asset and buy 2 ATM calls.

Risk: Limited.

Profit: Unlimited.

Time Decay Effect: Detrimental.

Situation: Look for a market where you expect volatility to increase. This is a delta neutral, nondirectional trade.

Profit: Unlimited above break-even points. Adjustments can provide increased profits.

Risk: Limited to the net debit of the options.

Upside Break-even: Price of underlying asset plus net debit paid for options.

Downside Break-even: Price of underlying asset minus net debit paid for options.

Figure 12.14   Strategy Review—Long Synthetic Straddle

options or $4000 ($2 \times \$2000 = \$4000$). Total risk is only assumed if you hold the position to expiration and the underlying asset does not move (or you fall asleep and never make an adjustment). Maximum profit is unlimited.

A long synthetic straddle combines long or short futures or stocks and long put or call options in such a way as to maximize profits regardless of which direction the market moves. (See Figure 12.14.) The upside break-even of a long synthetic straddle is calculated by adding the net debit paid for the options to the price of the underlying asset. In this case, the upside break-even is 113^23 (109^23 + 4^00 = 113^23). The downside break-even is calculated by subtracting the net debit paid for the options from the price of the underlying asset. In this trade, the downside break-even is 105.23 (109^23 − 4^00 = 105^23). Therefore, this trade makes money if the price of the underlying moves above 113^23 or below 105^23 assuming you make no adjustments on the trade. Long synthetic straddles are best employed when you expect a significant move in the price of the underlying in either direction.

SHORT SYNTHETIC STRADDLE

A short synthetic straddle combines a long or short futures contract (or stock) and short options. It is best placed in a stable market where very little price movement is anticipated. For example, we can buy 1 Sep T-Bond Futures @ 113 and sell 2 Sep ATM 113 Calls @ 3.16. The risk profile for this trade is shown in Figure 12.15.

The short synthetic straddle's risk profile resembles a short straddle's risk graph. (See Figure 12.16.) The maximum reward is limited to the net credit received from the option premiums, in this case $6500 [(2 × $3^{16}/_{64}$) = $6^{32}/_{64}$ = (6 × $1000) + (32 × $15.625) = $6500]. This amount is earned over time as the options lose value. However, your risk is unlimited and dangerous if the market moves quickly in either direction. The upside break-even is equal to the price of the underlying asset plus the net credit received on the option

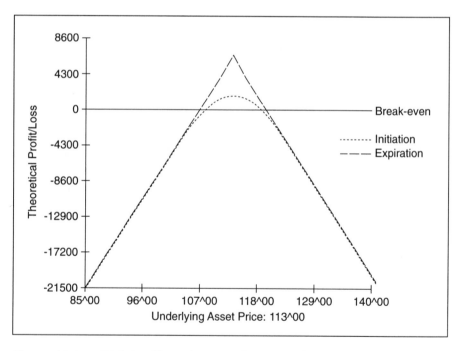

Figure 12.15 Risk Profile—Short Synthetic Straddle (Long 1 Sep T-Bond Futures @ 113^00, Short 2 Sep T-Bond Futures 113 Calls @ 3^16)

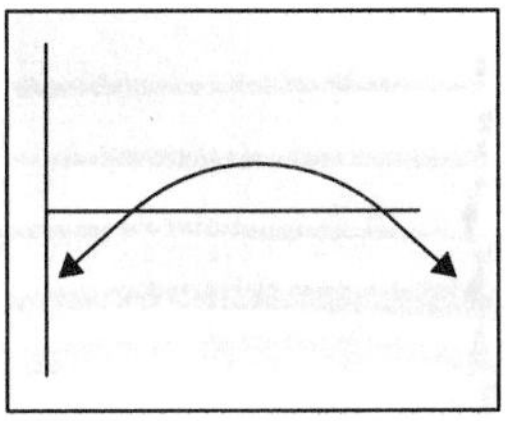

Strategy: Sell 1 underlying asset. Sell 2 ATM puts. OR Buy 1 underlying asset. Sell 2 ATM calls.

Risk: Unlimited.

Profit: Limited.

Time Decay Effect: Helpful.

Situation: Look for a market with high volatility which is expected to slow and trade in a range. Not a highly recommended trade due to high risk.

Profit: Limited to the net credit received.

Risk: Unlimited risk beyond the break-even points.

Upside Break-even: Price of underlying asset plus net credit received on short options.

Downside Break-even: Price of underlying asset minus net credit received on short options.

Figure 12.16 Strategy Review—Short Synthetic Straddle

premiums. In this case, the upside break-even is $119^{16}/_{32}$ ($113 + 6^{32}/_{64} = 119^{32}/_{64} = 119^{16}/_{32}$). The downside break-even is equal to the price of the underlying asset minus the net credit received on the option premiums. In this trade, the downside break-even is equal to $106^{16}/_{32}$ ($113 - 6^{32}/_{64} = 106^{32}/_{64} = 106^{16}/_{32}$). To make a profit, the T-bond market must stay in between 119^16 and 106^16.

CONCLUSION

When you put on a long synthetic straddle, you are placing a hedge trade. All you are paying for is the cost of the options. If your broker requires you to have margin on the futures or stock side, then try to find someone who will give you a cross margin account. There are companies out there that offer cross margining, although it is a relatively new concept to the public.

Putting on a synthetic straddle is not new; just the concept of looking at it as a low-risk trade from the brokerage firm side is new.

These trades are referred to as synthetic primarily because the two ATM options behave like an underlying futures contract or stock (two ATM options = +100 or −100 deltas). They create a synthetic instrument that moves as the underlying asset changes. When you initiate the position, you are completely offsetting the other side to create a perfect delta neutral trade. As the market moves, you will gain more on the winning side of the trade or in adjustment profits than you will relinquish on the losing portions of the trade. It works because you are combining a fixed delta with a variable delta. Adjustments can be made when the market makes a move. If the market moves so that the overall trade is +100 deltas, then you can sell a futures contract or 100 shares of stock. If the market moves and the overall position delta becomes −100, you can buy another futures contract or 100 shares of stock. Either way, the trade returns to delta neutral.

To be successful at this game, you have to understand how the strike prices work in the market you are placing a trade in. Don't be fooled. Every market is different. For example, S&P strike prices are every 5. In contrast, bonds are every 2. However, in the last month, bond strike prices go to increments of 1. This information can be found on our Web site (www.MarketScoreboard.com) or by checking with your broker.

Each trade has a unique risk-and-reward scenario. You can create straddles and strangles by buying or selling options. Each strategy has a chance of making a profit regardless of market direction. Choosing the right strategy is directly related to your experience and knowledge of specific markets. At this point in my trading career, I usually check out which way is less expensive and let that be my guide.

As a beginner, you should play it safe and place trades that offer limited risk. Although it may be tempting to go short options since a sale places money directly in your trading account over time, I do not recommend selling options until you are truly well-versed in delta neutral trading. Remember that when you sell options you do get a credit, but you earn this credit as the options lose value over time.

13

Advanced Delta
Neutral Strategies

Understanding the mechanics of a variety of delta neutral strategies is the key to profitable nondirectional trading. Instead of being overwhelmed by the complex nature of market dynamics, you can implement a delta neutral strategy that takes advantage of market conditions. Determining which strategy best fits the situation can easily be deduced through the use of risk profiles and relatively easy mathematical calculations. Delta neutral trading is all about empowering traders to maximize their returns and minimize their losses. Delta neutral strategies have been used on the major exchanges for years by professional traders, but off-floor traders are rarely aware of these strategies.

We have already explored the basic delta neutral trading techniques. It's time to turn the spotlight on some advanced strategies: ratio spreads and ratio backspreads. Ratio spreads are interesting strategies that provide a wide profit zone; however, they also have unlimited risk. Ratio backspreads, on the other hand, offer limited risk with unlimited reward potential.

RATIO SPREADS

A ratio spread is a strategy in which an uneven number of contracts with the same underlying instrument are bought and sold. Unlike straddles and strangles, which use a 1-to-1 ratio of the same kind of options, ratio spreads off-set an uneven number of different types of options. For example, you can buy 1 Oct S&P 500 Futures ATM 950 Call @ 10.80 and sell 2 Oct S&P 500 Futures OTM 960 Calls @ 5.55 against it to create a ratio call spread.

This trade will not cost you any money to place. You're spending 10.80 which translates to $2700 (10.8 × $250 = $2700) to buy the 950 call and receiving 11.10 points of credit (11.10 × 250 = $2775) for selling the 960 calls. (The $250 point value for the S&P 500 futures became standard in November 1997.) A debit is where you are spending more than you are taking in (i.e., you are paying money out of your pocket) and a credit is where the money is deposited in your account. In this trade, you are receiving a credit of $75 to place the trade. However, you still have unlimited risk. One of the short October OTM 960 calls is covered by the long 950 call. If the market goes to 970, you would make 20 points on the long call, lose 10 on the first call, to lock in a net profit of 10 points. However, the second 960 call is uncovered and even though it was an OTM option when the trade was initiated, there is some margin and risk on it. If the market rises to 970, the second 960 call loses 10 points, reducing the net profit to 0 points (20 − 10 − 10 = 0). Many traders are willing to take the risk involved in shorting OTM options because they believe that the probability of the market moving that much is slim. Meanwhile, they are taking in a lot of premium. However, in volatile markets such as the S&P 500 futures, a market can easily move enough to lose money on the uncovered short option.

Although a ratio spread simply involves the buying and selling of an uneven number of contracts, there are a variety of complex ways to implement this strategy. The previous trade was a ratio call spread, which involves buying a lower-strike call option and selling a greater number of OTM higher-strike call options. For example, you can buy one OTM call option and sell two call options that are even further out-of-the-money. You can also use a different ratio other than 1 to 2. For instance, you might buy two ATM options and sell three OTM options. A ratio call spread is useful when a trader sees a slight rise in a market followed by a sell-off. If this trade is done at a credit, this increases the chance of success. The risk graph shown in Figure 13.1 details the following trade: long 1 Mar Silver Futures 475 Call @ 10, short 2 Mar Silver Futures 500 Calls @ 7 (net credit received = 4 points = $200).

The maximum profit of a ratio call spread is calculated by multiplying the

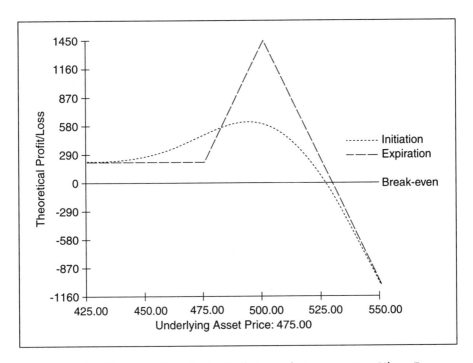

Figure 13.1 Risk Profile—Ratio Call Spread (Long 1 Mar Silver Futures 475 Call @ 10.00, Short 2 Mar Silver Futures 500 Calls @ 7.00)

difference in strikes by the value per point and then adding the net credit received or subtracting the net debit paid. In this trade, the maximum profit is limited to $1450 [(500 − 475) × $50 + $200 = $1450]. The risk is unlimited to the upside, beyond the break-even point. The upside break-even is calculated by dividing the difference in strike prices times the number of short contracts by the number of short contracts minus the number of long contracts and adding that amount to the lower call strike price. Then add the credit received or minus the net debit paid. (See Figure 13.2.) In this case, the upside break-even is equal to 475 + [(500 − 475) × 2 ÷ (2 − 1)] + 2 = 475 + 50 + 2 = 527. There is no risk to the downside because the trade was entered as a credit. This trade is best entered during times of high volatility with expectation of decreasing volatility.

A ratio put spread should be implemented in a bullish market. It involves

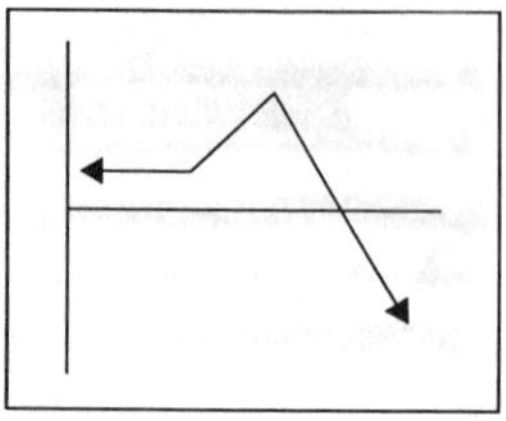

> **Strategy:** Buy lower strike call. Sell greater number of higher strike calls.
>
> **Risk:** Unlimited.
>
> **Profit:** Limited.
>
> **Time Decay Effect:** Mixed.
>
> **Situation:** Look for a market where you expect a decline (to keep the net credit) or a slight rise not to exceed the strike price of the short options.
>
> **Profit:** Limited (difference in strike prices times value per point, plus net credit or minus net debit).
>
> **Risk:** Unlimited to the upside above break-even.
>
> **Upside Break-even:** Lower strike price call plus (difference in strike prices times number of short contracts) ÷ (number of short contracts less number of long contracts) plus net credit received or minus net debit paid.

Figure 13.2   Strategy Review—Ratio Call Spread

buying a higher-strike put option and selling a greater number of lower-strike OTM put options. For example, let's buy 1 Oct S&P 500 Futures 955 Put @ 9.80 and sell 2 Oct S&P 500 Futures 940 Puts @ 5.60. This gives us a net credit of 1.40 or $350 (2 × 5.60 = 11.20 − 9.80 = 1.40 × $250 per point = $350). The risk graph for this trade is shown in Figure 13.3.

The maximum profit of a ratio put spread is calculated by multiplying the difference in strike prices by the value per point and then adding the net credit received. In this trade, the maximum profit is limited to $4100 [(955 − 940) × $250 + $350 = $4100]. The maximum risk is unlimited to the downside.

The downside break-even is calculated by dividing the difference in strike prices times the number of short contracts by the number of short contracts minus the number of long contracts and subtracting that number from the higher put strike price. Then, subtract the net credit received or add the net

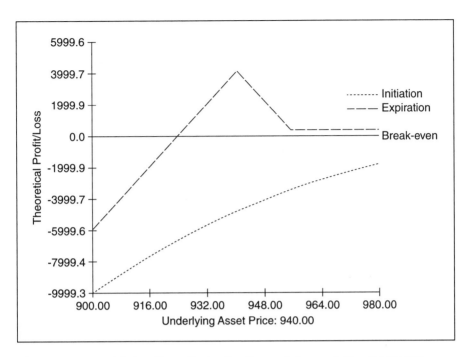

Figure 13.3 Risk Profile—Ratio Put Spread (Long 1 Oct S&P 500 Futures 955 Put @ 9.80, Short 2 Oct S&P 500 Futures 940 Puts @ 5.60)

debit paid. In this example the downside break-even is 923.60 (955 − {[(955 − 940) × 2] ÷ (2 − 1)} − 1.40) = (955 − 30 − 1.40 = 923.60). (See Figure 13.4.)

A ratio put spread can be implemented when a slight fall in the market is anticipated followed by a sharp rise. This strategy works well in the stock market, as stocks generally tend to move up in price. However, it is important to place this trade on only high-quality stocks. If the company has reported lower than expected earnings or bad news is released, exit the position. A ratio put spread also works well in many futures markets, especially during seasonal periods when prices tend to go up (such as heating oil in the winter months).

The main risk in ratio spreads comes from the uncovered short call or put. These options have unlimited risk. Watch the market closely and exit or adjust the trade if the market moves into the price strike of the short options.

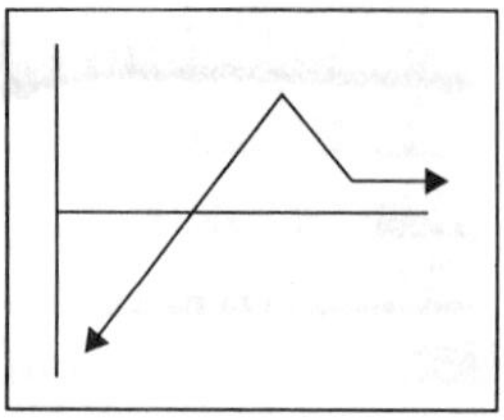

Strategy: Buy higher strike put. Sell greater number of lower strike puts.

Risk: Unlimited.

Profit: Limited.

Time Decay Effect: Mixed.

Situation: Look for a market where you expect a rise or a slight fall not to exceed the strike price of the short put options.

Profit: Limited (difference in strike prices times value per point, plus net credit or minus net debit).

Risk: Unlimited to the downside.

Downside Break-even: Higher strike price (difference in strikes times the number of short contracts ÷ the number of short contracts minus long contracts) minus the net credit received *or* plus the net debit paid.

Figure 13.4 Strategy Review—Ratio Put Spread

RATIO BACKSPREADS

Ratio backspreads are one of my favorite strategies for volatile markets. They are very powerful strategies that will enable you to limit your risk and receive unlimited potential profits. These strategies do not have to be monitored very closely as long as you buy and sell options with at least 30 days (the longer the better) until expiration. I call them "vacation trades" because I can place a ratio backspread, go on vacation, and not even worry about it. Some traders find ratio backspread opportunities hard to find. Perhaps they are looking in the wrong places. It is difficult to find ratio backspread opportunities in highly volatile markets with expensive stocks or futures. For example, you will rarely find them in the S&P 500 futures market. This index is simply too volatile and the options are too expensive. Focus on medium-priced stocks (between $25 and $75) or futures. These trades can be quite profitable, so be persistent. They're out there—just keep looking.

A ratio backspread strategy involves buying one leg and selling another in a disproportionate ratio that does not create a net debit. The following seven rules must be diligently observed to create an optimal ratio backspread trade:

1. Choose markets where volatility is expected to increase in the direction of your trade.

2. Avoid markets with consistent low volatility. If you really want to place a ratio backspread in a market that does not move, pay close attention to rule #4.

3. Do not use ratios greater than .67—use ratios that are multiples of 1 to 2 or 2 to 3.

4. If you choose to trade a slow market, a .75 ratio or higher is acceptable only by buying the lower strike and selling the higher. However, there is more risk.

5. To create a call ratio backspread, sell the lower-strike call and buy a greater number of higher-strike calls.

6. To create a put ratio backspread, sell the higher-strike put and buy a greater number of lower-strike puts.

7. Avoid debit trades. But, if you do place a ratio backspread with a debit, you must be able to lose that amount.

Let's take a look at the mechanics of a call ratio backspread. As previously stated, a call ratio backspread involves selling the lower-strike call and buying a greater number of higher-strike calls. For example, let's pick a fictitious market (it doesn't matter which market as long as it is highly volatile) with strikes starting at 80, 90, 100, 110, 120, and 130. The ATM calls are at 100, which means that the current price of the underlying market equals 100 also. Now, according to rule #5, the first part of this strategy is to sell the lower-strike call. Which is the lowest-strike call here? The 80 is the lowest-strike call.

Let's say this is the digital phone market. One phone costs approximately 100. However, I can purchase the option to buy this phone for a variety of strike prices from 80 to 130. If one digital phone is currently worth 100, but I could buy it for 80, what do you think I'm going to do? I'll buy it for 80 and sell it to someone else for 100 and make 20. In other words, all the strike prices that give me the right to buy something at a lower price than it's currently trading for are in-the-money. Therefore, the 80 and 90 prices are in-the-money.

Now, the other part of the rule tells me to buy a greater number of higher-strike calls. I am going to buy an option to buy this phone at 130 because I think the market is going to reach 140. Am I going to pay less for this call, or more? I'm going to pay less because now I'm speculating that the market mood is bullish. Speculating on market direction is one of the main reasons why many people lose money trading options. However, I'm going to go ahead and speculate that the market is going to go to 140, even though it's only at 100 right now. Furthermore, I'm going to pay less for a 130 option than a 120, 110, 100, 90, or an 80. As the strike price goes up, the premiums of the ITM options also go up because they become more and more valuable. If our phone market is currently trading at 100 but it's starting to rise, the price of the 130 option will also rise.

Let's introduce the delta into this situation. The delta is the probability of an option closing at expiration in-the-money. If 100 is at-the-money, which way can the market go? The market can move in either direction, which means there is a 50 percent probability of it closing in-the-money. Obviously, a price that's already in-the-money has a higher probability of closing in-the-money than something that's out-of-the-money. Therefore, the delta for an ITM option is higher than the delta for the ATM option or an OTM option. The higher the probability an option has of closing in-the-money, the higher its premium. This relationship enables a trader to create trades that are virtually free of charge. Ratio backspreads take full advantage of this relationship. It's a very simple concept. As the underlying instrument's price changes, the option deltas change accordingly. For example, our 80 option has a higher delta than a 90, and therefore has a higher premium.

Let's set up a call ratio backspread using the digital phone market, which is trading at 100. To satisfy the rules, let's sell an 80 call and buy more of the 90 calls in a ratio of 2 to 3 or less. This trade would receive a credit on the short 80 call and a debit on the long 90 calls. We have limited the risk of the short 80 call by offsetting it with one of the long 90 calls and can still profit from the other long 90 call.

As previously stated, determining risk is the most important part of setting up any trade. The risk of this trade can be calculated using the following option premiums:

Call	Price
120	$ 60
110	$ 70
100	$ 80
90	$ 90
80	$100

If we sell one 80 call option and buy two of the 90 call options, we have a debit of $80. But if the prices rise, we make more money on the $90 calls than we have spent on the $80 call. If the market falls, the out-of-pocket cost of placing the trade is the maximum risk. The most we can lose is $80 (2 × $90 = $180 − $100 = $80). To avoid risk, the trick to creating an optimal trade is to use a ratio that makes this trade delta neutral. In this way, it is possible to place a trade for free at no net debit. That's right! You can create ratio backspreads that don't cost a penny (except for commissions) and still make healthy profits. You can do this by offsetting the credit side with the debit side so that they cancel each other out and you do not spend any money out-of-pocket. This is the best kind of trade to place (especially if you're 100 percent wrong about market direction), because you don't lose any money. In this case, as long as the market breaks down below the 80 call strike, both options expire worthless. However, there is some risk between the 80 and 90 strike prices because the trade could lose more than it profits.

To figure out the most effective ratio, you have to be able to accurately calculate the net credit of a trade. This can be accomplished by calculating the full credit realized from the short options and dividing it by the debit of one long option. You can then use up as much of the credit as you can to make the most profitable ratio.

- Credit = number of short contracts times short option premium times dollar value of each full point.

- Debit = number of long contracts times long option premium times dollar value of each full point.

This is why it is vital to understand the variables of the markets you are trading. Each market has a particular dollar value for each point and a unique number of tick moves in each point. For example, the S&Ps are worth $250 per point as of November 1997 and have 20 ticks per point. The minimum price move is 5. Bonds, on the other hand, are worth $1000 per point. Bond options have 64 ticks per point. That means that 1 long bond futures call at 2^34 would cost $2531.25 [(2 × $1000) + (34 × 15.625) = $2000 + $531.25 = $2531.25].

Once you have figured out the best ratio of the trade, you still have to calculate your risk.

- Risk = number of short contracts times difference in strike prices times dollar value of each full point plus any debit paid or less any credit received.

Let's use these equations to determine an optimal call ratio backspread using T-bonds currently trading at 113^19. Table 13.1 details the option prices at various expiration months.

Let's create a call ratio backspread by selling 2 Dec T-Bond Futures 112 Calls @ 2^02 and buying 1 Dec T-Bond Futures 114 Calls @ 1^31. Our short calls give us a credit of $2031.25 {2 × [(2 × $1000) + (2 × 15.625)] = 2 × $2031.25 = $4062.50}. One long call costs $1484.38. Unfortunately, these calculations do not offer much in the form of a credit trade. We cannot buy 3 of the 114 calls because it would cost more than the $4062.50 we received. We will have to increase our ratio substantially to be able to set up a virtually free trade.

With T-bonds trading at 109^26, let's look to the October options and see if we can find a better combination. Let's try selling 2 Oct T-bond Futures 112 Calls @ 1^18 and buying 3 Oct T-bond Futures 114 Calls @ ^53. This time, our credit is $2562.50 {2 × [(1 × $1000) + (18 × 15.625)] = 2 × $1281.25 = $2562.50}. Each long call costs $828.125. By dividing our credit by one long call, we can buy three of the long calls. This creates a ratio of 2 to 3, which satisfies rule #3. We have a slight net credit of $78.50 ($2562.50 − $2484.375 = $78.125) or ⁵⁄₆₄, which can go toward the cost of commissions. Now, let's calculate the risk on this trade: risk = (2 × 2 × $1000) − $78.125 = $3921.875.

The next step is to take a look at this trade's risk profile. This risk graph (Figure 13.5) shows the trade's unlimited potential reward. It also reveals that the maximum risk of $3921.875 is realized only if the underlying instrument at expiration is at the strike price of the long option (114). The upside break-even of this example is calculated by dividing the difference in strike prices times the number of short contracts by the number of long calls minus short calls and adding that number to the higher call strike price. Then, subtract the net credit or add the net debit. In this case, the upside

Table 13.1 Option Prices

Asset	E Cost	E Cost Units	H Units	H Cost Units	Last	Change	Volatility	Time	Date
US U7 0	N/A	0	N/A	0	113^19		8.1708	11:38 29 AM	8/15

Options	Description	Last	Theoretical	Change	Probability/TM	UV/OV
US U7C116	U7 Sep 116.00C	^01	^01	+.00	3.20	Overvalued
US U7C115	U7 Sep 115.00C	^04	^06	−.01	13.84	Undervalued
US V7C112	U7 Oct 112.00C	1^18	1^29	+^18	58.20	Undervalued
US V7C114	U7 Oct 114.00C	^53	^61	+^12	44.39	Undervalued
US V7C116	U7 Oct 116.00C	^31	^37	+^07	31.34	Undervalued
US V7C118	U7 Oct 118.00C	^16	^21	+^03	20.37	Undervalued
US V7C120	U7 Oct 120.00C	^07	^11	^00	12.15	Undervalued
US Z7C112	U7 Dec 112.00C	2^02	2^08	+29	55.11	Undervalued
US Z7C114	U7 Dec 114.00C	1^31	1^41	+12	46.51	Undervalued
US Z7C116	U7 Dec 116.00C	1^10	1^14	−18	38.51	Undervalued
US Z7C118	U7 Dec 118.00C	^53	^57	N/A	30.37	Undervalued
US Z7C120	U7 Dec 120.00C	^38	^41	+09	23.45	Undervalued

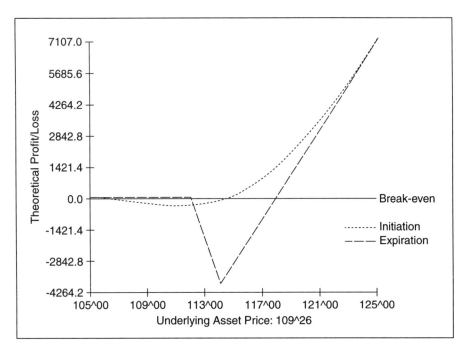

Figure 13.5 Risk Profile—Call Ratio Backspread (Short 2 Oct T-Bond Futures 112 Calls @ 1^18 and Long 3 Oct T-Bond Futures 114 Calls @ ^53)

break-even is $117^{29.5}/_{32}$ $(114 + \{[(114 - 112) \times 2] \div (3 - 2)\} - 78^{5}/_{64}) = (114 + 4 - {}^{5}/_{64}) = 117^{59}/_{64} = 117^{29.5}/_{32})$. The downside break-even is the strike price of the short options plus the net credit or minus the net debit. In this trade, the downside break-even is $112^{2.5}/_{32}$ $(112 + {}^{5}/_{64} = 112^{5}/_{64} = 112^{2.5}/_{32})$. That means this trade makes money as long as the price of the underlying closes above the upside break-even. Call ratio backspreads are best implemented during periods of low volatility in a highly volatile market that shows signs of increasing activity to the upside. (See Figure 13.6.)

Let's take a look at the mechanics of a put ratio backspread. In a put ratio backspread, you sell a higher-strike put and buy a greater number of lower-strike puts. This strategy is best implemented at periods of low volatility in a highly volatile market when you anticipate increasing market activity to the downside (bearish).

To reduce confusion, let's use the same numbers as the initial digital phone

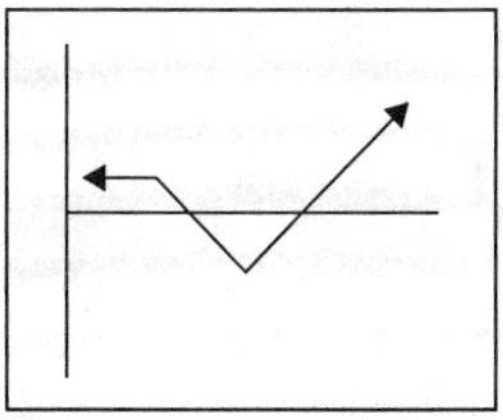

Strategy: Sell lower strike calls. Buy greater number higher strike calls. (The ratio must be less than .67.)

~~Risk: Limited.~~

~~Profit: Unlimited.~~

Time Decay Effect: Mixed.

Situation: Look for a market that rises sharply with increasing volatility. Should be placed as a credit or at-even.

Profit: Unlimited to the upside.

Risk: Limited (number of short calls times difference in strikes, times value per point minus net credit received or plus net debit paid).

Upside Break-even: Higher strike calls, plus (difference in strikes times number of short calls), divided by (number of long calls less short calls) minus net credit or plus net debit paid.

Downside Break-even: Strike price of the short options plus net credit or minus net debit.

Figure 13.6   Strategy Review—Call Ratio Backspread

example to demonstrate a put ratio backspread. Using this strategy, we'll sell a higher-strike put and buy a greater number of lower-strike puts. The strikes are the same as before: 80, 90, 100, 110, 120. Which is the highest-strike price? The 120 is the highest with the most intrinsic value. If I have an option that gives me a right to sell the phone at 120, it's different than an option that gives me the right to sell it at 110, 100, 90, or 80. In other words, 120 is the highest strike here and 80 is the lowest.

Using this scenario, I could place a wide variety of put ratio backspreads. To further complicate the situation, I could do different ratios on each combination. For this example, I'm going to sell the higher 120 put and buy a greater number of 110 puts. If the market crashes, I'll lose money to the 110 point; but below 110 I'll be making more on the 110 puts than I lose on the 120 puts since I have more of the 110 puts.

This actually happened to me once in the S&P 500 futures market. If you think the S&P 500 futures market is moving into lofty levels and you don't

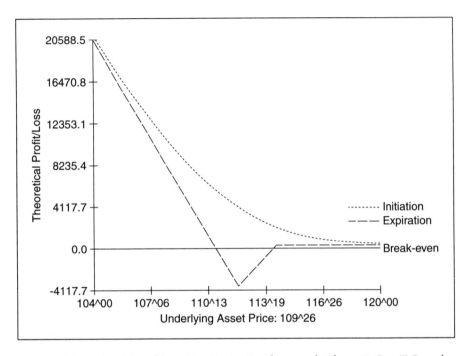

Figure 13.7 Risk Profile—Put Ratio Backspread (Short 2 Oct T-Bond Futures 114 Puts @ 1^21 and Long 5 Oct T-Bond Futures 112 Puts @ ^31)

want to gamble a lot, you could do a put ratio backspread. I was lucky. The market moved down so fast that month that I made a lot of money. Similarly, if you had placed a put ratio backspread the day the market crashed back in 1987, you wouldn't need to read this book. You'd be in Aruba, the Bahamas, or somewhere equally as relaxing. You'd be laughing all the way to the bank because you would have made big-time bucks on a trade with minimal risk.

In placing these kind of trades, it is essential to create the most effective ratio in markets with increasing volatility, liquidity, and flexibility. Let's create a new put ratio backspread trade using T-bonds trading at 113^19. The T-bond options on futures trade at every 2^00 points until approximately 30 days prior to expiration, at which time they will trade at every 1^00 point. For example, with the bonds trading at 113^19, the available strikes are 110, 112, 114, 116, and so on. Any put options with strikes above 113^19 are in-the-money, and put options with strikes below 113^19 are out-of-the-money.

Let's create a put ratio backspread by selling 2 Oct T-Bond Futures 114 Puts @ 1^21 and buying 5 Oct T-Bond Futures 112 Puts @ ^31. The short puts give me a credit of \$2656.25 {2 × [(1 × \$1000) + (21 × 15.625)] = 2 × \$1328 = \$2656.25}. The long puts only cost \$484.375 each. If we divide \$2656.25 by \$484.375, we can afford to purchase five long put options and still have net credit of \$234.375 or $^{15}/_{64}$ [\$2656.25 − (5 × \$484.375) = \$234.375]. This gives us a ratio of 2 to 5, which satisfies the rule of creating ratios less than .67. To calculate the risk, multiply the number of short contracts (2) by the difference in strike prices (2) by the dollar value of each full point (\$1000) plus any debit paid (0) or minus any credit received (\$234.375). This gives us a maximum risk of \$3765.625 {[(2 × 2) × 1000] − 234.375 = \$3765.625}. The risk profile of this trade is shown in Figure 13.7, and the strategy is reviewed in Figure 13.8.

You can see that we have created a trade with unlimited reward and a maximum risk of \$3765.625. Once again, the maximum risk will be realized only if the underlying futures contract at the time of expiration is equal to

---

Strategy: Sell higher strike put. Buy greater number of lower strike puts. (The ratio must be less than .67.)

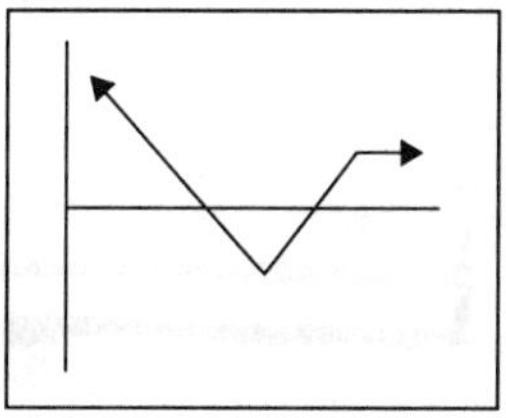

Risk: ~~Limited.~~

~~**Profit:** Unlimited.~~

Time Decay Effect: Mixed.

Situation: Look for a market where you expect a sharp decline with increased volatility. Should be placed as a credit or at-even.

Profit: Unlimited to the downside.

Risk: Limited (number of short puts times difference in strike prices times value per point) minus net credit received or plus net debit paid.

Upside Break-even: Higher strike put option minus net credit received.

Downside Break-even: Lower strike price minus [(number of short puts times difference in strike prices) divided by (number of long puts less number of short puts)] plus net credit received or minus net debit paid.

Figure 13.8   Strategy Review—Put Ratio Backspread

the long strike price. The upside break-even is the higher-strike put option minus the net credit received translated into points. In this case, the upside break-even is $113^{24.5}/_{32}$ ($114 - {}^{15}/_{64} = 113^{49}/_{64} = 113^{24.5}/_{32}$). If the market closes above 114, all options expire worthless, but you can keep the credit. The downside break-even is calculated by multiplying the number of short contracts times the difference in strike prices and dividing that amount by the number of long options minus the number of short options and subtracting that amount from the lower strike price. Then add the net credit or minus the net debit. In this trade, the downside break-even is $110^{29}/_{32}$ ($112 - \{[(114 - 112) \times 2] \div (5 - 2)\} + {}^{15}/_{64} = 112 - {}^{4}/_{3} + {}^{15}/_{64} = 110^{58}/_{64} = 110^{29}/_{32}$). This trade makes money as long as the price of the underlying closes below the downside break-even.

This trade works because the further the market gets away from the strike where you originally purchased the options, the more money the trade will make. As each level of option gets further in-the-money, the delta of the options purchased will become greater than the delta of the options sold. In other words, the further an option is in-the-money, the more it acts like a futures contract.

CONCLUSION

Correctly forecasting market direction is not essential to making money using advanced delta neutral strategies. However, having a good feel for volatility is an important part of being able to pick the right market and the optimal strategy. Markets that go up rapidly most likely will come down fast. The faster they go down, the faster they go up. If you are in a market that is going straight to the moon, start looking for opportunities for put ratio backspreads. Why? When the markets are going straight up, traders pump up the call prices because of increased volatility. This also means that the market may very well be positioning itself for a severe correction to the downside. Many times you can get better prices on the put side of a trade, because people tend to buy calls when volatility increases. There is simply a greater demand for calls in a fast-moving market to the upside. If the market is going down and you expect continuation, do a put ratio backspread. If you expect a reversal, do a call ratio backspread.

14

Trading Techniques
for Range-Bound Markets

Not all markets trend upward or downward. In fact, a large percentage of markets in both stocks and futures trend sideways within a consistent trading range during a year. In many cases, you may find stocks or futures that have been trading sideways for some time. These markets provide an opportunity to employ strategies that allow you as a trader to exploit the sideways movement and the time value of options (otherwise known as the time premium).

As previously discussed, option pricing includes time value and intrinsic value. The intrinsic value of an option is the value an in-the-money (ITM) option has if it were exercised at that point. For example, if I own an IBM 100 December call option, and IBM is trading at $120, the option has $20 of intrinsic value. This is due to the fact that the strike price of the call option is below the current trading price of the underlying asset. If the option has a market price of $22, then the remaining $2 of the call option is the time value.

Furthermore, if an IBM 130 put option costs $13, it would have $10 of intrinsic value and $3 of time value. Intrinsic value is not lost due to the passage of time. Intrinsic value is lost only when the underlying asset—in this case IBM—moves against your option's position. In this example, if IBM moves down, the call options lose intrinsic value. If the market moves up, the put options lose intrinsic value.

Time value is lost due to time decay (also referred to as the theta decay) of the option. Options lose the most time value in the last 30 days of the life of the option—the closer the expiration date, the faster the theta decay. Therefore, the last day will have the fastest loss of value due to time.

Since options lose value over time if markets do not move, this basic option characteristic can be used to create strategies that work in markets that are moving sideways. Before we can explore the specific strategies, you need to be able to spot a sideways (or range-bound) market.

A sideways market is a market that has traded between two numbers for a specified period of time. The minimum time frame I prefer to use is two months. However, for our purposes, a longer time frame can mean a more stable sideways market. As previously reviewed, these two numbers are referred to as the support and resistance levels. For example, if every time IBM dips to around $100 per share, the market rebounds, this would establish the support. If IBM would then trade up in price to reach $130 and then sell off again, this would establish the resistance. These two levels can then be used to employ an effective options strategy that would allow us to collect time premium.

How do I find these range-bound markets? I look at charts. I scan all the futures and stock markets and basically just eyeball the charts. If I spot a market that appears to be going sideways, I take a ruler and try to draw a support and resistance line. If this is easily accomplished, I then look for the most effective options strategy to take advantage of the given market. Three of my favorite sideways strategies are the long butterfly, long condor, and long iron butterfly spreads. However, I will review six market strategies in this chapter, although I prefer to focus my trading on the three mentioned above.

BUTTERFLY SPREAD

The butterfly trade is one of the most popular strategies, probably due to its widespread mention in many options trading books. There are two basic butterfly trades: the short butterfly and the long butterfly. Both consist of three options: the body and the two wings. The body contains an option with the strike price in between the support and resistance levels. The wings are composed of options with the strike prices at both ends of the trading range. For example, let's create a butterfly in the gold futures market with the 320,

330, and 340 December call options. In this example, the body is the 330 call and the wings are the 320 and 340 call options.

LONG BUTTERFLY

To create a long butterfly, you would go long (buy) the wings and go short (sell) the body (the middle strike options). A long butterfly trade consists of selling more options in the body than are bought individually in each wing. Using the gold example, you would buy one 320 call, sell two 330 calls, and buy one 340 call. The risk profile of the trade is shown in Figure 14.1.

The basis of this trade is to purchase as many option contracts as you sell, except that you are selling more of the body and separate the rest in the wings. You make money when the market closes in between the wings. Your

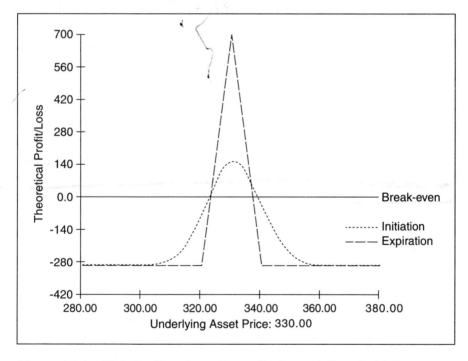

Figure 14.1   Risk Profile—Long Butterfly (Long 1 Dec Gold Futures 320 Call @ 13, Short 2 Dec Gold Futures 330 Calls @ 8, Long 1 Dec Gold Futures 340 Call @ 6)

total risk is the net debit paid for the trade. In this trade, you paid a debit of three points [(13 + 6) – (8 + 8) = 3], or $300, which is your total risk. The maximum profit potential of the trade is calculated by taking the difference in the strike prices of the middle and lower strikes times the value per point less any debit paid. In this example, the maximum reward is $700 {[(330 – 320) × $100] – $300 = ($1000 – $300) = $700}.

Your downside break-even for the trade is calculated by adding the strike price of the lower option strike (in this case 320) to the net debit of the trade (in this case 3). Therefore, the downside break-even for this trade is 323. The upside break-even is calculated by taking the higher strike wing (340) and subtracting the net debit (3). The upside break-even is 337. Therefore, the break-even range for this trade is between 323 and 337, and the maximum reward kicks in at 330, the strike price of the middle options (the body). Refer to Table 14.1 for a tabular representation of the value of the call options based on the initial investment as determined at expiration.

Here you can find the value of each option's position at expiration. For example, if gold closes at 330 per ounce at expiration, the 320 call that cost $1300 would now be worth $1000 for a loss of $300. However, you would get to keep the $1600 credit received from selling the two 330 calls because they expired at-the-money. Finally, you would incur a loss of $600 for the 340 call for an overall profit of $700.

The long butterfly trade is a very popular strategy that captures time premium as the market trades back and forth between the wings. (See Figure 14.2.) Since the premise for this trade is to capture time premium, you need to use this strategy in the optimal time decay zone, which is the last 30 days of life of the option. If you find a market that has been going sideways for a long time, the options premium you receive may be very low due to a decreased volatility premium attached to the options. Therefore, when you

Table 14.1   Value of Gold Futures Call Options—Long Butterfly

	Gold Market at Expiration				
Calls	310	320	330	340	350
320 (Debit: 13)	(1300)	(1300)	(300)	700	1700
330 (Credit: 16)	1600	1600	1600	(400)	(2400)
340 (Debit: 6)	(600)	(600)	(600)	(600)	400
Profit/(Loss)	(300)	(300)	700	(300)	(300)

Strategy: Buy lower strike (call or put). Sell two higher strike (calls or puts). Buy higher strike (call or put). Use all calls or all puts.

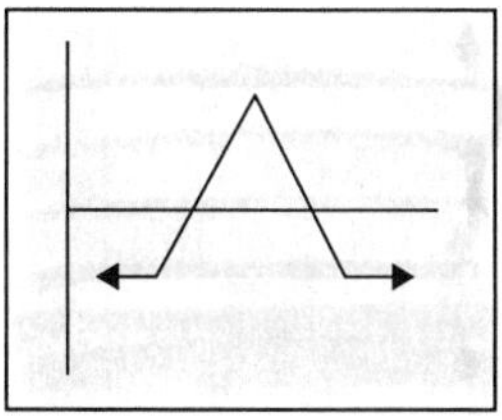

Risk: Limited.

Profit: Limited.

Time Decay Effect: Helpful.

Situation: Look for a sideways market that is expected to stay between the break-even points.

Profit: Limited (difference in strike prices times value per point, minus net debit paid). Profit exists between break-evens.

Risk: Limited to the net debit paid.

Upside Break-even: Highest strike price minus net debit paid.

Downside Break-even: Lowest strike price plus net debit paid.

Figure 14.2   Strategy Review—Long Butterfly

sell the body of the butterfly you will receive less of a premium for time than in a market that has higher volatility. You will likely have to go out at least another 30 days in the expiration cycle to make the trade reasonably profitable.

SHORT BUTTERFLY

In a short butterfly spread, you will go short (sell) more options at the body strike and go long (buy) the wings of the option. This strategy is applied when you expect a breakout above or below the wings or the market is already outside the wings. It is not used as a range trading strategy, but is included here because it is an interesting strategy to use when a market is hovering near the equilibrium level and you expect a sharp move in either direction (above the upper strike price or below the lower strike price of the wings). For example, let's create a delta neutral short butterfly trade by going short 1 Gold Futures 340 Call @ 12.6, long 2 Gold Futures 330 Calls @ 20.7, and short 1 Gold

Futures 320 Call @ 30. The net credit for this trade is $120 [(12.6 + 30) − (2 × 20.7) = (42.6 − 41.4) = 1.20 × 100 = $120]. The risk profile for this trade is shown in Figure 14.3, and the strategy is reviewed in Figure 14.4.

The risk for a short butterfly spread is the difference between strikes (body and wings) times the value per point minus the net credit received. In this case, the maximum risk would be $880 {[(340 − 330) × $100] − 120 = $880}. The maximum profit for this spread is the net credit which in this trade is only $120 [(30 + 12.6) − (2 × 20.7) = 1.2 × $100 = $120). The upside break-even equals the highest strike price minus the net credit. In this trade, the upside break-even would be 338.80 (340 − 1.2 = 338.80). The downside break-even equals the lowest strike price plus the net credit which in this case would be 321.20 (320 + 1.20 = 321.20). This trade has a profit range below 321.20 and above 338.80. Since your reward is the net credit of the trade, it is essential to find markets with appropriate option premiums

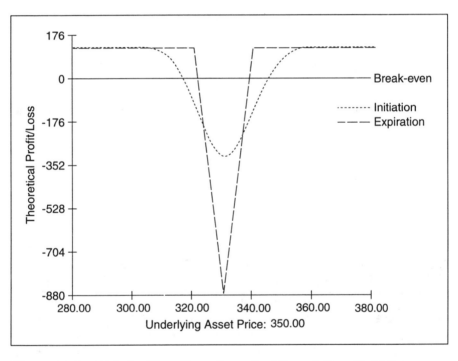

Figure 14.3   Risk Profile—Short Butterfly (Short 1 Dec Gold Futures 340 Call @ 12.6, Long 2 Dec Gold Futures 330 Calls @ 20.7, Short 1 Dec Gold Futures 320 Call @ 30)

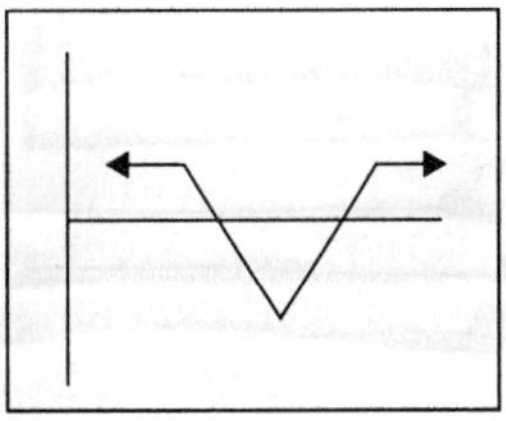

Strategy: Sell lower strike (call or put). Buy two higher strike (calls or puts). Sell higher strike (call or put). Use all calls or all puts.

Risk: Limited.

Profit: Limited.

Time Decay Effect: Detrimental.

Situation: Look for a market ready to break out above the highest strike price or below the lowest strike price.

Profit: Limited to the net credit received.

Risk: Limited (difference of middle and lower strike prices times value per point minus net credit received).

Upside Break-even: Highest strike price minus net credit received.

Downside Break-even: Lowest strike price plus net credit received.

Figure 14.4 Strategy Review—Short Butterfly

that make the trade worth the risk. It is best placed no earlier than four weeks before expiration.

LONG CONDOR

The long condor is one of my favorite nontrending market strategies. The long condor can be thought of as a butterfly spread split apart. In a long condor, you use the body of the butterfly but instead of one strike for the body, there are multiple strikes. For example, let's use the gold market again, this time with 310, 320, 330, and 340 strikes. If you believe gold will continue in a trading range between 310 and 340, then you can create a long condor by going long 1 Dec Gold Futures 340 Call, short 1 Dec Gold Futures 330 Call, short 1 Dec Gold Futures 320 Call, and long 1 Dec Gold Futures 310 Call with gold trading at 315. In a long condor, you need to go short (sell) the two inner option strikes that make up the body of the condor and go long (buy) the wings. You are selling the middle options to collect time premium as the gold market continues to trade in between the wings. The risk profile of this long condor trade is shown in Figure 14.5. This is usually a net debit transaction and that debit paid is also your maximum risk. (See Figure 14.6.) In this trade, the net debit is $590 [(40 + 12.6) – (17.7 + 29) = 52.6 – 46.7 = 5.9 × 100 = $590].

This strategy makes money with the passage of time if the market trades in between the wings. The maximum reward is the difference in the strike prices of the lower short option and the lower long option multiplied by the value for each point less the net debit paid or plus the net credit received (if a credit was received). A net debit is the most likely scenario. In this case, the maximum reward is $410 {[(320 – 310) × $100] – $590 = $410}. The maximum risk is the net debit paid of $590. The upside break-even is equal to the highest strike price minus the net debit. In this example, the upside break-even is 334.10 (340 – 5.90 = 334.10). The downside break-even is equal to the lowest strike price plus the net debit. In this example, the downside break-even is equal to 315.90 (310 + 5.90 = 315.90). The profit range is therefore in between 315.90 and 334.10, perfect for a sideways market.

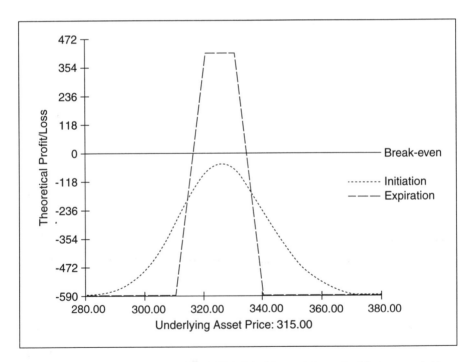

Figure 14.5   Risk Profile—Long Condor (Long 1 Dec Gold Futures 340 Call @ 12.6, Short 1 Dec Gold Futures 330 Call @ 17.7, Short 1 Dec Gold Futures 320 Call @ 29.0, Long 1 Dec Gold Futures 310 Call @ 40.0)

Strategy: Buy lower strike (call or put). Sell one higher strike (call or put). Sell one higher strike (call or put). Buy one higher strike (call or put). Use all calls or all puts.

~~Risk: Limited.~~

~~Profit: Limited.~~

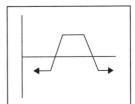

Time Decay Effect: Beneficial.

Situation: Look for a sideways market that is expected to remain between the break-even of the condor.

Profit: Limited (difference between highest and next higher strike prices times value per point) minus net debit paid.

Risk: Limited to the net debit paid.

Upside Break-even: Highest long strike price minus net debit paid.

Downside Break-even: Lowest long strike price plus net debit paid.

Figure 14.6 Strategy Review—Long Condor

A long condor is actually a combination of a bull call spread (310/320 spread) and a bear call spread (330/340 spread). Thus the risk and reward are calculated in a similar fashion as with these strategies.

Is the following trade still a long condor?: long 1 Gold Futures 350 Call, short 1 Gold Futures 340 Call, short 1 Gold Futures 320 Call, and long 1 Gold Futures 310 Call. Yes, it is. As long as you sell the body and buy the wings, you are creating a long condor that may be appropriate in a nontrending market. It must be noted that by opening the condor, you are increasing the profit area (now between 350 minus the debit and 310 plus the debit paid). However, if you buy a deeper ITM option and thereby pay a higher debit, you reduce the profit.

SHORT CONDOR

In a short condor you go long the body and short the wings in anticipation of a breakout beyond the trading range. Therefore, it is not an appropriate strategy for a nontrending market trade. For example, you could create a short condor in which you go short 1 Dec Gold Futures 340 Call @ 12.6, long 1 Dec Gold Futures 330 Call @ 20.7, long 1 Dec Gold Futures 320 Call @ 30.0 and short 1 Dec Gold Futures 310 Call @ 40.0. The risk profile for this trade is shown in Figure 14.7, and the strategy is reviewed in Figure 14.8.

The maximum risk for a short condor equals the difference between the strikes, less the net credit. In this trade, the maximum risk is $810 [(340 − 330) × $100 = $1000 − $190 = $810]. The maximum profit is the net credit from the spread. In this trade, you would have a maximum profit of $190 [(12.6 + 40) − (20.7 + 30.0) = 52.6 − 50.7 = 1.9 × $100 = $190]. Once again, you need to look for markets where the reward is worth the risk.

Since the profit depends on the underlying market breaking beyond the normal trading range, look for a market where you anticipate a sharp increase of volatility. The upside break-even equals the highest strike price minus the net credit. In this case, the upside break-even is 338.10 (340 −

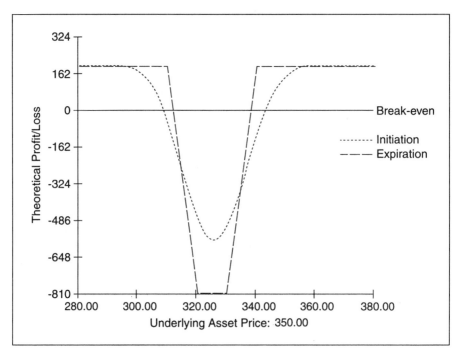

Figure 14.7   Risk Profile—Short Condor (Short 1 Dec Gold Futures 340 Call @ 12.6, Long 1 Dec Gold Futures 330 Call @ 20.7, Long 1 Dec Gold Futures 320 Call @ 30.0, Short 1 Dec Gold Futures 310 Call @ 40.0)

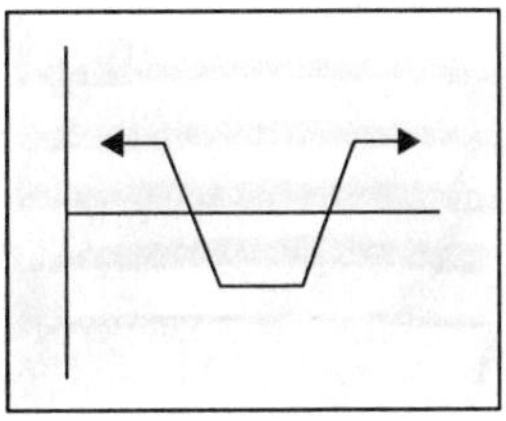

Strategy: Sell one lower strike (call or put). Buy one higher strike (call or put). Buy one higher strike (call or put). Sell one higher strike (call or put). Use all calls or all puts.

Risk: Limited.

Profit: Limited.

Time Decay Effect: Detrimental.

Situation: Look for a market ready to break out above the highest strike price or below the lowest strike price.

Profit: Limited to the net credit received.

Risk: Limited (difference between lowest and next higher strike prices times value per point) minus net credit received.

Upside Break-even: Highest short strike price minus net credit received.

Downside Break-even: Lowest short strike price plus net credit received.

Figure 14.8 Strategy Review—Short Condor

1.90 = 338.10). The downside break-even is equal to the lowest strike price plus the net credit, which is 311.90 (310 + 1.90 = 311.90) in this trade. To make a profit, you need the market to break above 338.10 or below 311.90. It is best to place this trade with less than 30 days till expiration.

LONG IRON BUTTERFLY

The long iron butterfly spread is the third strategy that can be used in a sideways market. It combines two more basic option strategies: the bear call spread (short lower call and long higher call) and the bull put spread (long lower put and short higher put). It is similar to a long condor, but has a particular twist. This shift is illustrated in Table 14.2.

As you can see, the long iron butterfly is created by shifting one of the spreads. In this case, we shifted the 320/330 calls and made them puts instead. Using this market, we can create a long iron butterfly by going long 1 Dec Gold Futures 350 Call @ 7.5, short 1 Dec Gold Futures 340 Call @ 12.6, short 1 Dec Gold Futures 330 Put @ 9.8, and long 1 Dec Gold Futures

Table 14.2   Shift from Condor to Iron Butterfly

	Long Condor	Long Iron Butterfly	
Strike Price	Calls	Calls	Puts
350	Buy 1	Buy 1	
340	Sell 1	Sell 1	
330	Sell 1		Sell 1
320	Buy 1		Buy 1

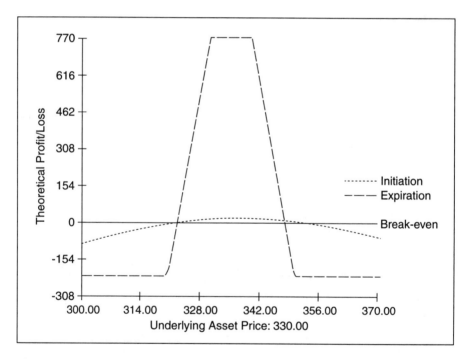

Figure 14.9   Risk Profile—Long Iron Butterfly (Long 1 Dec Gold Futures 350 Call @ 7.5, Short 1 Dec Gold Futures 340 Call @ 12.6, Short 1 Dec Gold Futures 330 Put @ 9.8, Long 1 Dec Gold Futures 320 Put @ 7.2)

320 Put @ 7.2. The risk curve for this trade is shown in Figure 14.9, and the strategy is reviewed in Figure 14.10.

This risk graph strongly resembles the risk profile of a long condor. Maximum reward is simply the net credit of the spread. In this example, the maximum reward is $770 [(12.6 + 9.8) − (7.2 + 7.5) = 22.4 − 14.7 = 7.7 × $100 = $770]. Maximum risk is equal to the difference between the strikes times the value per point minus the net credit received. In this case, the maximum risk is $230 {[(350 − 340) × $100] − $770 = $1000 − $770 = $230}. The upside break-even is equal to the middle call option strike price plus the net credit received. In this example, the upside break-even is 347.70 (340 + 7.7). The downside break-even is equal to the middle put strike price minus the net credit received, or 322.30 (330 − 7.7 = 322.30). Therefore, the profit range for this trade is between 322.30 and 347.70.

I prefer to place an iron butterfly instead of a condor if my calculations show an increased reward-to-risk ratio. This often happens when the puts and calls

---

Strategy: Buy one higher-strike call. Sell one lower-strike call (ATM or other). Sell one higher-strike put (ATM or other). Buy one lower-strike put.

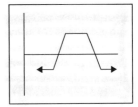

Risk: Limited.

Profit: Limited.

Time Decay Effect: Mixed.

Situation: Look for a sideways market that you expect to close between the wings of the iron butterfly.

Profit: Limited to the net credit received.

Risk: Limited (difference between long and short strikes times value per point, minus net credit received).

Upside Break-even: Strike price of middle short call plus the net credit received.

Downside Break-even: Strike price of middle short put minus net credit received.

Figure 14.10 Strategy Review—Long Iron Butterfly

have different implied volatilities. This difference can make one trade better than the other. As a rule, I go for the trade with the best reward-to-risk ratio.

SHORT IRON BUTTERFLY

A short iron butterfly is not appropriate for a sideways market. It is more appropriate for a market ready to break out of its normal trading range. A short iron butterfly is the combination of a bull call spread (long lower call and short higher call) and a bear put spread (long higher put and short lower put). Typically the straddle is purchased at-the-money and the strangle is sold. For example, we can create a short iron butterfly by going short 1 Dec Gold Futures 330 Call @ 3.0, long 1 Dec Gold Futures 320 Call @ 7.0, long 1 Dec Gold Futures 320 Put @ 6.8, and short 1 Dec Gold Futures 310 Put @

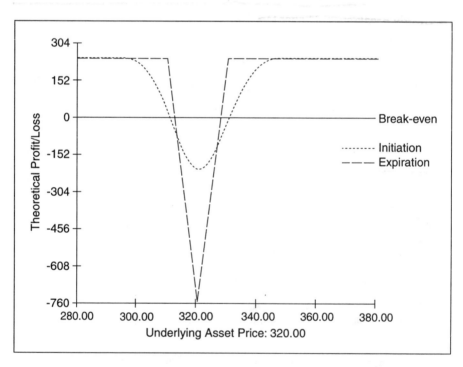

Figure 14.11   Risk Profile—Short Iron Butterfly (Short 1 Dec Gold Futures 330 Call @ 3.0, Long 1 Dec Gold Futures 320 Call @ 7.0, Long 1 Dec Gold Futures 320 Put @ 6.8, Short 1 Dec Gold Futures 310 Put @ 3.2)

Strategy: Sell one higher strike call. Buy one lower strike call (ATM or other). Buy one higher strike put (ATM or other). Sell one lower strike put.

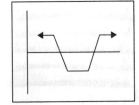

Risk: Limited.

Profit: Limited.

Time Decay Effect: Mixed.

Situation: Look for a market ready to break out from the break-even points.

Profit: Limited (difference between long and short strikes times value per point minus net debit paid).

Risk: Limited to the net debit paid.

Upside Break-even: Higher long call strike price plus net debit paid.

Downside Break-even: Lower long put strike price less net debit paid.

Figure 14.12   Strategy Review—Short Iron Butterfly

3.2. The risk profile for this trade is shown in Figure 14.11, and the strategy is reviewed in Figure 14.12.

The maximum risk is net debit paid for the trade, or in this case, $760 [(7 + 6.8) – (3 + 3.2) = (13.8 – 6.2) = 7.6 × 100 = $760]. The maximum reward is limited to the difference in the strikes of the long options and the short options multiplied by the value per point minus the net debit paid. In this case, the maximum reward is $240 {[(320 – 310) × $100] – [(7 + 6.8) – (3 + 3.2) × $100] = $1000 – $760 = $240}. The upside break-even is equal to the strike price of the higher long call option plus the net debit paid. In this trade, the upside break-even is 327.6 (320 + 7.6 = 327.6). The downside break-even is equal to the strike price of the lower long put option minus the net debit. In this example, the downside break-even is 312.4 (320 – 7.6 = 312.4). Therefore, to make a profit the underlying market would have to climb above 327.60 or fall below 312.40. It is very important to calculate the break-evens on all short trades so that you can fully understand just how much the market has to move for the trade to be profitable.

CONCLUSION

A butterfly or condor spread can be constructed using all calls or all puts. I usually base my selections by calculating the best possible reward-to-risk ratios. To accurately assess the situation, you have to be willing to do the calculations. I prefer long condors to long butterfly spreads because it is easier to widen the maximum profit zone by spreading the condor out. I look for the right market by scanning charts until I locate one with strong support and resistance levels.

When I see a market with a strong support and resistance line, I take a ruler and draw the lines before choosing which options to buy and sell. In many cases, I am willing to accept a lower profit potential for an expanded profit zone. Although you can calculate these risk/reward scenarios by hand, a good options analysis program is worth the investment. It will save you a great deal of time and avoid costly errors. Besides, one good trade could certainly pay for the software.

These strategies can be exited by simply doing the opposite of the original trade. If you bought options, you sell them and if you sold options, you buy them back. If you are exiting at expiration, then you can let the short options that are worthless simply expire. If any of the short options have value, you can buy them back for a profit. Try to limit your commissions when you are placing and exiting these trades, as commissions can be a big part of the cost of trading.

Trading sideways markets can be a very conservative specialty. If you decide to trade markets that have established strong support and resistance levels, never forget that markets can change erratically. Always be vigilant to the changing nature of the markets you are trading. If the market starts to move above the options strikes you purchased, make a bullish adjustment. If the market appears to be making a real move downward, make a bearish adjustment. Learn to be flexible in your trading. This will lead to longer-term success.

15

Increasing Your Profits
with Adjustments

You can create the best trade in the world, but what you do after the trade is placed is crucial to your success. When you put on a trade that is perfectly delta neutral and the market makes a move, it changes your overall position delta. Your trade is no longer delta neutral. At this point, you can choose to maintain or exit the trade, or return to delta neutral by making adjustments. An adjustment can be made by buying or selling options and futures (or stocks) to offset your position to bring it back to delta neutral. Determining which adjustment to make is a decision dependent on critical thinking and market experience.

In general, delta neutral trading experience fosters market insight, which guides your decision-making process regarding when and how to make an adjustment to your position. To a certain extent, adjustments are the real meat of delta neutral trading. As you become more experienced in the adjustment arena, your profits will reflect your increased proficiency. This is where the professional floor trader needs to excel to survive. Off-floor traders have more time to think about and execute the optimal hedge.

When you are trading delta neutral, it can be helpful to think of one side of the trade as your hedge and the other side as your directional bet. In many cases, even if you are 100 percent wrong about market direction you can still make a profit. I prefer to hedge with the options and bet on the direction of the futures or the stock. Theoretically speaking, if the market moves 10 points up or down, you should be able to squeeze the same amount of profit out of the trade. However, when you start factoring in things like time decay and volatility, this figure may change.

As previously mentioned, there are two different types of deltas: fixed deltas and variable deltas. A fixed delta means something that never changes, something that always stays the same. For example, if you buy a futures contract at 925 and sell it for 930, you will have 5 points deposited into your account. Conversely, if you buy a 925 futures contract and it goes down to 920, you lose 5 points. This 5 points will be drained out of your brokerage account. Either way, the delta of the futures remains the same. This is a fixed delta. Buying and selling futures and stocks are also examples of fixed deltas. The deltas will remain at +100 for each one futures contract or each 100 shares of stock you are long and −100 for short positions.

What is a variable delta? Deltas change because of the passing of time and due to market movement, which modifies prices. Options at different strikes have different deltas that vary as the underlying security changes.

If you buy five futures and sell five futures at 925, your overall position is delta neutral. But there's something faulty in this reasoning. This kind of trade goes flat. Can you buy a September S&P 500 futures and sell a December S&P 500 futures? Yes, you can. Is this trade delta neutral? Yes, it creates an overall position delta of zero. However, since both deltas are fixed, this trade cannot be adjusted. Options, on the other hand, have variable deltas that change as the underlying price moves. When the overall position delta moves away from zero, you can apply adjustments to bring the trade back to delta neutral and thereby incur additional profits.

As we have already discussed, deltas are the cornerstone of learning delta neutral trading. As previously shown, one future or 100 shares of stock has a fixed delta of plus or minus 100 while ATM options have a delta of plus or minus 50. If you buy two futures contracts for a delta of +200, you can buy four ATM puts or sell four ATM calls to create a delta neutral trade. The type of options you choose determines whether your focus is on a long or a short strategy. The plus or minus sign depends on which direction best takes advantage of the market circumstances. Buying a call or selling a put takes advantage of a rising market and therefore has a corresponding plus sign. Buying a put or selling a call takes advantage of a decreasing market and therefore has a minus sign.

Mathematically, this is quite easy to understand. But why do deltas act the way they do? Perhaps a simple analogy will convey the meaning of a delta. When you slam on the brakes of your car, the process from the time you hit the brakes until the time your car stops is like a delta curve. Near the end of the stopping, you tend to stop more quickly than when you first hit the brakes—even with antilock brakes. Right at the precise point where you completely stop, everybody kind of jogs forward a bit for a little whiplash action. This is exactly like the movement of a delta at expiration.

LONG SYNTHETIC STRADDLES

You can create a long synthetic straddle by selling 5 Jun T-Bond Futures @ 110 and buying 10 Jun T-Bond Futures 110 ATM Calls @ 2^20. If you are selling a future, this trade is still a long synthetic straddle because you are buying the option side of the trade to create an imitation straddle. You're putting on a trade where you are hedged both ways to make money on the long side. As long as you have long options, be it puts or calls, you have a long synthetic straddle. The name of this trade (long) is based on the options.

I prefer to use ATM options because they have high liquidity and are easy to work with. High liquidity increases the probability of profit and fosters better pricing because the spreads are thinner. Price spreads are the difference between the bid price and the ask price for which you, as a trader, can buy and sell options, futures, or stocks. As an off-floor trader you will typically buy at the higher price (the ask) and sell at the lower price (the bid). Meanwhile, floor traders typically make their money by buying from you at the bid, and selling to someone else at the ask, or vice versa. In other words, when we refer to spreads, we are really talking about the bid and ask price.

An ATM option in the last 30 days before expiration is actually the most liquid option out there. In most cases, ATM options have the highest liquidity. Liquidity tends to taper off like a bell curve the further out-of-the-money or deeper in-the-money you go because there is less buying and selling. The spreads become a lot wider. You can look at something that is two strikes out-of-the-money and there could be half a point difference between buying and selling it. This means that you are automatically in the hole half a point before you even initiate a trade. You should—in almost every case—use ATM options to offset your futures or stock positions when you initiate a delta neutral trade.

Let's return to your synthetic straddle created by selling 5 Jun T-Bond

Futures @ 110 and buying 10 Jun T-Bond Futures 110 ATM Calls @ 2^20. In this trade, you have –500 (5 × –100) deltas on the futures side and +500 (10 × +50) deltas on the options side for an overall position delta of zero. If the futures moves up 5 points, the futures delta is still –500. It doesn't change, because it's fixed. The only time it changes is when you change it by adding another future, or taking one off. The variable deltas are your option deltas. The ATM calls are +50 each. If the underlying futures move up 5 points, the calls become in-the-money with a higher delta of approximately +70 each for a total of +700 deltas. This means that your overall position delta is +200. To bring the trade back to delta neutral, you can make an adjustment by either selling two additional futures or selling three of the ITM calls you already own. Either choice realizes an increased credit into your account. If the market makes another move, you will be able to make another adjustment to increase your profit even more. This adjustment process locks in profits.

Let's do a stock trade using Intel. On April 11, you see that Intel is breaking out of its all-time high of 90. You elect to try a delta neutral trade. After looking at the prices of options you see the following: Intel stock is at 90; the July 90 calls are priced at $3^3/_4$ and the July 90 puts are priced at $2^3/_4$. You decide to initiate a 5 × 10 position with Intel (i.e., 500 shares of Intel stock and 10 Intel options). Once again, you have to choose which options have a better profit potential: puts or calls. To avoid unlimited risk, you purchase the stock and buy ATM puts. On the stock side, you have +500 deltas, which will be offset by 10 long ATM Jul 90 Puts for a total of –500. The overall position delta going into this trade is a perfect zero. (See Figure 15.1.) My total risk is the premium paid for the 10 put options of $2750.

On April 14, Intel closes at $95. The July 90 calls close at $6^7/_8$ and the July 90 puts close at 2.00. The positive delta is still +500. Since you are one strike out-of-the-money, the negative deltas have moved to –35 each for a total deltas of –350. Your overall position delta is now +150. You make an adjustment to get back to delta neutral by selling 150 Intel shares for a profit. Now, you own 350 shares of Intel and the 10 puts originally purchased. (See Figure 15.2.)

What is your cash settlement up to this point? Right now, it is relatively easy to calculate the cash settlement. You started with 500 shares of Intel at 90. Then the price went up 5 points and you sold 150 shares for a $750 profit. The puts are now at 2.00. You lost $3/_4$ points on the puts, which equals

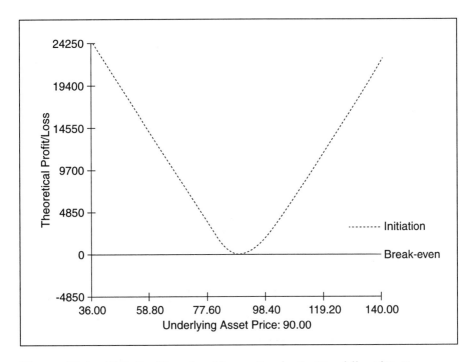

Figure 15.1 Risk Profile—Intel Long Synthetic Straddle 4/11 (Long 500 Shares of Intel Stock @ 90, Long 10 Jul Intel Stock 90 Puts @ $2^3/_4$)

$750. That means you have broken even on this trade so far, but still have 350 shares of Intel @ 90 showing an open position profit of $1750.

On April 26, Intel hits 105 a share. The July 90 calls are now at 11.5 and the July 90 puts are now going for $1^5/_8$. Your 350 Intel shares have a positive delta of 350. The puts are now at –250 because you're 3 strikes out or –25 each. That gives you a position delta of +100. Let's make another adjustment by selling 100 more shares of Intel at 105. (See Figure 15.3.)

What is your cash settlement to date? You started with 500 shares of Intel at 90. You sold 150 at 95. You made $750 on that one trade. You still own a lot more that have incurred profits as well. You just haven't sold them yet. Then, you sold another 100 shares at 105 making 15 points on each. That gives you another $1500. Now, you are still holding 250 shares of Intel stock at 90. If you bought 250 at 90 and now it is at 105, you have $3750 in an open position profit. This adds up to $6000 on the stock side. Let's take a look at the put side of the trade. You bought the

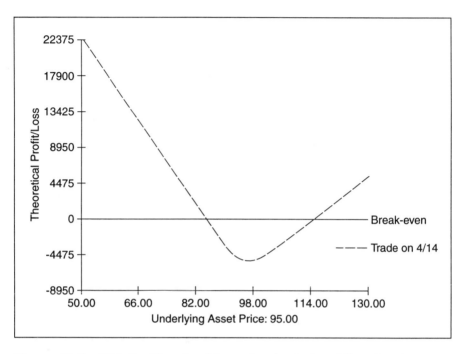

Figure 15.2   Risk Profile—Intel Long Synthetic Straddle 4/14 (Long 350 Shares of Intel Stock @ 90, Long 10 Jul Intel Stock 90 Puts @ 2.00)

puts for $2^3/_4$, which translates to $2750. They are worth only $1625 now, which means you have lost $1125. That creates a net profit of $4875, which is a pretty good trade.

Market Opportunity: On April 11, Intel breaks out of its all-time high of 90.

Strategy: Long Synthetic Straddle—Limited risk and unlimited profit potential.

Initial Trade: Long 500 Shares of Intel Stock @ 90, 10 Long Jul Intel Stock 90 Puts @ $2^3/_4$.

Initial Deltas: +500 and –500 = Zero.

Move #1: April 14—Intel moves to 95. Jul 90 puts close at 2.00.

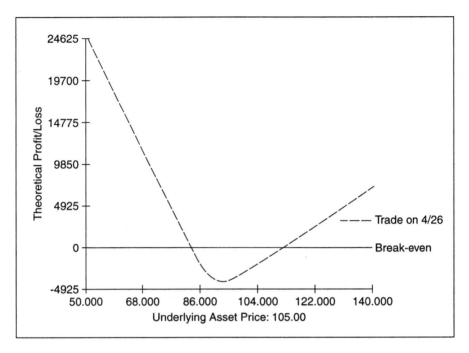

Figure 15.3 Risk Profile—Intel Long Synthetic Straddle 4/26 (Long 250 Shares of Intel Stock @ 90, 10 Long Jul Intel Stock 90 Puts @ 1⁵/₈)

Consequence #1: Puts are now 1 strike out-of-the-money for a total of −350 deltas. Overall position is now +150 deltas.

Adjustment #1: Sell 150 shares of Intel @ 95.

Cash Settlement: Selling 150 Intel shares @ 95 translates to a profit of $750. The long puts are now at 2.00, which is a loss of ³/₄ each. This equates to a loss of $750. The total cash profit so far is zero; however, the 350 shares of Intel @ 90 do have an open position profit of $1750.

Move #2: On April 26, Intel hits $105 a share. Jul 90 puts close at 1⁵/₈.

Consequence #2: Puts are now 3 strikes out-of-the-money for a total of −250 deltas. Overall position delta is now +100.

Adjustment #2: Sell 100 shares of Intel at 105.

Cash Settlement: Selling 100 Intel shares @ 105 translates to a profit of $1500. The 10 long puts are now at $1^5/_8$, which translates to $1625, a net loss of $1125.

Total Cash: The additional open position profit on the 250 shares purchased at 90 that are now worth 105 translates to $3750 profit. Adding this to the previous profits creates a total of $6000. The total put loss is $1125. The total profit on this trade equals $4875.

Since this is a stock trade, you have to remember that your margins are going to be quite a bit higher—in most cases—because you are talking about buying stock, which does not have the same leverage as futures (500 shares at 90 each is a whopping $45,000; you will be required to put up $^1/_2$ the amount). Luckily, the margin agreements that you can get with certain brokerage firms when you trade delta neutral are significantly lower than that.

Let's try a 10×20 long synthetic straddle using gold futures. With a large trade ratio, we will be able to make even more adjustments. On March 25, we initiate the following trade: short 10 Jun Gold Futures @ 330 and long 20 Jun Gold Futures 330 Calls @ $3^1/_2$. Since we are doing a long synthetic straddle, we do not have to post a margin requirement for the futures. Although we do not receive a direct credit into our account for selling futures, it will reflect profits as the market moves. Each futures point movement equals $100. Each call option costs $350 ($3^1/_2 \times 100$) for a total debit of $7000 ($350 \times 20$). (See Figure 15.4.)

Four days later, the market moves to 335. The calls are now worth 11.25 each and are now one strike in-the-money. This means that the 20 long calls now have a total delta of +1300, creating an overall position delta of +300. To make an adjustment, we sell three futures. We have returned to a delta neutral position that is short 13 futures and long 20 calls. (See Figure 15.5.)

Two days later, the market goes up to 340. Once again, our long deltas increase again another +300. We sell three futures to adjust the trade back to delta neutral. That gives us an open position of long 20 calls @ 19.00, short 10 futures at 330, short three futures at 335, and short three futures at 340. (See Figure 15.6.)

Let's take a look at the cash settlement to date. We originally sold 10 futures, incurring a loss of $10,000. We made our first adjustment by selling three more at 335 for a loss of $1500. We also sold three more futures at 340, but since futures are still at 340, we have not incurred a profit or a loss

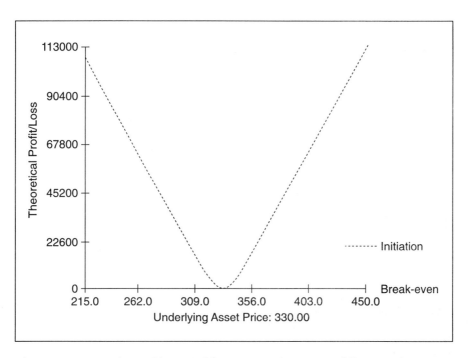

Figure 15.4   Risk Profile—Gold Long Synthetic Straddle #1 (Short 10 Jun Gold Futures @ 330, Long 20 Jun Gold Futures 330 Calls @ 3½)

yet. This creates a total loss of $11,500. The long calls originally cost us $350 each for a total debit of $7000. They have increased in value to 19.00 or $1900 each. That gives us a total of $38,000 for a profit on the call side of $31,000. If we reconcile this with our loss on the futures side, we have total profit of $19,500 ($31,000 − $11,500 = $19,500).

Market Opportunity: On March 25, Gold is ready for a break-out above 330.

Strategy: Long Synthetic Straddle—Limited risk and unlimited profit potential.

Initial Trade: Short 10 Jun Gold Futures @ 330, Long 20 Jun Gold Futures 330 Calls @ 3½. Total debit = $7000.

Initial Deltas: −1000 and +1000 = Zero.

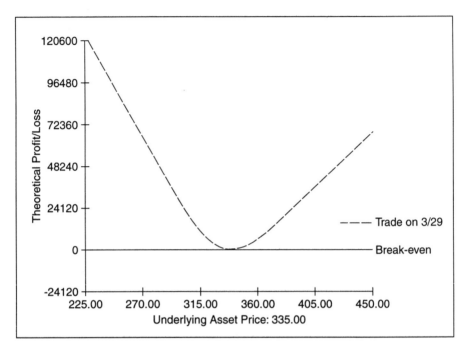

Figure 15.5   Risk Profile—Gold Long Synthetic Straddle #2 (Short 10 Jun Gold Futures @ 330, Short 3 Jun Gold Futures @ 335, Long 20 Jun Gold Futures 330 Calls @ 11.25)

Move #1: March 29, Gold moves to 335.

Consequence #1: The calls are now 1 strike in-the-money, which means that the 20 long calls now have a total delta of +1300. Overall position delta is now +300.

Adjustment #1: To make an adjustment, sell 3 Gold futures @ 335. The trade is now short 13 futures and long 20 calls.

Move #2: On April 1, Gold moves to 340.

Consequence #2: Long call deltas increase another +300.

Adjustment #2: Sell 3 Gold futures @ 340. The trade is now long 20 Gold futures 300 calls @ 19.00, short 10 Gold futures @ 330, short 3 Gold futures @ 335, and short 3 Gold futures @ 340.

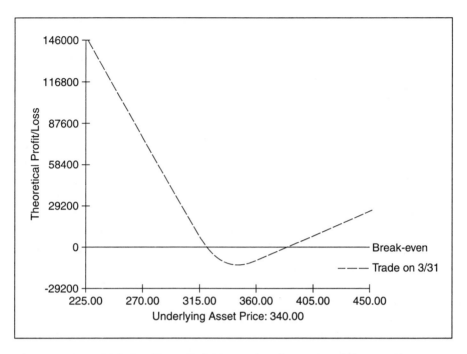

Figure 15.6 Risk Profile—Gold Long Synthetic Straddle #3 (Short 10 Jun Gold Futures @ 330, Short 3 Jun Gold Futures @ 335, Short 3 Jun Gold Futures @ 340, Long 20 Jun Gold Futures 330 Calls @ 19.00)

Total Cash: We originally sold 10 futures, incurring a loss of $10,000. We made our first adjustment by selling three more at 335 for a loss of $1500. We also sold 3 more futures at 340, but since futures are still at 340, we have not incurred a profit or a loss yet. This creates a total loss of $11,500. The long calls originally cost us $350 each for a total debit of $7000. They have increased in value to 19.00 or $1900 each. That gives us a total of $38,000 for a profit on the call side of $31,000. If we reconcile this with our losses on the futures side, we have total profit of $19,500 ($31,000 − $11,500 = $19,500).

Can you make adjustments on 1 × 2 trades? Approximately 90 percent of the time, a 1 × 2 trader will not make any adjustments. The trade is simply placed and exited when the market moves. If an adjustment is possible, it will most likely be made on the option side.

Frequently, when the market moves up fast and you see a dramatic increase in volatility, it can be better to get out of the trade altogether. Why? Because when you have an increase in the volatility, the premium on an option is going to pump up. I recommend exiting the trade, waiting for volatility to collapse a little, and then getting back in.

For example, if you have a 1 × 2 (1 future or 100 shares of stock × 2 options) or 2 × 4 (2 futures or 200 shares of stock × 4 options) trade, you have to have some decent-sized market movement, and a good profit (i.e., 20 percent), before you even consider making an adjustment. Why make an adjustment at all when you can just get out of the trade and then get back into the trade when the market calms down? If you can make a 20 percent return on your risk capital, you are on your way to consistent profits.

What determines whether you initially go short the underlying contract (stock or futures) or long the underlying contract with the corresponding long two puts or long two calls? The way to decide is to look at the prices of the puts and calls and buy the ATM options that are the cheapest. You could be looking at a computer or you could be looking at the newspaper at the end of the night. Let us say S&P 500 futures calls are going for $10^1/_2$ and the 500 puts are $11^1/_4$. There is a $.75 difference between the price of the puts and the price of the calls. Therefore, I would rather pay $10^1/_2$ for the calls and buy two for each S&P futures I sell.

It really doesn't matter which way you go to get to delta neutral. It is safe to assume that you want to take the less expensive of the two options and thereby pay less money out-of-pocket. Taking less money out of your account initially is a good technique to use if you want to dramatically increase your account size. That's where the real buried treasure lies and it's just waiting for you to discover it.

CONCLUSION

The more contracts you have to buy and sell (i.e., 2 × 3, 3 × 5, 5 × 10), the more profitable adjustments you can make. It's somewhat like being in Atlantic City or the racetrack. If you are betting on a horse with 2 to 1 odds, you know you have a pretty decent chance of winning. If you bet on a horse that has 100 to 1 odds, your chances of winning are slim, but the payoff would be enormous.

Consistent returns on your investments lead to the gradual accumulation of wealth. The accounts we trade have increased dramatically over the years because we take profits on a consistent basis. You, too, will be able to increase your account size dramatically. Did you ever lose everything you had in the futures or stock market? I have, more than once. But, I persevered in the face of what seemed impossible odds and bounced back into prosperity. It can happen to anybody. With delta neutral trading, you have a much better chance of succeeding. I tell a lot of traders that if they cannot trade delta neutral, then it's better not to trade at all. I believe that trading without visualizing the risk and subsequently limiting that risk is akin to gambling at a Las Vegas craps table—the house eventually wins.

16

Processing Your Trade

Stocks, futures, and options are traded on organized exchanges throughout the world, 24 hours a day. These exchanges establish rules and procedures which foster a safe and fair method of determining the price of a security. They also provide an arena for the trading of securities. Over the years, the various exchanges have had to update themselves with the ever-increasing demands made by huge increases in trading volume. The New York Stock Exchange (NYSE)—probably the best known of the exchanges—not too long ago traded 100 million shares as a high. Today we see 200, 300, 400, and even 500 million share days. At some time in the future 1 billion share days will be the norm.

Stock, futures, and options exchanges are businesses. They provide the public with a place to trade. Each exchange has a unique personality and competes with other exchanges for business. This competitiveness keeps the exchanges on their toes. Exchanges sell memberships on the exchange floor to brokerage firms and specialists. They must be able to react to the demands of the marketplace with innovative products, services, and technological innovations. If everyone does his or her job, then you won't even know where your trade was executed.

In addition, exchanges all over the world are linked together regardless of different time zones. Prices shift as trading ends in one time zone, moving activity to the next. This global dynamic explains why stocks close at one price and open the next day at a completely different price at the same exchange. With the increased use of electronic trading in global markets, these price movements are more unpredictable than ever before.

The primary U.S. stock exchanges are the New York Stock Exchange (NYSE), the American Stock Exchange (AMEX), and NASDAQ (over-the-counter stock market). There is a host of others that do not get as much publicity as the big three. However, each exchange certainly produces its share of activity. These include the Pacific Stock Exchange in San Francisco, the Chicago Stock Exchange, the Boston Stock Exchange, and the Philadelphia Stock Exchange. The major international exchanges are in Tokyo, London, Frankfurt, Johannesburg, Sydney, Hong Kong, and Singapore.

In the United States, exchanges are regulated by the Securities and Exchange Commission (SEC). The Commission was created by Congress in 1934 during the Depression. It is composed of five commissioners appointed by the President of the United States and approved by the Senate and a team of lawyers, investigators, and accountants. The SEC is charged with making sure that security markets operate fairly and with protecting investors. Among other acts, they enforce the Securities Act of 1933, the Securities Exchange Act of 1934, the Trust Indenture Act of 1939, the Investment Company Act of 1940, and the Investment Advisers Act of 1940.

The SEC also monitors insider trading. This is a form of trading in which corporate officers buy and sell stock within their own companies. This type of trading is widely influenced by inside information that only corporate officers have access to. Many off-floor traders keep track of insider trading to gauge the movement of a specific stock. In addition, there are a myriad of regulations aimed at preventing corporate officers from profiting from information not released to the general public during mergers or takeovers.

The primary commodities exchanges include: Chicago Mercantile Exchange (CME); Chicago Board of Trade (CBOT); New York Mercantile Exchange (NYMEX); COMEX (New York); Kansas City Board of Trade; Coffee, Cocoa and Sugar Exchange (New York); and the Commodity Exchange (CEC). The Commodities Futures Trading Commission (CFTC) and the National Futures Association (NFA) currently regulate the nation's commodity futures industry. Created by the Commodity Futures Trading Commission Act of 1974, the CFTC has five futures markets commissioners who are appointed by the President and subject to Senate approval. The rules of the SEC and the CFTC differ in some areas, but their goals remain similar. They are both charged with ensuring the open and efficient operation of exchanges.

Most investors never realize the number of steps required for a transaction to occur and the incredible speed involved. Technology has made this process almost unnoticeable to the average investor. When you contact your stock or commodity broker, you begin a process that—in many cases—can be completed in 10 seconds or less, depending on the type of trade you want to execute. There are various types of orders that are placed between customers and brokerage firms. (There is list of types of orders in the Appendixes.) The faster technology becomes, the faster a trader's order gets filled. Let's take a closer look at what happens when you place an order.

STOCK AND STOCK OPTION ORDERS

If you are playing the stock market, you begin by placing an order with your broker, who passes it along to a floor broker who then takes it to the appropriate specialist. At this time, the floor broker may or may not find another floor broker who wants to buy or sell your order. If your broker cannot fill your order, it is left with the specialist who keeps a list of all the unfilled orders, matching them up as prices fluctuate. In this way, specialists are brokers to the floor brokers and receive a commission for every transaction they carry out. Groups of specialists trading similar markets are located near one another. These areas are referred to as trading pits.

Once your order has been filled, the floor trader contacts your broker, who in turn calls you to confirm that your order has been placed. The amazing part of this process is that a market order—one that is to be executed immediately—can take only seconds to complete. As the information superhighway speeds up, this transaction process will evolve beyond our wildest imaginings. In addition, computerized trading is used for smaller orders. More than 50 percent of a day's trades use the Designated Order Turnaround (DOT) system.

Your broker—as your intermediary—is paid a fee (commission) for his or her efforts. Each completed trade is called a round turn (buy/sell) and costs $30 on the low end and $100 (or more) on the high end. Stock commissions may also be based on a percentage value of the securities bought or sold. Remember, your broker should be in the business of looking after your interests, not generating commissions for the broker's own pockets. Since your chief concern as a trader should be to get the transactions executed as you desire and at the best price possible, choosing the right broker is essential to your success.

Let's review the stock market order process. The seven steps are as follows:

1. You call your broker.

2. The broker writes your order.

3. Broker transmits your order via DOT (Designated Order Turnaround system) machine to stock exchange floor (NYSE, AMEX, etc.) or by wire to a floor broker, or to the NASDAQ (computerized matching system) computer.

4. Floor broker tries to immediately fill your order or takes it to a specialist.

5. A specialist matches your order.
   • If your order is placed as a market order, you get an (almost) immediate fill.
   • If placed as a limit order, you have to wait until you get the price you want.

6. Fill is sent back to the broker.

7. Broker contacts you to confirm that your order has been executed.

This is the process for most transactions. In addition to the specialists, there are also market makers who are there to create liquidity and narrow the spread. Market makers trade for themselves or for a firm. Once an order "hits the floor," the market makers can participate with the other players on a competitive basis.

In contrast, NASDAQ—also referred to as the over-the-counter (OTC) market—is an electronic computerized matching system that lists over 5000 companies, including a large number of high-tech firms. Brokers can trade directly from their offices using telephones and continuously revised computerized prices. Since they completely bypass the floor traders, they get to keep more of their commissions. There are no specialists, either; but, there are market makers. Their role is to bid and offer certain shares they specialize in, thereby creating liquidity. They make their money on the spread—the difference between the bid price and the offer price—as well as on longer-term plays. This difference may be only $.25 ($1/4$ point) or less. However, when you trade a large number of shares this adds up very quickly.

FUTURES (COMMODITY) ORDERS

Futures contracts are traded at commodity exchanges. The exchanges are divided into trading pits that are sometimes subdivided into sections of smaller commodities. Individual trades are recorded on trading cards that are turned in to the pit recorder, who time-stamps and keys the transaction into a computer. Some exchanges prefer the use of handheld computers that instantly record the transactions.

Orders are filled using an open outcry system in which the buyers (who make bids) and the sellers (who make offers, otherwise known as the ask) come together to execute trades. For example, in the gold market, if gold is trading at $300 per ounce, you may get a price of $299.50 to $300.50. This means that you would be buying the gold futures contract at $300.50 and you would be selling at $299.50. You may ask, "Why can't I buy for the lower price and sell for the higher price?" You can try, but the trade will probably not be executed. The floor traders make their living off this spread. They won't want to give it up to you.

Let's review the futures market order process. The six steps are as follows:

1. Call your commodity broker (or call direct to the trading floor for large accounts).

2. The broker writes an order ticket or sends your order via computer or calls the trading floor.

3. Floor broker will bid or offer.

4. When your order is matched, the fill is signaled to the desk.

5. The desk calls your broker.

6. Broker contacts you to confirm execution.

Floor traders primarily make their money on the bid/ask spread. They are the ones who spend (in many cases) thousands of dollars each month for the privilege of being on the floor of the exchange (or hundreds of thousands to buy a seat). They can either lease the seats—gaining the right to trade as an exchange member—or purchase the seats. In addition, they spend each and every day creating liquidity for the investor who is not trading on the exchange floor. For this they want something in return—the right to make money on the spread. The money to be made on the spread comes from the difference between the bid and offer price. In the gold example, the reward is $1.00 ($300.50 − $299.50 = $1.00).

In addition, being right where the action is allows them to see the order flow. Order flow is the buying and selling happening around them. They can spot when large traders are trading. This does give them an advantage, but there are negatives. These include the following aspects:

- High monthly expenses.

- The need to always be in the market to cover costs.

- Sometimes getting caught up in emotion, not fact.

- Missing opportunities in other markets.

- Very physically and mentally demanding work.

You probably have watched scenes of the trading pits on television or in movies. You see lots of people yelling and screaming. Is this the way it really is? Yes, when there is action in the market, it can be extremely volatile. If it is slow, you will find people reading newspapers or just staying away. I do suggest that you visit the commodity exchanges. It is very exciting and enlightening to experience what really goes on there.

Commodity exchanges have to provide safeguards for the public trader. For every buyer there is a matching seller. Clearing firms—where the funds are held—must guarantee that each person trading through them has the available funds to meet that trader's financial obligations, or they are responsible for the integrity of the transaction. This system of checks and balances has never failed, no matter how crazy the markets have become. Public investors can feel secure that they will not lose their money due to the system failing.

OPTION ORDERS

Just as the stock and commodity exchanges provide safe arenas for the sale and purchase of stocks and futures, options trading has a similar arena. Options exchanges provide a place for buyers and sellers to meet and thereby establish the price of options. The primary stock options exchanges include: Chicago Board Options Exchange (CBOE), Pacific Stock Exchange (San

Francisco), and the American Stock Exchange (New York). Individual futures exchanges also have options trading pits.

Placing option orders is very similar to that of placing futures orders. In many cases, if you are trading both futures and options, your order will be guided to an exchange that can process both. However, since they are individual orders, you will be charged a commission on both orders. Luckily, you will only be charged one time for the option round-turns, unlike stocks that have a charge to get in to and to exit a position.

The CBOE handles the majority of the options volume on stock options. The American Stock Exchange and the Pacific Stock Exchange round out the big three in the stock options arena. Many of the largest companies have options that you can trade, and many fast-growing companies have options to trade. Throughout the book, I have tried to acquaint you with the wide variety of techniques you can use to locate companies that have options that may provide explosive returns.

CONCLUSION

The progression of an order through the trading system is a fascinating process. It has come a long way from the days in the early 1800s when traders met under a buttonwood tree on Wall Street. Today's floor traders run an average of 12 miles each trading day just to get the job done. Although many traders never set foot in an exchange, it is important to understand the process your order goes through before returning to you as a profit or a loss. As we cross into the 21st century, this process will become more and more electronically synchronized. As the information superhighway speeds up, it will be very interesting to see how it changes the nature of the trading game.

17

Placing Orders

It is absolutely essential to master the art of placing orders. Clarity is a rarity and clear communication is imperative to successful trading. It is likely that the order process sounds more complicated than it really is. Don't waste time worrying about all the steps—just contact your broker with what you want to do. However, it is important to realize that each step outlined in the previous chapter leaves room for error to occur. You can't control all the steps; however, you can control which broker you've selected to help you. Remember, a good broker is an asset and a bad broker is a liability. Take the selection process very seriously. Don't let your broker make you broker!

A major mistake many people make when they first begin investing is to listen to their brokers. Why do they do this? Perhaps because many people have been brainwashed to believe that just because a broker has a license, he or she must know how to make top-notch investment decisions. As in any profession, there are top-notch professionals as well as others who have missed their calling and should not be offering their services. The best advice I can give you is to be very selective in finding your broker.

A broker is an individual who is licensed to buy and sell marketplace securities and/or derivatives to traders and investors. In addition, brokerage firms must also be licensed and insured to accept customer deposits. A word of caution: It is a major misconception to believe that just because someone is licensed to take an order they have the knowledge to invest your money wisely. A good broker is worth a great deal, especially if he or she understands a wide variety of markets and your trading strategies. Remember, successful traders develop profitable trading strategies that require a broker who can execute orders with precision. Brokers are the intermediaries of trading. Building profits is the name of the game. The broker makes money whether you win or lose—the brokerage commissions will always be paid. Many traders choose to trade with discount brokers; this can be profitable as long as they are getting good fills and timely exits. Brokers get paid to place and execute your orders and protect your interests. Many investors, especially beginners, try to find a broker with the lowest commission cost. However, an inexpensive broker can become an expensive broker overnight if mistakes lose money each time the broker places your trade. It is imperative to match low cost with prompt service and good execution.

There are several levels of brokers: full-service, discount, and deep-discount. All brokers get paid a commission each time you place a trade. The amount of this commission depends on what kind of service they provide. Full-service brokers have higher commissions because they spend a lot of time researching markets in order to advise their clients. Discount brokers have lower commissions because they simply act as an agent placing the trader's order as well as facilitating the exit. Deep-discount brokers primarily trade for investors who trade in large blocks. They offer the lowest commission rates of the three. However, with the advent of the Internet, electronic brokers are becoming more accessible than ever. They offer low commission costs and easy access via computer. Since they have only recently been introduced, it is too early to be able to measure their competence. It will probably be a while until Internet trading services can handle the more complicated orders that delta neutral strategies employ. You might want to go online and search the net to see what this kind of brokering provides.

In stock trades, your broker will charge you for each transaction. In futures, brokers charge only one time per round-turn, which opens and closes a position. Commission fees vary from around $30 on the low end to more than $100 on the high end. You don't have to pay more to get good service and accurate information. There are a number of good brokerage firms that provide excellent service and plenty of useful information at a fair rate of commission. Stock commissions are usually based on a percentage value of the securities bought or sold. Do not fret over a couple of dollars of commission when evaluating brokers; remember, a one tick difference in execution will cost you a great deal more than that. Commissions are decreasing steadily due to increased competition and the use of the Internet to place orders. It is best to select a broker through recommendation of other traders.

Remember, your broker is in the business of looking after your interests. Make sure you find a broker that is licensed to execute stock, futures, and options transactions. Your chief concern as a trader should be to get the transaction executed as you desired and at the best price possible. Choosing the right broker is essential to your success. But how do you find the right one? When choosing a broker, review the following four points:

1. *Does your broker* really *know more that you?*   Your broker should be an asset to you, should have sufficient knowledge of the markets you trade and invest in, and be able to make first-rate suggestions to help you increase your profitability. As a novice investor, be very careful with your broker selection. Look for a broker who has knowledge about a wide variety of option markets including margins, spread strategies, volatility, points, strikes, and so on. Interview potential brokers by presenting a specific trade to see if she or he can talk intelligently about it. Can she or he define the market conditions, risk, potential return, break-evens, and so on? Ask the broker how much of a percentage of their revenue comes from options. Look for a broker with a similar risk profile as you. Most importantly, make sure your personality fits the your broker's personality—you really have to be comfortable with their style and time availability. You should also find out if your broker's backup assistants understand options as well. Inevitably, you will end up dealing with assistants and they need to be knowledgeable about options or you will find frustration down the road.

2. *Invest your own account.*   Information from your broker should be viewed as a potential opportunity, not as advice. Once again, ask your broker for suggestions, not advice. It is very important that you always take responsibility for your own profitability.

3. *Do your own homework.*   Study, study, study. Continue to do your homework even after you've achieved success, because the learning process never ends when you're in the investment field. The day you think you have learned it all is the day you should retire. Overconfidence leads to complacency and losses.

4. *Always listen and digest before making any investment decisions. Remember, you can always call your broker back.*   When you call, listen to what your broker has to say, but never make an investment while still on the

phone. Put the phone down. Think about the information you have received and then do an analysis of risk and reward. If you still find the suggestion to be valuable, then call back and make the investment. My biggest mistakes were hasty investment decisions.

When you call your broker to place an order, it is a good idea to have all of the important information written down in front of you. What factors are important to this process? You have to know the quantity, the month, and the commodity. If there are options, you have to know the strike price, whether you want calls or puts, and if there is a price. A fill refers to the price at which an order is executed. Important items that need to be specified depending on the type of order you are placing include:

- What kind of order you wish to place.

- The exchange—where the order is to be placed (for futures and options).

- Quantity—number of contracts.

- Buy/sell—puts or calls (also include the strike price and expiration).

- Contract—name of the contract (e.g., T-Bond Futures).

- Month—expiration month of the contract.

- Price—instructions regarding price execution.

How is a delta neutral trade placed? To demonstrate this process, let's take a look at a delta neutral spread order using September S&P 500 futures trading at 938. To place an order, you would say, "I have a spread. I want to buy one September S&P 500 futures at 938. I want to buy two September S&P 500 futures 940 puts." When you do this as a spread on one ticket, it can only be entered at-the-market. A market order must be executed immediately at the best available price. It is the only order that guarantees execution. In contrast, a limit order is an order to buy or sell a stock, futures, or option contract at, below, or above a specified price. You cannot put a limit order or a price order on this type of trade, as there is no spread market that goes between the futures and the options. This order must be done as a market order.

If you want a limit order, you are going to have to do the futures separately at a limit. You can also do the options separately at a limit. However, if you do that, you run the risk of getting filled on one side and not the other;

and there goes your risk curve. If you are going to do this, you need to carefully pick some period of low volatility in the middle of a very fast market. You need to wait until things settle down a little bit.

Those of you who have traded before probably already know why clarity is so important. Most orders consist of buying the futures and selling the puts. This buy-sell combination on a spread is pretty normal. You have to be explicit when you place an order to make sure you get what you want. Before calling your broker, always write orders down on paper or better yet, in a trading journal. Every order you place with a broker is recorded on tape. If you make a mistake in the order process, you are responsible for that trade no matter what. By writing down exactly what you are going to say to your broker, you can avoid making costly mistakes. In addition, keeping a trading journal is an excellent way of learning from your successes and mistakes as well as staying organized.

Let's place an order where we sell one future and buy two calls. You would say, "I'd like to sell one September S&P 500 futures and buy two September S&P 500 calls." Now, what's missing from this order? You have to be careful; you cannot just say "buy two September S&P 500 calls." In fact, it is incorrect to say "buy two ATM September S&P 500 calls." People do this all the time. What happens if your chosen market is between two strike prices? Be clear! State the strike prices you want. Place the order by saying, "I have a delta neutral spread order. Futures with options. I am buying two September S&P 500 futures 940 calls at 14.25. I am selling one September S&P 500 futures at the market." You also want to request that the order be placed as one ticket to give you a better chance of execution. If you use ATM calls and ATM futures, your fills probably will not be as good or tight as a spread placed on one ticket performed simultaneously.

These examples are simply guides for entering delta neutral trades. Remember, the ratio does not make any difference. You could be doing two calls and one futures or 20 calls and 10 futures. Although you need to specify the number, all the other important factors remain the same.

Let's go over these examples one more time. If you have a delta neutral spread order, and you want to buy two September S&P 500 futures 940 calls, how would you place the order? You would usually say, "I want to buy two September/Labor Day S&P 500 futures 940 calls at 14.25 and sell one September/Labor Day S&P 500 futures at-the-market." We say "Labor Day" because "September" and "December" sometimes sound alike, especially when spoken loudly.

Again, it does not make a difference what kind of order you wish to enter. Just specify the quantity, the month, the commodity, then if there is an option, what kind and the price. These examples are basic market orders. Let's switch gears and try something a little more complicated.

A plain old bull call spread will enable you to understand the debit and credit side of a trade. Let's buy one September S&P 500 futures 935 call and sell one September S&P 500 futures 940 call. We are going to do this one as a limit order. We are not going to do it at-the-market. Just for a little calculation, let's say the premium on the buy side was 13.95 and the premium on the sell side was 11.05. This is where they closed. We come in and want to do it at whatever price they closed at. On the buy side, we are out-of-pocket paying 13.95; and on the sell side, we are receiving 11.05. What is the point difference? We are paying 2.90 more than we are getting. If you were placing this order, you would say, "I have a spread order. I am buying one September S&P 500 futures 935 call and selling one September S&P 500 futures 940 call at a debit of 2.90 to the buy side." This is just an ordinary bull call spread where we buy the lower call and sell the call further away. The trick is to figure out the premium on the buy side (debit) and the premium on the sell side (credit).

This process is pretty easy and would be the same if you were doing a 10 × 10, a 20 × 20, a 100 × 100, or a 2 × 2, as long as it is a one-to-one ratio. There is no other calculation than just doing the simple math. This would be the same process if you were doing a put spread. You would need to determine both the debit and the credit and net them out. If you are taking money out-of-pocket, it is a debit to the buy side. If you are receiving money, it is a credit to the sell side.

Never pick up the phone and call your broker without first writing out your order completely. By the time the information in your head gets to your mouth and over phone lines, it can be similar to the gossip or telephone games: The final outcome might only vaguely resemble your original thought. If you don't write it down, you may wind up placing a trade you never dreamed possible. Always remember that all your conversations with the broker will be on tape. Therefore, if you place the wrong trade and it goes awry, you are still stuck with it.

Let's take a look at a ratio backspread. We want to buy 2 September S&P Futures 935 Puts at 11.05 and sell 1 September S&P Futures 940 Put @ 13.95. The risk profile for this trade is shown in Figure 17.1.

How would this order be entered in terms of the premium? Since this is a ratio, we're going to have to do some multiplication. The sell side is easy be-

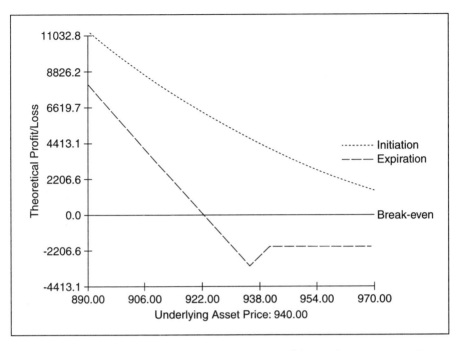

Figure 17.1 Risk Profile—S&P Put Ratio Backspread #1 (Long 2 Sep S&P 500 Futures 935 Puts @ 11.05, Short 1 Sep S&P 500 Futures 940 Put @ 13.95)

cause we only have one of them. We are taking in 13.95 points. On the buy side, we need to multiply 11.05 times 2, which equals 22.10. Now, we subtract the 13.95 from the 22.10 for a debit of 8.15 to the buy side. This is the formula for any 2 × 1 ratio trade. Regardless of the size of the order (i.e., a 4 × 2, an 8 × 4, a 10 × 5, or a 20 × 10), as long as the ratio is 2 to 1, this is what you will use. Even a 100 × 50 will have a debit of 8.15 to the buy side. This can be confusing. Just remember to always figure the spread using the minimum ratio, which in this case is 2 to 1. If you were placing a 10 × 5 order, you would say, "I am buying ten September S&P 500 futures 935 puts at 11.05. I am selling five September S&P 500 futures 940 puts at 13.95 for a 8.15 debit to the buy side."

Perhaps you have a specific idea—particularly when you are doing ratios—of a certain price you are willing to pay. Maybe this spread is trading at 8.15 but you are only willing to pay 7.50. You can put that order in; however, it may not get filled. The point is that you can enter a trade at whatever prices you like. The previous prices were just used to demonstrate the calculations.

If you are debiting the buy side, you don't say "credit" because you are actually taking money out-of-pocket. This is a debit. A credit means that you are taking money in. It is something that goes on the sell side of the ticket. A debit means that you are taking money out. It is something you are paying on the buy side.

Let us create another trade—a 3 × 2—using the same prices as the previous trade. (See Figure 17.2.) Let's buy three September S&P 500 futures 935 puts and sell two of the 940 puts. Using the same prices (13.95 and 11.05), take a minute to do the calculations and write down the order. Again, when you do a spread, you have to calculate the differential between the two sides. You cannot say, "I want to buy the buy side at 11.05 and sell the sell side at 13.95." You cannot put price or limit orders in on each side. You can

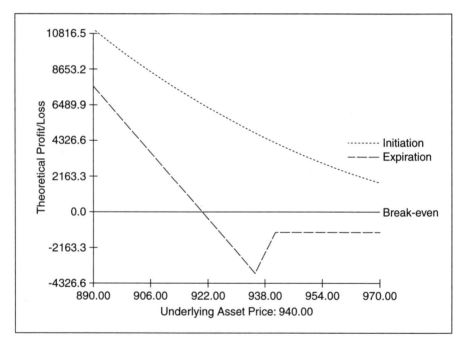

Figure 17.2 Risk Profile—S&P Put Ratio Backspread #2 (Long 3 Sep S&P 500 Futures 935 Puts @ 11.05, Short 2 Sep S&P 500 Futures 940 Puts @ 13.95)

only work the spread between the two premiums. Don't worry about the prices. Just make sure you get the right spread to make the trade work the way you want it to. If you want to do a credit of five, do you care whether you do it at 15 and 20 or 5 and 10? No, you do not care what those prices are. All you care about is the differential. The floor will not fill a limit order if you give them premium prices on each side.

Let's calculate this trade. With a 3×2, we need to multiply 11.05 times 3, which would be 33.15. Then multiply 13.95 times 2, which equals 27.90. You subtract them from one another and get 5.25 (33.15 − 27.90 = 5.25). You can now call your broker and say, "I have a ratio spread. I want to buy three September S&P 500 futures 935 puts and sell two September S&P 500 futures 940 puts at 5.25 debit to the buy side."

Let's shift gears and take a look at placing a short iron butterfly spread order. There are strikes at 280, 285, 290, 295, and 300 options. Gold is at 290. In this case, let's say we think gold's going to try for 305, so we'll choose a 285 option. Since this is a short iron butterfly spread, we are buying three straddles at 285 (long a 285 call and long a 285 put at the same strike price). What else do we need to do to complete the trade? We need to sell the wings of the butterfly by selling three of the 280 puts and three of the 290 calls.

Now we're ready to place the trade. Always write the order on paper prior to calling your broker. In addition, write the order in a "trading journal," to keep an accurate account of every trade you make and glean as much knowledge as possible from your trading experiences.

The typical brokerage firm ticket has the buy side of the trade on the left and the sell on the right. Generally, we would always start from left to right, writing down your buy side first. You would say, "I have a spread order. I am going to buy three of the October gold 285 straddles and sell three of the October gold 290/280 strangles at —— price." The blank would be filled in with "at-the-market," "at-even," or with a certain number of ticks or points.

With a spread order, always give the quantity, the month, the underlying instrument, the price, and the strategy: "I am buying three (quantity) October (month) gold (instrument) 285 (price) straddles (strategy)." The other half of the order would be, "I am selling three October gold 290/280 strangles."

Now we have to calculate the price. It is either a debit, a credit, or at-even. If it is at-even, you do not want to receive a debit or a credit. You want to stay at net cost of zero. I like to do my trades at-even or better. In this way I do not pay or receive cash in my account.

If you are not comfortable with the specific language of straddles and spreads, then state each part of the trade instead. Tell your broker, "I want to buy three of the October gold 285 puts. I want to buy three of the October gold 285 calls." Spell out the whole thing if you are more comfortable doing it that way. In fact, you don't even have to say "straddle" and "strangle" if you are not comfortable with those terms. In the beginning, it is a good idea to be specific about each leg to make sure you get it right. Once you have experience in these types of trades, it will become second nature to properly state your orders.

If you are trying to get a credit, do not state the credit as a dollar value. You do not say, "I want $200." You specify the credit, if that is what you desire, at the point level you want. For example, it may be at $^{32}/_{64}$ (in tick values) or .5 points. You need to specify the trade in the terminology used by the floor. Most importantly, it has to always be in tick values or point values, not in dollar terms of how much you want to spend or take in.

You can go into any market at whatever price you want. The floor will either execute the trade at that price or will not. You could say that you want the trade at-even, but if the market is not at-even, your order will not get filled. At one point during the day, perhaps the market does get to even and you finally get what you want. Bottom line: If you don't enter, you can't win.

If you want it at a certain price, put the order in the market. Then wait to see if you get the trade filled. If you do not get your credit price or even, try the trade at some other time. Do not chase the trade.

The more volatile the market is, the wider the bid/ask spread will be. If the market is pretty quiet that day, the bid/ask spread will be smaller. The bid/ask will be smaller for the ATMs and for the body of the trade and greater for the wings. Floor prices primarily depend on volatility and liquidity. In addition, the longer the time your options have until expiration, the wider the spread. Floor traders will widen the spread when there is a greater chance of their being wrong due to time, volatility, and volume.

CONCLUSION

You must be absolutely clear and correct when you are placing an order. Let's review the eight guidelines:

1. Always place an order by stating whether you want to buy or sell, the quantity, the month, and the commodity or stock. If there are options, state whether you are buying or selling, the price, what kind of option (whether you want calls or puts), and the credit/debit in point value.

2. Always state the month first when you are placing an order even though most quote machines go commodity, month.

3. It is really good practice to say, "a credit to the sell side or a debit to the buy side," because it doubly reinforces the side you want the trade on. Many times people get confused and put a debit on the sell side. For stocks, it is customary to just use the words debit or credit.

4. As long as the ratio remains the same, the differential will remain the same.

5. Do not specify the year. Order takers assume you mean the current year unless you specify otherwise.

6. Do not call and give orders in symbols, because symbols are not used consistently. Different quote services use different symbols.

7. Be clear. Write everything down before you place an order.

8. Keep a journal and record every trade you place so that you can learn from your mistakes and your successes.

18

Final Summary

This book has reviewed a variety of strategies that can be applied in various markets. It has avoided trying to forecast market direction or analyzing charts with detailed market patterns, and has not referenced highly technical data or difficult-to-interpret fundamental information. Although these trading tools may have their place in your trading arsenal, they are exhaustively studied in many other publications. The purpose of this book is to focus on unique trading strategies and to demonstrate how professionals trade without overanalyzing the markets. When traders get bogged down in trying to process too much information, the result is what I like to call "analysis paralysis."

I have tried to make the information contained in this book as straightforward as possible. Learning to trade can be quite difficult and perplexing. Each strategy has an infinite number of possibilities when applied to the markets. Each trade is unique and your task as a trader is to learn from your achievements and your mistakes. There are no absolutes in trading.

However, I do believe that you will be able to build a solid trading foundation based on the delta neutral strategies explored in this book. This approach to trading comes from years of experience from my trading team and my own endeavors. To become successful, it's up to you to take a systematic approach to becoming confident in the markets. You must be willing to spend the time it takes to study the markets and learn to trade.

In late October of 1997, the Dow Jones Industrial Average dropped 554 points or 7 percent. By most people's standards, this constitutes a minicrash. It was not as severe as the 1987 crash when there was a 22 percent drop, but it definitely shook up the markets. Throughout the day of the minicrash, I talked with a number of traders and investors to discuss our views on this market decline. At many brokerage firms, clients were being forced to meet margin calls as their positions declined. Eventually, there were more sell orders than the markets could bear and trading closed early at the New York Stock Exchange. Unlike the millions of individuals who lost a great deal of money, traders who were using the strategies included in this book fared much better. They knew how to hedge their positions and either made money or at least minimized the losses to their accounts. This approach to trading offers protection and enables players to keep playing the game.

To get started, find one market you like and get to know it very well. How many shares of contracts are traded? What is the tick value? What are the support and resistance levels? What are the strike prices of the available options? How many months of options should be analyzed? Is this a volatile market? Does it have high liquidity? Do you have enough capital to play this market?

Once you determine the right market for you, focus your efforts on evaluating which strategies best take advantage of this market's unique characteristics. This can be accomplished by paying close attention to market movement trends. For example, stocks have a natural tendency to go up in price over the long run. This means that in many cases I take a bullish bias over the long run in top stocks. Since many futures markets go sideways, I like to apply the appropriate strategies for range-bound markets.

By concentrating your attention on one market, you will become familiar with that market's personality. When change occurs, this familiarity will enable you to profit the most from the change. Practice these strategies by paper trading your market until you get the hang of it. I recommend three months of paper trading before investing a dime. For every great trade you missed, there will be mistakes that could have wiped out your whole account. Take small steps up the ladder of experience and you'll learn what you need to master along the way.

In addition, you need to determine what influences a specific market. Markets have spheres of influences. You need to get to know what internal and external forces drive your chosen market. For example, the bond market affects the S&Ps. What affects Dell Computer, Intel, Microsoft, gold, silver, and other markets? All of this research combines to increase your overall knowledge of trading, which will help to make you a successful trader in the years to come.

During one of my two-day Optionetics seminars, I kept saying that very few traders and investors really know what is going on in the markets. The very next day, as if by magic, the following article appeared in *USA Today*. I promptly revealed it to the students at my seminar.

GARBAGEMEN GOOD AT PREDICTING ECONOMY

In December of 1994, the economists sent a questionnaire to four chairmen of multinational companies, former finance ministers from four countries, four Oxford University students, and four garbagemen. They were asked to predict average economic prospects including world economic growth, inflation, the price of oil, and the pound's exchange rate against the dollar in the ten years following 1994. The economists said the garbagemen and company bosses tied for first with the predictions. The finance ministers came in last.

So, let me get this straight. Politicians supposedly run entire countries, right? Then how come their own finance ministers cannot beat garbagemen at predicting economic prospects? This only emphasizes the point that the markets are great equalizers of education. It is irrelevant whether you have an MBA or a PhD or are a rocket scientist. High school dropouts can do just as well, if not better, if they are disciplined and have the skills and knowledge to succeed. It is actually easier for me to train individuals with very little experience or none whatsoever than those who have years of experience. This is due to the fact that many experienced traders have developed bad habits that need to be broken.

Approximately 99 percent of the time that I trade delta neutral, I am able to manage my risk on entering the trade and monitor it each day as the market moves. Delta neutral trading is a scientific system that significantly reduces your stress level. It provides you with the means to limit your risk and make a consistent profit. It directs you to take advantage of market movement by making adjustments. By learning to trade using delta neutral strategies, traders have the opportunity to maximize profits and make consistent returns.

On a cautionary note, avoid high commissions, brokers soliciting business, and software that promises or boasts impossible results. High turnaround fees can really eat into your profits. Remember, nothing beats your own ability to trade effectively and no one takes better care of your money than you do.

The markets by their very nature have multiple personalities. Perhaps the only way to beat them is to get to know their personalities and use the appropriate weapons to win the war. These weapons include knowledge, experience, patience, and perseverance. By reading this book, you have been armed with the knowledge you need to become successful. Now you need to foster your own confidence and develop real trading savvy by practicing these skills and applying these techniques in the marketplace.

APPENDIXES

Trading Media Sources

FUTURES MAGAZINE

Top-notch monthly magazine superb for finding great investment opportunities, understanding the markets, and learning all aspects of successful futures trading. Excellent editorial staff. A must read for commodity traders. Telephone Number: (800) 972-9316.

TECHNICAL ANALYSIS OF STOCKS & COMMODITIES

Good cross section of stock and commodity information. More technical than other periodicals, but a very good source of interesting trading ideas. Telephone Number: (206) 938-0570.

COMMODITY PRICE CHARTS

Exceptional information to base commodity trading decisions on and to locate excellent trading opportunities. Keeps you abreast of the markets with easy-to-read charts and timely market information. Telephone Number: (800) 972-9316.

THE WALL STREET JOURNAL

It is a rare event to find anyone who has not heard of the *Wall Street Journal* (the *Journal*). This publication seems to have been around forever and will undoubtedly be around for many years to come. With worldwide distribution and a wide readership in the United States, it has the ability to influence the markets. If a company is mentioned in the *Wall Street Journal*, it is news. The *Journal* is packed with information—some useful to the investor, some not. The following areas are the most useful for spotting investment opportunities, as well as providing a perspective of what is happening in the markets.

What's News—Business and Finance (Front Page)

This section is the first read of the day. In just a few minutes, you can scan summaries of the most important information you need. You can then turn to the detailed article if you find something that interests you.

Money & Investing (Main Investment Section)

On the first page of this section, you will find the following series of graphs: stocks, international stocks, bonds, interest, U.S. dollar, commodities (Markets Diary on next page). These six charts are placed here purposely. A knowledgeable investor can look at these charts individually and collectively to get a very good idea as to the outlook for the U.S. economy, the stock market's strengths or weaknesses, and even what the world may think of U.S. economic prospects.

The second page of this section provides some valuable information that many investors tend to overlook. This includes the following:

Most Active Issues (Various Exchanges).   Many stocks show up here day after day. To spot profitable trade opportunities, you want to locate those that are new to the list. For example, you may see Wal-Mart and Intel on the list each day, but you must concentrate on finding the new stocks. These new stocks have increased in volume for a reason. You may also ask your broker if any new stocks came out. If there isn't anything new, then this may be a good momentum investment time since there may be news that hasn't leaked out yet. Does this happen? Yes. It happens all the time, even though it's not supposed to happen.

Price Percentage Gainers . . . and Losers.   This is my favorite column. If there were only two pieces of information I could look at to make a smart investment, I would pick these two because they reveal the stocks with the greatest momentum (up or down). The best investments are based on momentum, at least in the short-term. I watch these stocks like a hawk to see if they have momentum that is continuing (good or bad) or momentum that is slowing and reversing. I look for a chance to do the opposite on fast movers down (price percentage losers) by looking for buying opportunities. I also like to buy on a fast mover up (price percentage gainers). If a move up is missed, I look to sell as soon as the momentum starts slowing or reversing.

For example, one day while I was watching this column, a company—Syquest (SYQT)—caught my eye. It was an inexpensive stock (less than $10), so I bought call options. The stock was trading at around $6 per share. I bought the $7\frac{1}{2}$ calls very inexpensively, at around $87 ($\frac{7}{8}$) apiece (100 shares). The very next day the options doubled in value. I sold these options for over $500—a 400 percent return—a short time thereafter. Have you ever been able to do this?

Why did I buy an option instead of buying the stock? To get more value for my dollar. In this case, I controlled 100 shares of the stock for $87. If I bought the stock, I would have had to pay $600 (100 shares times $6 per share). When the stock doubled in value, my options went up four times in value. Therefore, my return on invested capital was twice as much using the options versus the stocks.

Note: This is very important. Please review the concept of options versus shares until you grasp it. Then focus on the information in the Price Percentage Gainers . . . and Losers columns and learn how to use it intelligently (as described in this course) to make money.

Volume Percentage Leaders.   Volume percentage leaders represent those with the highest trading records. However, they are not as important as percentage gainers and losers or new additions (see previous discussion of most active issues).

Marketplace (Review Front Page)

This column can be used effectively if you scan for news that is dramatically bullish (good news that should help a stock price go up) or excessively bearish (bad news that should make a stock price go down). The best way to use much of this information is to do the opposite of the crowd. This is called the contrarian approach to investing. The theory behind this approach is that the majority of the investors will be wrong a majority of the time—most people lose money when they invest. Look for information that sounds very optimistic or very pessimistic. Then watch these stocks to see how they react once the information is in the marketplace.

Stock Page Headings

Many people look at these tiny numbers and become overwhelmed. This section of the paper is easier to read once you know which information is important to focus on.

52 Weeks Hi/Lo: High and Low Prices for the Past 52 Weeks. Important: This figure tells you the price change of a stock over the past year. The difference between the high and low is called the range. If a stock has moved only $1 in the past year, it is likely to stay in this range. Also, if a stock is at its 52-week high, it may be ready to make new highs. This is one you want to look at as a potential buy. If a stock is at a 52-week low, it could break down and go lower, which may be a selling opportunity (going short). It is generally stated on Wall Street that strength leads to strength and weakness leads to weakness. Since many investors use this information to make investment decisions, it can have great influence on the directions of many stocks.

Stock: Name of the Company. Important: Obviously, you need to know the name of the company and its abbreviation to trade it.

Yld Div/%: Dividend Yield. Not Too Important: Unless you are buying stocks based on dividend yield (the return you make on a dividend payout) and earnings, this is not a critical number. If you are building a long-term portfolio based on yields, then you will want to compare one stock versus another using this information. Many stocks—especially high-tech stocks—will have a low dividend yield yet still be good investments.

PE: Price-to-Earnings Ratio. Important: The price-to-earnings ratio tells you how many times the earnings a stock is trading at. For example, a stock with earnings of $1 per share and a price of $20 has a PE of 20. If the industry average is a PE of 40, then this stock may be undervalued. If the stock is trading at a PE of 100 ($100 per share) with the industry average being a PE of 40, then the stock is likely overvalued; on any sign of weakness, the stock will come tumbling down.

Brokerage firm analysts establish guidelines for each industry. For example, a slow-growth industry, such as the steel industry, may have a PE of only 10, while a high-growth industry, such as the Internet businesses, may have a PE of 40 or higher. These range significantly. There are a number of publications that list this information, including *Value Line*.

Vol: Number of Shares of Stock Traded per Day.   *Important:* This number is important when the volume is increasing significantly. For example, when a stock has an average share volume of 100,000 shares and the stock trades five times that (500,000) this information is useful. If the stock has a high trading volume and is found on the Price Percentage Gainers . . . and Losers list, then you have a confirmation signal that the stock is making a move. When volume is decreasing or stable, the stock will likely go nowhere as interest in the stock is dwindling. It is important to watch the volume of the stocks you own or are trading to see whether there is a momentum increase or decrease.

Hi/Lo: High and Low Prices Yesterday.   *Not Critical:* Unless you are day trading (going in and out during one trading session), this information is not critical. Investors and traders look at this information to signal if stock traders will be running stops. This technique can also be used to look for orders from public traders. For example, if a trader sold a stock yesterday, he or she may place a buy stop (to cover losses) above yesterday's high. This is referred to as a resistance point. If the trader bought a stock, he or she may place a sell stop (to sell the stock purchased) below yesterday's low. This is referred to as a support point. These techniques are used frequently for protection if the market moves against the original position.

Note: The technique of running stops is used by many investors and traders; however, it is not what I recommend. I prefer to use options to protect my investments, because I find them to be more profitable and safer in the long run.

Close: Closing Price Yesterday; Net Chg: Change in Price Yesterday.
Important: These two points are important as they represent the dollar value
a stock has changed. The net change value is based on where the price of the
stock is today relative to yesterday's close. If a stock is trading at $10 today,
and it closed yesterday at $8, then the stock has a net change of +$2. This 20
percent increase is significant (30 percent is even better). If a stock is trading today at $10 and closed yesterday at $20, this $10 drop in value (50 per-
cent) is very significant.

Futures Page Headings

The information you use for futures analysis is similar to the data used for
looking at stock prices. The biggest difference is the time frame. When trading futures versus stocks, the time frame is much shorter. For example, you
may very well have a portfolio of stocks that you hold for years; however,
when you trade futures, positions may last months, days, or hours. Although
it is possible to hold futures trades for years, it is not their nature. Futures
have a defined length of existence (the expiration date). You may move from
one expiration month to another; but in most cases you will trade the front
month (the contract closest to you being traded). The front-month contract
will have the most liquidity, as most traders focus on this contract to trade.
Let's take a look at the information you will find when you look at futures in
the newspaper.

Open: Yesterday's Opening Price.   Not So Important: This is a reference
point for short-term traders because it establishes the starting point for
where the futures contract traded. Although many traders—especially day
traders—use this as a critical level, you should focus on longer-term indicators, which will be discussed below. Short-term traders find this information
significant because if a futures contract trades high (prices go up) and then
breaks below where the future opened, they look at this as a sign of weakness and begin to sell the contract.

High: Yesterday's High Price; Low: Yesterday's Low Price.   Impor-
tant: First reread the information as noted on stocks highs and lows. The
same information applies; however, for futures this category has an *im-*
portant rating. In futures trading the high price and low price yesterday

has more meaning than in stock trading as the traders are much shorter-term–oriented. This means that these resistance (high price) and support (low price) levels become more important. As futures trading is much shorter-term–oriented, these are important reference points. When trading futures on a longer-term basis (as I prefer) these levels become less important.

Settle: Yesterday's Closing Price Changed Compared to the Previous Day's Close.   *Important:* Once again, reread the previous discussion for stocks. For the most part, the same holds true for futures trading. Most traders look at the change over a short one-day trading period for futures. However, as a longer-term trader, you want to take longer time frames.

Lifetime High/Low: Highest and Lowest Prices since Inception. *Very Important:* Once again the importance of a number is built by the traders who build this number up as being critical. As they say, "if enough people believe something, then it becomes true." This may not be exactly correct, but it's close. The same occurs in futures trading. If the lifetime high and low—also known as the contract high and low—create an important point of reference for the majority of traders, then they become very important. Contract highs and lows are very strong resistance (for highs) and support (for lows) levels. This means that when these numbers are in striking reach of the traders, an effort is usually made to reach these levels.

When a contract high is broken as new highs are being established, this is very important to the intelligent traders. This may lead to a large number of successive new highs as long as the market stays above the original contract high. A failure of this move up can signal a weak market and selling can ensue. In a similar vein, new contract lows could lead to a major sell-off in the instrument; however, unless the market rebounds above the original contract low, then the market will likely stay weak.

Open Interest: Contracts/Units Being Held.   *Not Important:* From my experience—although some traders may disagree with me on this point—I have found this number to be relatively unimportant. Many investors and traders don't realize that a great majority of the trading and open interest contracts are created by hedging practices primarily generated by large commercial traders and speculators. Large commercial traders actually use the end products such as soybeans and wheat while speculators tend to increase the open interest due to their own hedging activities. In addition, floor traders are also hedging longer-term positions.

I have found open interest data to be difficult to utilize and assimilate into intelligent trading decisions even though the numbers appear to be easily broken and classified correctly.

Strike. *Very Important:* For options, the price at which the underlying asset is sold or bought if exercised. The strike price is used to determine the available contracts which can be traded and to develop strategies that meet specific investment objectives.

Exp.: Expiration Months. *Important:* For options, the months corresponding to the expiration of the options that were bought or sold. This information is vital to determining the available contracts that can be traded and to develop the strategies that meet investment objectives.

Note: The *Wall Street Journal* contains a great deal of information. Each day, I scan the newspaper and look for clues to make intelligent investment decisions. If you make an effort to learn to use the *Wall Street Journal* to its fullest, you will have made a significant investment in your own trading education.

INVESTOR'S BUSINESS DAILY—DAILY GRAPHS

Investor's Business Daily (IBD) was started with the intent to add a new dimension of information to the investment community. *IBD* focuses on concise investment news information—including sophisticated charts, tables, and analytical tools—with the hope of adding valuable information that the *Wall Street Journal* may not provide. As the name implies, *Investor's Business Daily* is published for the investor. *IBD* is an exceptional newspaper for an investor to use to learn about the markets and locate profitable investment opportunities. It is excellent for spotting stock patterns that can produce excellent trading profits. It's well worth the investment. Telephone Number: (800) 831-2525.

Note: Since some of the information included in *IBD* has already been explained in the previous *Wall Street Journal* description, I will refer to this information when applicable.

Executive News Summary

Located on the very first page, this section is a brief, yet useful summary of the important news of the day. Once again, you want to focus on news events that are either extremely bullish (positive for the market or an individual stock) or very bearish (negative for the market or an individual stock). If you find an article worth exploring, you can go to the details within the article.

Stock Tables: Intelligent Tables

One of the very interesting features in *IBD* is its "Intelligent" Tables developed for the major stock markets. These contain some of the most important information on stocks based on a number of technical indicators. (A technical indicator is a numerical calculation of a specific equation that is used to determine a specific event.) *IBD* uses a number of standard technical indicators that will be reviewed in detail.

Note: Once again, you need to focus on the movers and shakers in the market. If you focus on ordinary stocks you will produce ordinary financial returns. As discussed in the *Wall Street Journal* section, you need to focus on the stocks that have a reason to move. Stocks move on momentum either due to technical factors or because they are being watched by a large number of investors.

You will find Intelligent Tables that list selected stocks with the following indicators:

- Greatest % Rise in Volume.

- Most Active.

- Most % Up in Price.

- Most % Down in Price.

You will also find Intelligent Tables for the three major exchanges:

- New York Stock Exchange (NYSE).

- NASDAQ over-the-counter issues.

- American Stock Exchange (AMEX).

Table Column Headings

EPS Rnk.: Earnings per Share Growth Rank.   Important: This number is calculated as an average of five-year earnings per share growth and stability and the EPS growth the last two quarters. The resulting number is compared to other companies in the table and given a rank of 1 (lowest) to 99 (highest).

Focus on companies with an EPS ranking of 95 or better when buying and 20 or lower when selling (i.e., buy stocks with the greatest strength and sell the weakest). It is a good idea to track the EPS rank of your stocks on at least a weekly basis so you have a chance to make changes to your portfolio if there is a dramatic change in the character of your investments.

Rel. Str.: Relative Price Strength.   Important: A relative strength weighting is used to compare one company to another, or one industry to another. This *IBD* table is an analysis of a stock's price change relative to other stocks in the table over a 12-month period. When buying options I focus on stocks with a relative strength weighting of 80 or better, and 40 or lower when selling stock (shorting stock).

Acc. Dis.: Accumulation Distribution Rating.   Important: This indicator reflects the percentage change of a stock's price and its volume, two of the most important indicators of strength or weakness in a stock. *IBD* uses the rating A (strongest) to E (weakest). I like to focus on As only for buying and Es only for selling stock short or taking a bearish perspective on the stock.

Vol. % Chg.: Percent Change in Volume.   Important: This is an interesting addition to the table of information. *IBD* highlights stocks that have prices greater than $10 when the volume increases by 50 percent or greater than the average volume over the last 50 trading days. Why is this important? Volatility. Always look for large increases in volume. I look for increases that at least double (200 percent) in average volume, because the larger the increase in volume the more likely something important may be happening. This is a typical signal of momentum change indicating strong impending moves either up or down in the price of a stock.

Note: Look for stocks that are lower than $10 in price that have volume percentage changes of 200 percent or greater. These could signal the beginning of explosive growth in the price of a stock.

Other table column headings are:

- 52-Week High.
- 52-Week Low.
- Closing Price.
- Price Change.
- PE Ratio: price-to-earnings ratio.
- Float (mil): number of shares outstanding.
- Vol. (100s): number of hundreds of shares traded on the session.

INVESTOR'S BUSINESS DAILY—OPTION GUIDE FROM DAILY GRAPHS

Another exceptional publication to help you spot futures with options that can make a big move. Worth its weight in gold many times over once you understand the risks and rewards associated with options strategies, and the techniques used to maximize gain and minimize risk. Telephone Number: (800) 472-7479.

Miscellaneous IBD Information

In regard to table information, the commodity section in the *IBD* provides similar information as the *Wall Street Journal*. However, in Section B, you will also find price charts of popular futures trading. These important charts give you the opportunity to scan for potential investment opportunities. As stated earlier, markets go in one of three directions (up, down, or sideways). It is up to you to eyeball the charts and find the markets that appear to provide profitable opportunities. Which ones are these? In general you should look for the following: markets that make fast moves up; markets that make fast moves down; and, markets that go nowhere. All three of these types of markets have different strategies that work when trading and investing in commodities.

Data Service Providers

As an investor or trader, you can access sources of information that provide you with current data as to prices on stocks, futures, and options. In addition to prices, you can also receive up-to-the-minute news and market analyses. This information can be accessed in a variety of ways including cable, FM, satellite, and wireless networks. Which kind of service you need depends on what kind of trading you are involved with. Real-time data is as close to the actual prices as you can get. As the prices change at the exchange, the data is transmitted directly to you, thereby minimizing price discrepancies. Delayed prices are typically transmitted 15 to 20 minutes after the prices have changed at the exchanges. End-of-day prices are transmitted at the close of the market each day. The faster you receive your data, the more costly it is to obtain; however, the level of accuracy can be a significant contributing factor in the kind of trading you choose to pursue.

BONNEVILLE MARKET INFORMATION (BMI)

3 Triad Center, Suite 100
Salt Lake City, UT 84180
Phone: (800) 287-9520
Fax: (801) 539-4370

- Mix-and-match real-time and delayed information (simultaneously if needed).

- Fundamental information on over 150,000 stocks, futures, options, bonds, mutual funds, indexes, fixed income, FOREX, and statistics direct from the exchange floors.

- Compatibility with a wide variety of software packages.

- Discrimination between day and night sessions.

- Complete news stories on changes in market conditions.

- Data available via cable or satellite.

SIGNAL BROADCASTING (PRODUCT OF DBC)

Data Broadcasting Corporation
1900 South Norfolk Street
San Mateo, CA 94403
Phone: (800) 322-1320
Fax: (650) 596-1142
Internet: http://www.dbc.com

- Real-time, delayed, or end-of-day quotes 24 hours a day.

- Stock market information from NYSE, AMEX, NASDAQ, and regional exchanges.

- Commodity and futures option information from CBT, CME, CEC, NYMEX, KCBT, MGE, and MidAm.

- Quotes on stock and currency options from the Option Price Authority Exchange.

- Money market funds, mutual funds, and indexes direct from the exchange floors.

- A variety of news services including the Dow Jones News Service, NewsReal, and sports action.

- Market commentary, fundamental analysis, historical charting, and company research is prepared daily by experts and wire services.

- Compatibility with more than 100 analytical software packages.

- Data available via cable, satellite, or FM.

Types of Orders

The following list describes the kinds of orders that are available to be placed between customers and brokerage firms.

At-the-opening order   An order, not necessarily executed at the opening price, that specifically should be executed at the opening of the market or else it is to be canceled.

Day order   The order remains good only for the duration of the trading day that it is entered. It is canceled at the end of the trading day, if not executed.

Fill-or-kill (FOK)   The whole order must be executed immediately. If not, the entire order is canceled.

Good till canceled (GTC)   The order remains in effect until executed, explicitly canceled, or the contract expires.

Immediate or cancel (IOC)   The order must be executed immediately in whole or in part as soon as it is entered. Any part not executed is automatically canceled.

Limit order   An order specifying a maximum buying price or a minimum selling price. For a limit buy the specified limit must be below the current market price; for a limit sell the specified limit must be above the current market price.

Market on close   The order must be executed during the closing of trading.

Market on open   The order must be executed during the opening of trading.

Market order   This is the most common type of order. It must be executed when entered at the best price prevailing in the market.

Market-if-touched (MIT)   A combination of the market and limit orders, whereby the order becomes a market order when the options or futures reach a specified price. For a MIT buy the specified price must be below the current market price; for a MIT sell the specified price must be above the current market price.

Stop limit order   The activated order becomes a limit order when the options or futures reach a certain price.

Stop order   One of the most useful orders. Like MIT orders, stop orders become market orders when tche options or futures reach a certain price. However, in contrast to MIT orders, with buy stop orders the specified price must be above the current market price, and with sell stop orders the specified price must be below the current market price.

Options Delta Value Chart

At-the-Money Options

Long 1 ATM Call = +50

Short 1 ATM Call = –50

Long 1 ATM Put = –50

Short 1 ATM Put = +50

In-the-Money Options

Long 1 Strike ITM Call = +60 to +65

Short 1 Strike ITM Call = –60 to –65

Long 2 Strikes ITM Call = +70 to +75

Short 2 Strikes ITM Call = –70 to –75

Long 3 Strikes ITM Call = +80 to +85

Short 3 Strikes ITM Call = –80 to –85

Long 1 Strike ITM Put = –60 to –65

Short 1 Strike ITM Put = +60 to +65

Long 2 Strikes ITM Put = –70 to –75

Short 2 Strikes ITM Put = +70 to +75

Long 3 Strikes ITM Put = –80 to –85

Short 3 Strikes ITM Put = +80 to +85

Out-of-the-Money Options

Long 1 Strike OTM Call = +35 to +40

Short 1 Strike OTM Call = –35 to –40

Long 2 Strikes OTM Call = +25 to +30

Short 2 Strikes OTM Call = –25 to –30

Long 3 Strikes OTM Call = +15 to +20

Short 3 Strikes OTM Call = –15 to –20

Long 1 Strike OTM Put = –35 to –40
Short 1 Strike OTM Put = +35 to +40
Long 2 Strikes OTM Put = –25 to –30
Short 2 Strikes OTM Put = +25 to +30
Long 3 Strikes OTM Put = –15 to –20
Short 3 Strikes OTM Put = +15 to +20

Note: These are rough estimates. More exact estimates may be calculated using options analytic software programs.

Option Symbols

To understand quotes, you must be able to decipher option symbols. Option symbols vary depending on their source. However, all option symbols convey the following five items of information:

1. *Underlying financial instrument*—The stock, futures contract, index, or security on which an option is based.

2. *Root symbol*—The symbol used to identify the underlying financial instrument.

3. *Expiration month*—The month in which the option contract expires, represented by a letter of the alphabet. (Expiration Month Codes chart can be found on page 252.)

4. *Strike price*—The specific price the option gives the holder the right to buy or sell the underlying financial instrument. In futures, strike prices are usually numeric. In stocks, strike prices are represented by a letter of the alphabet.

5. *Option type*—In stock options, calls and puts have a letter designating their expiration. In the futures markets, calls are represented as a "C" and puts are represented as a "P."

Stock Example: INQ AA stands for the trade Intel Jan 105 Call (INQ = option symbol for Intel stock, first A = January call expiration, and second A = strike price of 5, 105, 205, 305, 405, 505, etc.).

Futures Example: SP M 8 P 950 stands for the trade S&P Jun 1998 950 Put (SP = Standard & Poor's 500 stock index futures, M = expiration in June, 8 = 1998, P = put option, and 950 = strike price of 950).

Market Expectations

Market	↑	↓	←→
Stocks	Buy	Sell	Stay out
Futures	Buy	Sell	Stay out
Calls	Buy	Sell	Sell
Puts	Sell	Buy	Sell

↑ = Market expectation bullish

↓ = Market expectation bearish

←→ = Market expectation sideways market

Note: Selling naked options is not advised because they offer unlimited risk.

Opportunity Chain

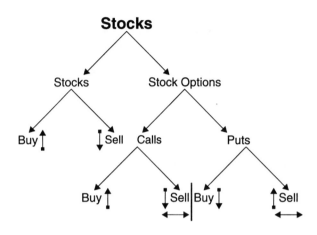

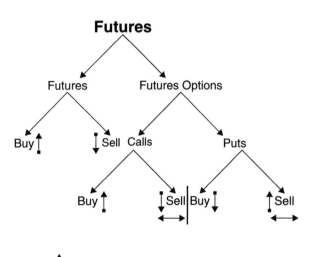

↑ = Market expectation bullish

↓ = Market expectation bearish

Intermarket Relationships

Interest Rates	Bond Prices	Stock Prices	U.S. Dollar
Rising	Falling	Falling	Rising
Falling	Rising	Rising	Falling
Stable	Stable	Up/stable*	Stable

Note: If these relationships do not hold then there is said to be a divergence. A good trader will look for reasons for a divergence and look for opportunities to make money under the circumstances.

---

*Stocks have an upward bias so in a stable interest rate market, stock prices have a tendency to want to move up.

Strike Price Codes for Stocks and Stock Options

JAN	FEB	MAR	APR	MAY	JUN	JUL	AUG
A	B	C	D	E	F	G	H
5	10	15	20	25	30	35	40
105	110	115	120	125	130	135	140
205	210	215	220	225	230	235	240
305	310	315	320	325	330	335	340
405	410	415	420	425	430	435	440
505	510	515	520	525	530	535	540

SEP	OCT	NOV	DEC	JAN	FEB	MAR	APR
I	J	K	L	M	N	O	P
45	50	55	60	65	70	75	80
145	150	155	160	165	170	175	180
245	250	255	260	265	270	275	280
345	350	355	360	365	370	375	380
445	450	455	460	465	470	475	480
545	550	555	560	565	570	575	580

MAY	JUN	JUL	AUG	SEP	OCT	NOV	DEC
Q	R	S	T	U	V	W	X
85	90	95	100	$7^1/_2$	$12^1/_2$	$17^1/_2$	$22^1/_2$
185	190	195	200				
285	290	295	300				
385	390	395	400				
485	490	495	500				
585	590	595	600				

Expiration Month Codes for Stocks and Stock Options

	Jan	Feb	Mar	Apr	May	Jun
Calls	A	B	C	D	E	F
Puts	M	N	O	P	Q	R

	Jul	Aug	Sep	Oct	Nov	Dec
Calls	G	H	I	J	K	L
Puts	S	T	U	V	W	X

Important Futures Values

This exhibit provides three important values of the major futures markets: margin requirements, tick fluctuation, and value per point. These values were accurate as of February 1998 and are subject to change. In particular, margin requirements change relative to perceived market risk by the exchanges and the clearing firms. Consult your broker for current market requirements or account requirements that are unique to your brokerage.

Changing margins signal changing market conditions which may signal risk or trading opportunities. As can be seen in this exhibit, the S&P 500 Stock Index Futures have the greatest perceived risk. Therefore, risk-averse traders should not trade this market unless delta hedged and willing to accept the volatility of the instrument.

Futures	*Margin*	*Chicago Mercantile* *Tick Fluctuation*	*Point Value*
S&P 500	$12,562	5 points = $12.50	1.00 = $250
Deutsche mark	$1,350	1 point = $12.50	1.00 = $1,250
Japanese yen	$2,565	1 point = $12.50	1.00 = $1,250
Swiss franc	$1,721	1 point = $12.50	1.00 = $1,250
British pound	$1,485	2 points = $12.50	1.00 = $625
Lean hogs	$810	2.5 points = $10.00	.01 = $400
Live cattle	$540	2.5 points = $10.00	.01 = $400
Pork bellies	$1,620	2.5 points = $10.00	.01 = $400

Futures	*Margin*	*Chicago Board of Trade* *Tick Fluctuation*	*Point Value*
Treasury bonds	$2,700	$1/32 = 31.25	1.00 = $1000
Ten-year notes	$1,485	$1/32 = 31.25	1.00 = $1000
Soybeans	$1,485	$1/4 = 12.50	.01 = $50

(*continued*)

Corn	$540	$^{1}/_{4} = \$12.50$	.01 = $50
Wheat	$675	$^{1}/_{4} = \$12.50$	.01 = $50
Soybean meal	$1,215	.10 = $10.00	1.00 = $100
Bean oil	$540	.0001/lbs. = $6.00	.01 = $600

New York Mercantile

Futures	*Margin*	*Tick Fluctuation*	*Point Value*
NYFE	$7,000	5 points = $25.00	1.00 = $500.00
Gold	$1,350	.10/oz = 10.00	1.00 = $100
Silver	$1,890	.005/oz = $25.00	.01 = $50
Copper	$2,160	.05/lb = $12.50	.01 = $250
Crude	$2,025	1 point = $10.00	1.00 = $1000
Coffee	$4,900	1 point = $3.75	1.00 = $375
Cocoa	$840	1 point = $10.00	1.00 = $10.00
Cotton	$997	1 point = $5.00	.01 = $500

Margin Commodity Table

Commodity	Spec Initial	Spec Maint.	Spec Spot I	Spec Spot M	Hedge Initial	Hedge Maint.	Hedge Spot I	Hedge Spot M
wheat	675	600	810	600	810	600	810	600
corn	540	400	540	400	540	400	540	400
soybeans	1,485	1,100	1,485	1,100	1,485	1,100	1,485	1,100
T-bonds	2,700	1,800	2,430	1,800	2,430	1,800	2,430	1,800
live cattle	540	400	540	400	540	400	607	450
lean hogs	810	800	1,080	800	1080	800	840	630
pork bellies	1,620	1,200	1,620	1,200	1,620	1,200	1,755	1,300
fdr cattle	843	625	843	625	843	625	843	625
mid beans	297	220	297	220	297	220	567	420
mid corn	108	80	108	80	108	80	108	80
mid C-dollar	253	188	253	188	253	188	253	188
mid S-franc	810	600	810	600	810	600	810	600
mid lean hogs	472	350	472	300	472	350	472	350
mid J-yen	1,215	900	1,215	900	1,215	900	1,215	900
mid live cattle	303	225	303	225	303	225	303	225
mid d-mark	607	450	607	450	607	450	607	450
mid T-bonds	1,215	900	1,215	900	1,215	900	1,215	900
soybean meal	1,215	900	1,215	900	1,215	900	1,215	900
soybean oil	540	500	675	500	675	500	675	500
mid wheat	162	120	162	120	162	120	162	120
rough rice	810	600	810	600	810	600	810	600
hg copper	2,160	1,600	2,160	1,600	2,160	1,600	2,160	1,600
Comex gold	1,350	750	1,012	750	1,012	750	1,012	750
Comex silver	1,890	1,400	1,890	1,400	1,890	1,400	1,890	1,400
cocoa	840	600	840	600	840	600	1000	750
coffee	4,900	4,000	5,600	4,000	5,600	4,000	5,600	4,000
sugar #11	560	400	560	400	560	400	1,250	900
lt. crude	2,025	1,500	2,025	1,500	2,025	1,500	6,075	4,500
heating oil	2,025	1,500	2,025	1,500	2,025	1,500	6,075	4,500

Commodity	Spec Initial	Spec Maint.	Spec Spot I	Spec Spot M	Hedge Initial	Hedge Maint.	Hedge Spot I	Hedge Spot M
unleaded gas	2,025	1,500	2,025	1,500	2,025	1,500	6,075	4,500
platinum	2,700	2,000	2,700	2,000	2,700	2,000	4,050	3,000
KC Value Line	7,500	6,000	7,500	6,000	7,500	6,000	7,500	6,000
mini Value Line	1,500	1,200	1,500	1,200	1,500	1,200	1,500	1,200
KC wheat	1,000	800	1,000	800	1,000	800	1,000	800
Mpls wheat	975	750	975	750	975	750	975	750
IPE crude	1,500	1,500	1,500	1,500	1,500	1,500	1,500	1,500
US dollar index	1,330	1,000	1,330	1,000	1,330	1,000	1,330	1,000
cotton	997	750	997	750	997	750	750	750
frozen oj	997	750	997	750	997	750	997	750
crb index	1,750	1,750	1,750	1,750	1,750	1,750	1,750	1,750
NYSE index	3,500	2,500	3,500	2,500	3,500	2,500	3,500	2,500
A-dollar	1,316	975	1,316	975	1,316	975	1,316	975
maj mkt	5,940	4,400	5,940	4,400	5,940	4,400	5,940	4,400
B-pound	1,485	1,400	1,890	1,400	1,890	1,400	1,890	1,400
C-dollar	540	400	540	400	540	400	540	400
d-mark	1,350	1,100	1,485	1,100	1,485	1,100	1,485	1,100
Eurodollar	472	350	472	350	472	350	472	350
S-franc	1,721	1,275	1,721	1,275	1,721	1,275	1,721	1,275
J-yen	2,565	2,250	3,037	2,250	3,037	2,250	3,037	2,250
S&P 500	12,562	17,500	21,000	17,500	21,000	17,500	21,000	17,500
T-bill	270	200	270	200	270	200	270	200
lumber 80	1,200	800	1,200	800	1,200	800	2,100	1,400

How a Trade Is Made

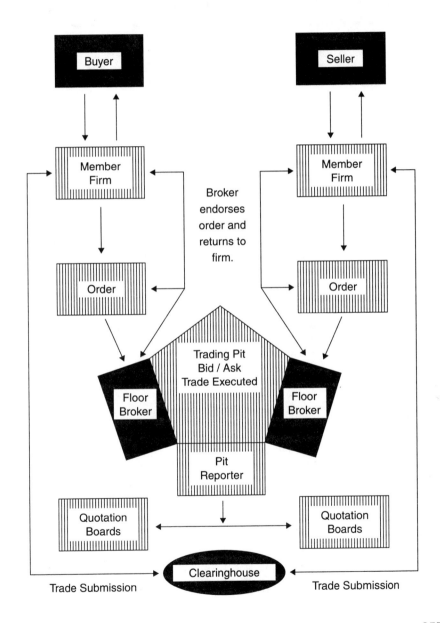

Options Strategy Quick Reference Guide

Strategy	Risk Profile	Trade	Market Outlook	Profit Potential	Risk Potential	Time Decay Effect
Long call	_/	B1-C	Bullish	Unlimited	Limited	Detrimental
Short call	⌐\	S1-C	Bearish	Limited	Unlimited	Helpful
Long put	_	B1-P	Bearish	Unlimited	Limited	Detrimental
Short put	/‾	S1-P	Bullish	Limited	Unlimited	Helpful
Covered call	/‾	B1-U S1-C	Slightly bullish to neutral	Limited	Unlimited	Helpful
Covered put	‾\	S1-U S1-P	Slightly bearish to neutral	Limited	Unlimited	Helpful
Bull call spread	_/‾	B1-LC S1-HC	Bullish	Limited	Limited	Mixed
Bull put spread	_/‾	B1-LP S1-HP	Bullish	Limited	Limited	Mixed
Bear call spread	‾_	S1-LC B1-HC	Bearish	Limited	Limited	Mixed
Bear put spread	‾_	B1-HP S1-LP	Bearish	Limited	Limited	Mixed
Long straddle	\/	B1-ATM-C B1-ATM-P	Volatile	Unlimited	Limited	Detrimental
Short straddle	/\	S1-ATM-C S1-ATM-P	Stable	Limited	Unlimited	Helpful
Long strangle	_/	B1-OTM-C B1-OTM-P	Volatile	Unlimited	Limited	Detrimental
Short strangle	/‾\	S1-OTM-C S1-OTM-P	Stable	Limited	Unlimited	Helpful
Long synthetic straddle	_/	B1-U/B2-ATM-P or S1-U/B2-ATM-C	Volatile	Unlimited	Limited	Detrimental

Key to Trade Codes

B—Buy
S—Sell
1—One contract
2—Two contracts
C—Call

P—Put
HC—Higher-strike call
LC—Lower-strike call
HP—Higher-strike put
LP—Lower-strike put

U—Underlying instrument
ATM—At-the-money
OTM—Out-of-the-money
ITM—In-the-money

Strategy	Risk Profile	Trade	Market Outlook	Profit Potential	Risk Potential	Time Decay Effect
Short synthetic straddle		B1-U/S2-ATM-C or S1-U/S2-ATM-P	Volatile	Limited	Unlimited	Helpful
Call ratio spread*		B1-LC S2-HC	Bearish Stable	Limited	Unlimited	Mixed
Put ratio spread*		B1-HP S2-LP	Bullish Stable	Limited	Unlimited	Mixed
Call ratio backspread*		S1-LC B2-HC	Very bullish	Unlimited	Limited	Mixed
Put ratio backspread*		S1-HP B2-LP	Very bearish	Unlimited	Limited	Mixed
Long butterfly		B1-LC S2-HC B1-HC or B1-LP S2-HP B1-HP	Stable	Limited	Limited	Helpful
Short butterfly		S1-LC B2-HC S1-HC or S1-HP B2-HP S1-HP	Bullish or bearish	Limited	Limited	Detrimental
Long condor		B1-LC S1-HC S1-HC B1-HC or B1-LP S1-HP S1-HP B1-HP	Stable	Limited	Limited	Helpful
Short condor		S1-LC B1-HC B1-HC S1-HC or S1-LP B1-HP B1-HP S1-HP	Bullish or bearish	Limited	Limited	Detrimental
Long iron butterfly		S1-ATM-C B1-OTM-C S1-ATM-P B1-OTM-P	Stable	Limited	Limited	Helpful
Short iron butterfly		B1-ATM-C S1-OTM-C B1-ATM-P S1-OTM-P	Bullish or bearish	Limited	Limited	Detrimental

Key to Trade Codes

B—Buy	P—Put	U—Underlying instrument
S—Sell	HC—Higher-strike call	ATM—At-the-money
1—One contract	LC—Lower-strike call	OTM—Out-of-the-money
2—Two contracts	HP—Higher-strike put	ITM—In-the-money
C—Call	LP—Lower-strike put	

*Follow ratio rule.

Options Strategy Handbook

Strategy: Buy a call option.

Risk: Limited.

Profit: Unlimited.

Time Decay Effect: Detrimental.

Situation: Bullish on the market. Expect a move above break-even.

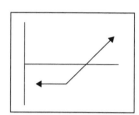

Profit: Unlimited with the increase of price in the underlying instrument.

Risk: Limited to the premium paid for the call option.

Break-even: Call strike price plus call premium.

Long Call

Strategy: Sell a call option.

Risk: Unlimited.

Profit: Limited.

Time Decay Effect: Helpful.

Situation: Bearish on the market. Expect falling or stable market.

Profit: Limited to the credit received for the call premium.

Risk: Unlimited as the price of the underlying instrument rises.

Break-even: Call option strike price plus call premium received.

Short Call

Strategy: Buy a put option.

Risk: Limited.

Profit: Unlimited.

Time Decay Effect: Detrimental.

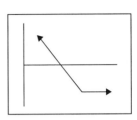

Situation: Bearish on the market. Look for a falling market.

Profit: Unlimited with the decline of the underlying instrument until the asset reaches 0.

Risk: Premium paid for the put option.

Break-even: Put option strike price minus put premium.

Long Put

Strategy: Sell a put option.

Risk: Unlimited.

Profit: Limited.

Time Decay Effect: Helpful.

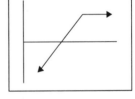

Situation: Bullish on the market. Expect rising or stable market.

Profit: Limited to the credit received for the put premium.

Risk: Unlimited as the price of the underlying instrument falls, until asset reaches 0.

Break-even: Put option strike price minus put premium received.

Short Put

Strategy: Buy the underlying security. Sell an OTM call option.

Risk: Unlimited.

Profit: Limited.

Time Decay Effect: Helpful.

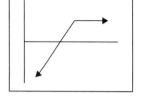

Situation: Slightly bullish to neutral. Look for a market where you expect a slow rise or stability in price with little risk of decline.

Profit: Limited to the credit received on the short call option plus (strike price of option sold less price of asset purchased) times value per point.

Risk: Unlimited as the underlying instrument falls to zero.

Break-even: Price of underlying security minus call premium received.

Covered Call

Strategy: Sell the underlying security. Sell an OTM put option.

Risk: Unlimited.

Profit: Limited.

Time Decay Effect: Helpful.

Situation: Slightly bearish to neutral. Look for a market where you expect a decline or stability in price with little risk of the market rising.

Profit: Limited to the credit received on the short put option plus (price of security sold less put option strike price) times value per point.

Risk: Unlimited as the price of the underlying increases above break-even.

Break-even: Price of underlying security plus put premium received.

Covered Put

Strategy: Buy a call at a lower strike price. Sell a call at a higher strike price. Both options must have identical expiration dates.

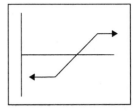

Risk: Limited.

Profit: Limited.

Time Decay Effect: Mixed.

Situation: Look for a moderately bullish to bullish market where you expect an increase in the price of the underlying asset above the price of the call option sold.

Profit: Limited (difference in strike prices times value per point, minus net debit paid). Profit results when the market closes above the strike price of the long call plus the net debit.

Risk: Limited to the net debit paid for the spread. Maximum risk results when the market closes at or below the strike price of the long call.

Break-even: Strike price of lower call plus net debit paid.

Bull Call Spread

Strategy: Buy a put at a lower strike price. Sell a put at a higher strike price. Both options must have identical expiration dates.

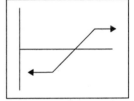

Risk: Limited.

Profit: Limited.

Time Decay Effect: Mixed.

Situation: Look for a moderately bullish to bullish market where you expect an increase in the price of the underlying asset above the strike price of the put option sold.

Profit: Limited to the net credit received. Profit is made when the market closes above the strike price of the short put option. This is a credit trade when initiated.

Risk: Limited (difference in strikes times the value per point, minus net credit).

Break-even: Strike price of higher put minus net credit received.

Bull Put Spread

Strategy: Buy a call at a higher strike price. Sell a call at a lower strike price. Both options must have identical expiration dates.

Risk: Limited.

Profit: Limited.

Time Decay Effect: Mixed.

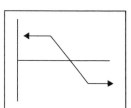

Situation: Look for a moderately bearish to bearish market where you expect a decrease in the price of the underlying asset below the strike price of the call option sold.

Profit: Limited to the net credit received. Maximum profit is made when the market closes below the strike price of the short call. This is a credit trade when initiated.

Risk: Limited (difference in strike prices times value per point, minus net credit). Maximum risk results when the market closes at or above the strike price of the long option.

Break-even: Strike price of lower call plus net credit received.

Bear Call Spread

Strategy: Buy a put at a higher strike price. Sell a put at a lower strike price. Both options must have identical expiration dates.

Risk: Limited.

Profit: Limited.

Time Decay Effect: Mixed.

Situation: Look for a moderately bearish to bearish market where you expect a decrease in the price of the underlying asset below the strike price of the put option sold.

Profit: Limited (difference in strike prices times value per point, minus net debit paid). Maximum profit results when the market closes at or below the strike price of the short put option.

Risk: Limited to the net debit paid for the spread. Maximum risk results when the market closes at or above the strike price of the long put.

Break-even: Strike price of higher put minus net debit paid.

Bear Put Spread

Strategy: Buy an ATM call and an ATM put with the same strike price and expiration date.

Risk: Limited.

Profit: Unlimited.

Time Decay Effect: Detrimental.

Situation: Look for a market with low volatility about to experience a sharp increase in volatility.

Profit: Unlimited. Profit requires sufficient market movement but does not depend on market direction.

Risk: Limited to the net debit paid. Margin is not required.

Upside Break-even: Strike price plus net debit paid.

Downside Break-even: Strike price minus net debit paid.

Long Straddle

Strategy: Sell an ATM call and an ATM put with the same strike price and expiration date.

Risk: Unlimited.

Profit: Limited.

Time Decay Effect: Helpful.

Situation: Look for a highly volatile market that seems to be entering a period of low volatility.

Profit: Limited to the net credit received. The less the market moves, the better chance you have of keeping the premiums.

Risk: Unlimited on both sides. Margin is required.

Upside Break-even: Strike price plus net credit received.

Downside Break-even: Strike price minus net credit received.

Short Straddle

Strategy: Buy an OTM call and an OTM put with the same expiration date.

Risk: Limited.

Profit: Unlimited.

Time Decay Effect: Detrimental.

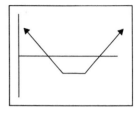

Situation: Look for a relatively stagnant market where you anticipate an explosion of volatility.

Profit: Unlimited. Profit requires expansive market movement but does not depend on market direction.

Risk: Limited to net debit paid. Loss is less than that of a straddle. Margin is not required.

Upside Break-even: Call strike price plus net debit paid.

Downside Break-even: Put strike price minus net debit paid.

Long Strangle

Strategy: Sell an OTM call and an OTM put with the same expiration date.

Risk: Unlimited.

Profit: Limited.

Time Decay Effect: Helpful.

Situation: Look for a highly volatile market which seems to be entering a period of low volatility or stagnation.

Profit: Limited to the net credit received. Profit does not depend on market direction.

Risk: Unlimited on both sides. However, market has to move significantly for loss to occur. Margin is required.

Upside Break-even: Call strike price plus net credit received.

Downside Break-even: Put strike price minus net credit received.

Short Strangle

Strategy: Buy 1 underlying asset and buy 2 ATM puts. OR Sell 1 underlying asset and buy 2 ATM calls.

Risk: Limited.

Profit: Unlimited.

Time Decay Effect: Detrimental.

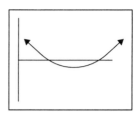

Situation: Look for a market where you expect volatility to increase. This is a delta neutral, nondirectional trade.

Profit: Unlimited above break-even points. Adjustments can provide increased profits.

Risk: Limited to the net debit of the options.

Upside Break-even: Price of underlying asset plus net debit paid for options.

Downside Break-even: Price of underlying asset minus net debit paid for options.

Long Synthetic Straddle

Strategy: Sell 1 underlying asset. Sell 2 ATM puts. OR Buy 1 underlying asset. Sell 2 ATM calls.

Risk: Unlimited.

Profit: Limited.

Time Decay Effect: Helpful.

Situation: Look for a market with high volatility which is expected to slow and trade in a range. Not a highly recommended trade due to high risk.

Profit: Limited to the net credit received.

Risk: Unlimited risk beyond the break-even points.

Upside Break-even: Price of underlying asset plus net credit received on short options.

Downside Break-even: Price of underlying asset minus net credit received on short options.

Short Synthetic Straddle

Strategy: Buy lower strike call. Sell greater number of higher strike calls.

Risk: Unlimited.

Profit: Limited.

Time Decay Effect: Mixed.

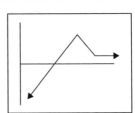

Situation: Look for a market where you expect a decline (to keep the net credit) or a slight rise not to exceed the strike price of the short options.

Profit: Limited (difference in strike prices times value per point, plus net credit or minus net debit).

Risk: Unlimited to the upside above break-even.

Upside Break-even: Lower strike price call plus (difference in strike prices times number of short contracts) ÷ (number of short contracts less number of long contracts) plus net credit received or minus net debit paid.

Ratio Call Spread

Strategy: Buy higher strike put. Sell greater number of lower strike puts.

Risk: Unlimited.

Profit: Limited.

Time Decay Effect: Mixed.

Situation: Look for a market where you expect a rise or a slight fall not to exceed the strike price of the short put options.

Profit: Limited (difference in strike prices times value per point, plus net credit or minus net debit).

Risk: Unlimited to the downside.

Downside Break-even: Higher strike price (difference in strikes times the number of short contracts ÷ the number of short contracts minus long contracts) minus the net credit received *or* plus the net debit paid.

Ratio Put Spread

Strategy: Sell lower strike calls. Buy greater number higher strike calls. (The ratio must be less than .67.)

Risk: Limited.

Profit: Unlimited.

Time Decay Effect: Mixed.

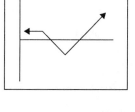

Situation: Look for a market that rises sharply with increasing volatility. Should be placed as a credit or at-even.

Profit: Unlimited to the upside.

Risk: Limited (number of short calls times difference in strikes, times value per point minus net credit received or plus net debit paid).

Upside Break-even: Higher strike calls, plus (difference in strikes times number of short calls), divided by (number of long calls less short calls) minus net credit or plus net debit paid.

Downside Break-even: Strike price of the short options plus net credit or minus net debit.

Call Ratio Backspread

Strategy: Sell higher strike put. Buy greater number of lower strike puts. (The ratio must be less than .67.)

Risk: Limited.

Profit: Unlimited.

Time Decay Effect: Mixed.

Situation: Look for a market where you expect a sharp decline with increased volatility. Should be placed as a credit or at-even.

Profit: Unlimited to the downside.

Risk: Limited (number of short puts times difference in strike prices times value per point) minus net credit received or plus net debit paid.

Upside Break-even: Higher strike put option minus net credit received.

Downside Break-even: Lower strike price minus [(number of short puts times difference in strike prices) divided by (number of long puts less number of short puts)] plus net credit received or minus net debit paid.

Put Ratio Backspread

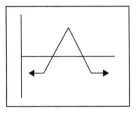

Strategy: Buy lower strike (call or put). Sell two higher strike (calls or puts). Buy higher strike (call or put). Use all calls or all puts.

Risk: Limited.

Profit: Limited.

Time Decay Effect: Helpful.

Situation: Look for a sideways market that is expected to stay between the break-even points.

Profit: Limited (difference in strike prices times value per point, minus net debit paid). Profit exists between break-evens.

Risk: Limited to the net debit paid.

Upside Break-even: Highest strike price minus net debit paid.

Downside Break-even: Lowest strike price plus net debit paid.

Long Butterfly

Strategy: Sell lower strike (call or put). Buy two higher strike (calls or puts). Sell higher strike (call or put). Use all calls or all puts.

Risk: Limited.

Profit: Limited.

Time Decay Effect: Detrimental.

Situation: Look for a market ready to break out above the highest strike price or below the lowest strike price.

Profit: Limited to the net credit received.

Risk: Limited (difference of middle and lower strike prices times value per point minus net credit received).

Upside Break-even: Highest strike price minus net credit received.

Downside Break-even: Lowest strike price plus net credit received.

Short Butterfly

Strategy: Buy lower strike (call or put). Sell one higher strike (call or put). Sell one higher strike (call or put). Buy one higher strike (call or put). Use all calls or all puts.

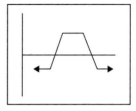

Risk: Limited.

Profit: Limited.

Time Decay Effect: Beneficial.

Situation: Look for a sideways market that is expected to remain between the break-even of the condor.

Profit: Limited (difference between highest and next higher strike prices times value per point) minus net debit paid.

Risk: Limited to the net debit paid.

Upside Break-even: Highest long strike price minus net debit paid.

Downside Break-even: Lowest long strike price plus net debit paid.

Long Condor

Strategy: Sell one lower strike (call or put). Buy one higher strike (call or put). Buy one higher strike (call or put). Sell one higher strike (call or put). Use all calls or all puts.

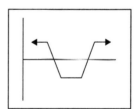

Risk: Limited.

Profit: Limited.

Time Decay Effect: Detrimental.

Situation: Look for a market ready to break out above the highest strike price or below the lowest strike price.

Profit: Limited to the net credit received.

Risk: Limited (difference between lowest and next higher strike prices times value per point) minus net credit received.

Upside Break-even: Highest short strike price minus net credit received.

Downside Break-even: Lowest short strike price plus net credit received.

Short Condor

Strategy: Buy one higher-strike call. Sell one lower-strike call (ATM or other). Sell one higher-strike put (ATM or other). Buy one lower-strike put.

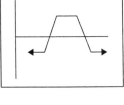

Risk: Limited.

Profit: Limited.

Time Decay Effect: Mixed.

Situation: Look for a sideways market that you expect to close between the wings of the iron butterfly.

Profit: Limited to the net credit received.

Risk: Limited (difference between long and short strikes times value per point, minus net credit received).

Upside Break-even: Strike price of middle short call plus the net credit received.

Downside Break-even: Strike price of middle short put minus net credit received.

Long Iron Butterfly

Strategy: Sell one higher strike call. Buy one lower strike call (ATM or other). Buy one higher strike put (ATM or other). Sell one lower strike put.

Risk: Limited.

Profit: Limited.

Time Decay Effect: Mixed.

Situation: Look for a market ready to break out from the break-even points.

Profit: Limited (difference between long and short strikes times value per point minus net debit paid).

Risk: Limited to the net debit paid.

Upside Break-even: Higher long call strike price plus net debit paid.

Downside Break-even: Lower long put strike price less net debit paid.

Short Iron Butterfly

Glossary

adjustment   The process of buying or selling instruments to bring a position delta back to zero and increase profits.

All Ordinaries Index   The major index of Australian stocks. This index represents 280 of the most active listed companies or the majority of the equity capitalization (excluding foreign companies) listed on the Australian Stock Exchange (ASX).

American Stock Exchange (AMEX)   A private, not-for-profit corporation, located in New York City, that handles approximately one-fifth of all securities trades within the United States.

American-style option   An option contract that can be exercised at any time between the date of purchase and the expiration date. Most exchange-traded options are American-style.

amortization   The paying off of debt in regular installments over a period of time.

analyst   Employee of a brokerage or fund management house who studies companies and makes buy and sell recommendations on their stocks. Most specialize in a specific industry.

annual earnings change (percent)   The historical earnings change between the most recently reported fiscal year earnings and the preceding year earnings.

annual net profit margin (percent)   The percentage that the company earned from gross sales for the most recently reported fiscal year.

annual percentage rate (APR)   The cost of credit that the consumer pays, expressed as a simple annual percentage.

annual report   A report issued by a company to its shareholders at the end of the fiscal year containing a description of the firm's operations and financial statements.

annual return   The simple rate of return earned by an investment for each year.

annuity   A series of constant payments at uniform time intervals (for example, periodic interest payments on a bond).

appreciation   The increase in value of an asset.

arbitrage   The simultaneous purchase and sale of identical financial instruments or commodity futures in order to make a profit where the selling price is higher than the buying price.

arbitrageur   An individual or company that takes advantage of momentary disparities in prices between markets to lock in profits because the selling price is higher than the buying price.

ask   The lowest price of a specific market that market makers, floor brokers, or specialists are willing to sell at.

at-the-money (ATM)   When the strike price of an option is the same as the current price of the underlying instrument.

at-the-opening order   An order that specifies execution at the opening of the market or else it is canceled.

auction market   A market in which buyers enter competitive bids and sellers enter competitive offers simultaneously. Most stock and bond markets, including those on the NYSE, function this way.

automatic exercise   The automatic exercise of an in-the-money option at expiration by the clearing firm.

average   An mathematical representation of the behavior of a specific sector or index of the market (for example, the Dow Jones Industrial Average).

back months   The futures or options on futures months being traded that are furthest from expiration.

backspread   A spread in which more options are purchased than sold and where all options have the same underlying asset and expiration date. Backspreads are usually delta neutral.

back-testing   The testing of a strategy based on historical data to see if the results are consistent.

bear   An investor who acts on the belief that a security or the market is falling or is expected to fall.

bear call spread   A strategy in which a trader sells a lower strike call and buys a higher strike call to create a trade with limited profit and limited risk. A fall in the price of the underlying asset increases the value of the spread. Net credit transaction; maximum loss = difference between the strike prices less credit; maximum gain = net credit; requires margin.

bear market   A declining stock market over a prolonged period of time usually caused by a weak economy and subsequent decreased corporate profits.

bear put spread   A strategy in which a trader sells a lower strike put and buys a higher strike put to create a trade with limited profit and limited risk. A fall in the price of the underlying asset increases the value of the spread. Net debit transaction;

maximum loss = difference between strike prices less the net debit; no margin required.

bid The highest price at which a floor broker, trader, or dealer is willing to buy a security or commodity for a specified time.

bid and asked The bid (the highest price a buyer is prepared to pay for a trading asset) and the asked (the lowest price acceptable to a prospective seller of the same security) together comprise a quotation, or quote.

bid-asked spread The difference between bid and asked prices constitute the bid-asked spread.

bid up Demand for an asset drives up the price paid by buyers.

block trade A trade so large (for example, 5000 shares of stock or $200,000 worth of bonds) that the normal auction market cannot absorb it in a reasonable time at a reasonable price.

blow-off top A steep and rapid increase in price followed by a steep and rapid drop in price. This indicator is often used in technical analysis.

blue chips This term is derived from poker where blue chips hold the most value. Blue chips in the stock market are stocks with the best market capitalization in the marketplace.

blue-chip stock A stock with solid value, good security, and a record of dividend payments or other desirable investment characteristics. Many times these stocks have a record of consistent dividend payments, receive extensive media coverage, and offer a host of other beneficial investment attributes. On the downside, blue-chip stocks tend to be quite expensive and often have little room for growth.

board lot The smallest quantity of shares traded on an exchange at standard commission rates.

bond Financial instruments representing debt obligations issued by the government or corporations traded in the futures market. A bond promises to pay its holders periodic interest at a fixed rate (the coupon), and to repay the principal of the loan at maturity. Bonds are issued with a par or face value of $1000 and are traded based on their interest rates—if the bond pays more interest than available elsewhere, its worth increases.

break-even (1) The point at which gains equal losses; (2) the market price that a stock or future must reach for an option to avoid loss if exercised; (3) for a call, the break-even equals the strike price plus the premium paid; (4) for a put, the break-even equals the strike price minus the premium paid.

breakout A rise in the price of an underlying instrument above its resistance level or a drop below the support level.

broad-based index   An index designed to reflect the movement of the market as a whole (for example, the S&P 100, the S&P 500, and the AMEX Major Market Index).

broker   An individual or firm that charges a commission for executing buy and sell orders.

bull   An investor who believes that a market is rising or is expected to rise.

bull call spread   A strategy in which a trader buys a lower strike call and sells a higher strike call to create a trade with limited profit and limited risk. A rise in the price of the underlying asset increases the value of the spread. Net debit transaction; maximum loss = debit; maximum gain = difference between strike prices less the net debit; no margin required.

bull market   A rising stock market over a prolonged period of time usually caused by a strong economy and subsequent increased corporate profits.

bull put spread   A strategy in which a trader sells a higher strike put and buys a lower strike put to create a trade with limited profit and limited risk. A rise in the price of the underlying asset increases the value of the spread. Net credit transaction; maximum loss = difference between strike prices less credit; maximum gain = net credit; requires margin.

butterfly spread   The sale (purchase) of two identical options, together with the purchase (sale) of one option with an immediately higher strike, and one option with an immediately lower strike. All options must be the same type, have the same underlying asset, and have the same expiration date.

buy on close   To buy at the end of a trading session at a price within the closing range.

buy on opening   To buy at the beginning of a trading session at a price within the opening range.

buy stop order   An order to purchase a security entered at a price above the current offering price triggered when the market hits a specified price.

CAC 40 Index   A broad-based index of 40 common stocks on the Paris Bourse.

calendar spread   A spread consisting of one long and one short option of the same type with the same exercise price, but which expire in different months.

call option   An option contract which gives the holder the right, but not the obligation, to buy a specified amount of an underlying security at a specified price within a specified time in exchange for paying a premium.

call premium   The amount a call option costs.

capital   The amount of money an individual or business has available.

capital gain The profit realized when a capital asset is sold for a higher price than the purchase price.

capitalization Refers to the current value of a corporation's outstanding shares in dollars.

capital loss The loss incurred when a capital asset is sold for a lower price than the purchase price.

capped-style option An option with an established profit cap or cap price.

cash account An account in which the customer is required to pay in full for all purchased securities.

cash dividend A dividend paid in cash to a shareholder out of a corporation's profits.

change The difference between the current price and the price of the previous day of a security.

Chicago Board Options Exchange (CBOE) The largest options exchange in the United States.

Chicago Board of Trade (CBOT) Established in 1886, the CBOT is the oldest commodity exchange in the United States and primarily lists grains, T-bonds and notes, metals, and indexes.

class of options Option contracts of the same type (call or put), style, and underlying security.

clearinghouse An institution established separately from the exchanges to ensure timely payment and delivery of securities.

close The price of the last transaction for a particular security each day.

closing purchase A transaction to eliminate a short position.

closing range The high and low prices recorded during the period designated as the official close.

closing sale A transaction to eliminate a long position.

commission A service charge assessed by a broker and his/her investment company in return for arranging the purchase or sale of a security.

commodity Any bulk good traded on an exchange (for example, metals, grains, and meats).

Commodity Futures Trading Commission (CFTC) The CFTC was created by the Commodity Futures Trading Commission Act of 1974 to ensure the open and efficient operation of the futures markets.

condor   The sale or purchase of two options with consecutive exercise prices, together with the sale or purchase of one option with an immediately lower exercise price and one option with an immediately higher exercise price.

consumer price index (CPI)   A measure of price changes in consumer goods and services. This index is used to identify periods of economic inflation or deflation.

contract   A unit of trading for a financial or commodity future, or option.

correction   A sudden decline in the price of a security after a period of market strength.

covered call   A short call option position against a long position in an underlying stock or futures.

covered put   A short put option position against a short position in an underlying stock or futures.

credit spread   The difference in value between two options, where the value of the short position exceeds the value of the long position.

cross rate   The current exchange rate between differing currencies.

daily range   The difference between the high and low price of a security in one trading day.

day order   An order to buy or sell a security which expires if not filled by the end of the day.

day trade   The purchase and sale of a position in the same day.

day trading   An approach to trading in which the same position is entered and exited within one day.

debit spread   The difference in value between two options, where the value of the long position exceeds the value of the short position.

deep in-the-money   A deep in-the-money call option has a strike price well below the current price of the underlying instrument. A deep in-the-money put option has a strike price well above the current price of the underlying instrument. Both primarily consist of intrinsic value.

delayed-time   Quotes from a data service provider that are delayed up to 20 minutes from real-time quotes.

delta   The amount by which the price (premium) of an option changes for every dollar move in the underlying instrument.

delta-hedged   An options strategy protecting an option against price changes in the option's underlying instrument by balancing the overall position delta to zero.

delta neutral   A position arranged by selecting a calculated ratio of short and long positions that balance out to an overall position delta of zero.

delta position   A measure of option or underlying securities delta.

derivative   Financial instruments based on the market value of an underlying asset.

discount brokers   Brokerage firms that offer lower commission rates than full-service brokers, but do not offer services such as advice, research, and portfolio planning.

divergence   When two or more averages or indexes fail to show confirming trends.

dividend   A sum of money paid out to a shareholder from the stock's profits.

Dow Jones Industrial Average (DJIA)   Used as an overall indicator of market performance, this average is composed of 30 blue-chip stocks that are traded daily on the New York Stock Exchange.

downside   The potential for prices to decrease.

downside break-even   The lower price at which a trade breaks even.

downside risk   The potential risk one takes if prices decrease in directional trading.

each way   The commission made by a broker for the purchase and sale sides of a trade.

end of day   The close of the trading day when market prices settle.

EPS Rank   An *Investor's Business Daily* list of companies ranked from 0 to 100 by the strength of each company's earnings per share.

equilibrium   A price level in a sideways market equidistant from the resistance and support levels.

Eurodollar   Dollars deposited in foreign banks, with the futures contract reflecting the rates offered between U.S. banks and foreign banks.

European-style option   An option contract that can be exercised only on the expiration date.

exchange   The location where an asset, option, future, stock, or derivative is bought and sold.

exchange rate   The price at which one country's currency can be converted into another country's currency.

execution   The process of completing an order to buy or sell securities.

exercise   Implementing an option's right to buy or sell the underlying security.

exercise price (strike price)   A price at which the stock or commodity underlying a call or put option can be purchased (call) or sold (put) over the specified period.

expiration   The date and time after which an option may no longer be exercised.

expiration date   The last day on which an option may be exercised.

explosive   An opportunity that can yield large profits with usually a limited risk in a short amount of time.

extrinsic value (time value)   The price of an option less its intrinsic value. An out-of-the-money option's worth consists of nothing but extrinsic or time value.

fade   Selling a rising price or buying a falling price.

fair market value   The value of an asset under normal conditions.

fair values   The theoretical value of what an option should be worth, usually generated by an option pricing model such as the Black-Scholes option pricing model.

fast market   A stock with so much volume that the order entry systems have difficulty processing all of the orders.

fill   An executed order.

fill order   An order that must be filled or canceled immediately.

fill or kill   Placing an order to buy or sell an exact number of units or none at all.

financial instruments   The term used for debt instruments.

fixed delta   A delta figure that does not change with the change in the underlying asset. A futures contract has a fixed delta of plus or minus 100.

floor broker   An exchange member who is paid a fee for executing orders.

floor ticket   A summary of the information on an order ticket.

floor trader   An exchange member who executes orders from the floor of the exchange only for his or her own account.

fluctuation   A variation in the market price of a security.

front month   The first expiration month in a series of months.

fundamental analysis   An approach to trading research to predict futures and stock price movements based on a balance sheet and income statements, past records of earnings, sales, assets, management, products, and services.

futures contract   Agreement to buy or sell a set number of shares of a commodity or financial instruments in a designated future month at a price agreed on by the buyer and seller.

gamma   The degree by which the delta changes with respect to changes in the underlying instrument's price.

gap   A day in which the daily range is completely above or below the previous day's daily range.

going ahead   Unethical brokerage activity whereby the broker trades first for his or her own account before filling the customer's order(s).

go long   To buy securities, options, or futures.

good till canceled order (GTC)   An order to buy or sell stock that is good until the trader cancels it.

go short   To sell securities, options, or futures.

guts   A strangle where the call and the put are in-the-money.

hammering the market   The intense selling of stocks by speculators who think the market is about to drop because they believe prices are inflated.

hedge   Reducing the risk of loss by taking a position through options or futures opposite to the current position they hold in the market.

high (hi)   The highest price that was paid for a stock during a certain period.

high and low   Refers to the high and low transactions prices that occur each trading day.

high flyer   A speculative high-priced stock that moves up and down sharply over a short period of time.

high-tech stock   Refers to the stock of companies involved in high technology industries, such as computers, biotechnology, robotics, electronics, and semiconductors.

historic volatility   A measurement of how much a contract's price has fluctuated over a period of time in the past; usually calculated by taking a standard deviation of price changes over a time period.

holder   One who purchases an option.

illiquid market   A market that has no volume; slippage is subsequently created due to lack of trading volume.

immediate/cancel   An order which must be filled immediately or canceled.

index   A group of stocks that can be traded as one portfolio, such as the S&P 500. Broad-based indexes cover a wide range of industries and companies and narrow-based indexes cover stocks in one industry or economic sector.

index options   Call options and put options on indexes of stocks are designed to reflect and fluctuate with market conditions. Index options allow investors to trade in a specific industry group or market without having to buy all the stocks individually.

interest rate   The charge for the privilege of borrowing money, usually expressed as an annual percentage rate.

interest rate–driven   Refers to a point in the business cycle when interest rates are declining and bond prices are rising.

intermarket analysis   Observing the price movement of one market for the purpose of evaluating a different market.

intermarket spread   A spread consisting of opposing positions in instruments with two different markets.

in-the-money (ITM)   If you were to exercise an option and it would generate a profit at the time, it is known to be in-the-money.

in-the-money (ITM) option   A call option is in-the-money if the strike price is less than the market price of the underlying security. A put option is in-the-money if the strike price is greater than the market price of the underlying security.

intrinsic value   The amount by which a market is in-the-money. Out-of-the-money options have no intrinsic value. Calls = underlying asset less strike price. Puts = strike price less underlying asset.

inverse relationship   Two or more markets that act totally opposite to one another, producing negative correlations.

investment   Any purchase of an asset to increase future income.

iron butterfly   The combination of a long (short) straddle and a short (long) strangle. All options must have the same underlying asset and the same expiration.

LEAPs   Long-term stock or index options that are available with expiration dates up to three years in the future.

leg   One side of a spread.

limit move   The maximum daily price limit for an exchange traded contract.

limit order   An order to buy a stock at or below a specified price or to sell a stock at or above a specified price.

limit up, limit down   Commodity exchange restrictions on the maximum upward or downward movements permitted in the price for a commodity during any trading session day.

liquidity   The ease with which an asset can be converted to cash in the marketplace. A large number of buyers and sellers and a high volume of trading activity provide high liquidity.

locked market   A market where trading has been halted because prices have reached their daily trading limit.

long   The term used to describe the buying of a security, contract, commodity, or option.

low (lo)   This is the lowest price paid for a stock during a certain period.

low-risk investing   A trade that is hedged for purposes of limiting price loss, as opposed to a directional trade where loss is unlimited.

make a market   A market maker stands ready to buy or sell a particular security for his or her own account to keep the market liquid.

margin   The margin amount is a deposit contributed by a customer as a percentage of the current market value of the securities held in a margin account. This amount changes as the price of the investment changes.

margin account   A customer account in which a brokerage firm lends the customer part of the purchase price of a trade.

margin call   A call from a broker signaling the need for a trader to deposit additional money into a margin account to maintain a trade.

margin requirements (options)   The amount of cash the writer of an uncovered (naked) option is required to deposit and maintain to cover his or her daily position price changes.

mark to market   The daily adjustment of margin accounts to reflect profits and losses. In this way, losses are never allowed to accumulate.

marked to market   At the end of each business day the open positions carried in an account held at a brokerage firm are credited or debited funds based on the settlement price of the open positions that day.

market   A specific asset, security, or commodity that is traded at an exchange.

market-if-touched (MIT)   A price order that automatically becomes a market order if the price is reached.

market maker   An independent trader or trading firm that is prepared to buy and sell shares or contracts in a designated market. Market makers must make a two-sided market (bid and ask) in order to facilitate trading.

market on close   An order specification that requires the broker to get the best price available on the close of trading, usually during the last five minutes of trading.

market on open   An order that must be executed during the opening of trading.

market order   Buying or selling securities at the price given at the time the order reaches the market. A market order is to be executed immediately at the best available price, and is the only order that guarantees execution.

market price   The most recent price at which a security transaction has taken place.

market value   The price at which investors buy or sell a share of common stock or a bond at a given time. Market value is determined by the interaction between buyers and sellers.

mid-cap stocks   Usually solidly established medium-growth firms with less than $100 billion in assets. They provide better growth potential than blue-chip stocks, but do not offer as wide a variety of investment attributes.

momentum   When a market continues in the same direction for a certain time frame, the market is said to have momentum.

momentum indicator   A technical indicator utilizing price and volume statistics for predicting the strength or weakness of a current market.

momentum trading   Investing with (or against) the momentum of the market in hopes of profiting from it.

moving average   The moving average is probably the best known, and most versatile, technical indicator. A mathematical procedure in which the sum of a value plus a selected number of previous values are divided by the total number of values. Used to smooth or eliminate the fluctuations in data and to assist in determining when to buy and sell.

mutual fund   An open-end investment company that pools investors' money to invest in a variety of stocks, bonds, or other securities.

naked option   An option written (sold) without an underlying hedge position.

naked position   A securities position not hedged from market risk.

narrowing the spread   The closing spread between the bid and asked prices of a security as a result of bidding and offering.

NASDAQ   National Association of Securities Dealers Automated Quotations system—a computerized system providing brokers and dealers with price quotations for securities traded over-the-counter as well as for many New York Stock Exchange–listed securities.

near-the-money   An option with a strike price close to the current price of the underlying tradable.

net change   The daily change from time frame to time frame. For example, the change from the close of yesterday to the close of today.

net profit   The overall profit of a trade.

New York Stock Exchange (NYSE)   The largest stock exchange in the United States.

note   A short-term debt security, usually maturing in five years or less.

OEX   This term, pronounced as three separate letters, is Wall Street shorthand for Standard & Poor's 100 stock index.

offer   The lowest price at which a person is willing to sell.

offer down   The change of the offer of the market related to a downward price movement at that specific time.

off-floor trader   A trader who does not trade on the actual floor of an organized futures of stock exchange.

offset   To liquidate a futures position by entering an equivalent but opposite transaction. Toffset a long position, a sale is made; to offset a short position, a purchase is made.

on-the-money (at-the-money)   The option in question is trading at its exercise price.

open order   An order to buy or sell a security at a specified price, valid until executed or canceled.

open outcry   A system of trading where an auction of verbal bids and offers is performed on the trading floor. This method is slowly disappearing as exchanges become automated.

open trade   A current trade that is still held active in a customer's account.

opening   The period at the beginning of the trading session at an exchange.

opening call   A period at the opening of a futures market in which the price for each contract is established by outcry.

opening price   The range of prices at which the first bids and offers are made or first transactions are completed.

opportunity costs   The theoretical cost of using capital for one investment versus another.

option   A security that represents the right, but not the obligation, to buy or sell a specified amount of an underlying security (stock, bond, futures contract, etc.) at a specified price within a specified time.

option holder   The buyer of either a call or a put option.

option premium   The price of an option.

option writer   The seller of either a call or a put option.

order   A ticket or voucher representing long or short securities and options.

order flow   The volume of orders being bought or sold on the exchanges.

out-of-the-money (OTM)   An option whose exercise price has no intrinsic value.

out-of-the-money (OTM) option   A call option is out-of-the-money if its exercise or strike price is above the current market price of the underlying security. A put option is out-of-the-money if its exercise or strike price is below the current market price of the underlying security.

overvalued   A term used to describe a security or option whose current price is not justified.

paper trading   Simulating a trade without actually putting up the money for the purpose of gaining additional trading experience.

par   The stated or nominal value of a bond (typically $1000) that is paid to the bondholder at maturity.

perceived risk   The theoretical risk of a trade in a specific time frame.

performance-based   A system of compensation in which a broker receives fees based on performance in the marketplace.

points   Points apply to security prices. In the case of shares, one point indicates $1 per share. For bonds, one point means 1 percent of par value. Commodities differ from market to market.

point spread   The price movement required for a security to go from one full point level to another (e.g., stock goes up or down $1).

position   The total of a trader's open contracts.

position delta   The sum of all positive and negative deltas in a hedged position.

position limit   The maximum number of open contracts in a single underlying instrument.

premium   The amount of cash that an option buyer pays to an option seller.

price   Price of a share of common stock on the date shown. Highs and lows are based on the highest and lowest intraday trading price.

price-earnings ratio (P/E)   A technical analysis tool for comparing the prices of different common stocks by assessing how much the market is willing to pay for a share of each corporation's earnings. P/E is calculated by dividing the current market price of a stock by the earnings per share.

principal   The initial purchase price of a bond on which interest is earned.

private company   A company that issues private stock and is not publicly traded.

public company   A company that issues stocks to be traded on the public market.

put option   An option contract giving the owner the right, but not the obligation, to sell a specified amount of an underlying security at a specified price within a specified time. The put option buyer hopes the price of the shares will drop by a specific date, while the put option seller (or writer) hopes that the price of the shares will rise, remain stable, or drop by an amount less than their profit on the premium by the specified date.

quickie   An order that must be filled as soon as it reaches the trading floor at the price specified, or be canceled immediately.

quote   The price being offered or bid by a market maker or broker-dealer for a particular security.

quoted price   Refers to the price at which the last sale and purchase of a particular security or commodity took place.

ratio backspread   A delta neutral spread where an uneven amount of contracts are bought and sold with a ratio less than 2 to 3. Optimally no net credit or net debit occurs.

ratio call spread   A bearish or stable strategy in which a trader sells two higher-strike calls and buys one lower-strike call. This strategy offers unlimited risk and limited profit potential.

ratio put spread   A bullish or stable strategy in which a trader buys one higher-strike put and sells two lower-strike puts. This strategy offers unlimited risk and limited profit potential.

real-time   Data received from a quote service as the prices change.

relative strength   A stock's price movement over the past year as compared to a market index.

Relative Strength Index (RSI)   An indicator used to identify price tops and bottoms.

resistance   A price level the market has a hard time breaking through to the upside.

return   The income profit made on an investment.

reversal stop   A stop that, when hit, is a signal to reverse the current trading position (i.e., from long to short); also known as stop and reverse.

rich   Priced higher than expected.

risk   The potential financial loss inherent in the investment.

risk graph   A graphic representation of risk and reward on a given trade as prices change.

risk manager   A person who manages risk of trades in a portfolio by hedging their trades.

risk profile   A graphic determination of risk on a trade. This would include the profit and loss of a trade at any given point for any given time frame.

risk-to-reward ratio   The mathematical relationship between the maximum potential risk and maximum potential reward of a trade.

round-turn   Procedure by which a long or short position is offset by an opposite transaction.

running stops   When quoted, floor traders use these to move the market. When stops are bunched together, traders may move the market in order to activate stop orders and propel the market further.

seasonal market   A market with a consistent but short-lived rise or drop in market activity due to predictable changes in climate or calendar.

seat   The traditional term for membership in a stock or futures exchange.

securities and commodities exchanges   Organized exchanges where securities, options, and futures contracts are traded.

Securities and Exchange Commission (SEC)   Commission created by Congress to regulate the securities markets and protect investors.

security   A trading instrument such as stocks, bonds, and short-term investments.

selling short   The practice of borrowing a stock, future, or option from a broker and selling it because the investor forecasts that the price of a stock is going down.

series (options)   All option contracts of the same class that also have the same unit of trade, expiration date, and exercise price.

shares   Certificates representing ownership of stock in a corporation or company.

short   The selling of a security, contract, or commodity not owned by the seller.

short premium   Expectation that a move of the underlying asset in either direction will result in a theoretical decrease of the value of an option.

short selling   The sale of shares or futures that a seller does not currently own. The seller borrows them (usually from a broker) and sells them with the intent to replace what he or she has sold through later repurchase in the market at a lower price.

small-cap stocks   Up-and-comer companies that offer big rewards and higher risks. They tend to cost less than mid-caps and have lower liquidity. However, small amounts of media coverage can prompt big gains.

smoothing   A mathematical technique that removes excess data in order to maintain a correct evaluation of the underlying trend.

specialist   A trader on the exchange floor assigned to fill bids/orders in a specific stock out of his or her own account.

speculator A trader who hopes to profit from a directional move in the underlying instrument. The speculator has no interest in making or taking delivery.

spike A sharp price rise in one or two days indicating the time for an immediate sale.

spread (1) The difference between the bid and the ask prices of a security. (2) A trading strategy in which a trader offsets the purchase of one trading unit against another.

Standard & Poor's Corporation (S&P) A company that rates stocks and corporate and municipal bonds according to risk profiles and that produces and tracks the S&P indexes.

stochastic indicator Based on the observation that as prices increase, closing prices tend to accumulate ever closer to the highs for the period.

stock A share of a company's stock translates into ownership of part of the company.

stock exchange or stock market An organized marketplace where buyers and sellers are brought together to buy and sell stocks.

stock split An increase in the number of a stock's shares that results in decreasing the par value of each share.

stops Buy stops are orders that are placed at a specified price over the current price of the market. Sell stops are orders that are placed with a specified price below the current price.

straddle A position consisting of a long (short) call and a long (short) put, where both options have the same strike price and expiration date.

strangle A position consisting of a long (short) call and a long (short) put where both options have the same underlying asset, the same expiration date, but different strike prices. Most strangles involve OTM options.

strike price (exercise price) A price at which the stock or commodity underlying a call or put option can be purchased (call) or sold (put) over the specified period.

support A historical price level at which falling prices have stopped falling and either moved sideways or reversed direction.

swings The measurement of price movement between extreme highs and lows.

synthetic long call A long put and a long stock or future.

synthetic long put A long call and a short stock or future.

synthetic long stock A short put and a long call.

synthetic short call A short put and a short stock or future.

synthetic short put   A short call and a long stock or future.

synthetic short stock   A short call and a long put.

synthetic straddle   Futures and options combined to create a delta neutral trade.

synthetic underlying   A long (short) call together with a short (long) put. Both options have the same underlying asset, the same strike price, and the same expiration date.

technical analysis   A method of evaluating securities and commodities by analyzing statistics generated by market activity, such as past prices, volume, momentum, and stochastics.

theoretical value   An option value generated by a mathematical option's pricing model to determine what an option is really worth.

theta   The Greek measurement of the time decay of an option.

tick   A minimum upward or downward movement in the price of a security. For example, bond futures trade in 32nds, while most stocks trade in eighths.

time decay   The amount of time premium movement within a certain time frame on an option due to the passage of time in relation to the expiration of the option itself.

time premium   The additional value of an option due to the volatility of the market and the time remaining until expiration.

time value (extrinsic value)   The amount that the current market price of a right, warrant, or option exceeds its intrinsic value.

trader   A client who buys and sells frequently with the objective of short-term profit.

trading account   An account opened with a brokerage firm from which to place trades.

Treasury bill (T-bill)   A short-term U.S. government security with a maturity of no more than a year.

Treasury bond (T-bond)   A fixed-interest U.S. government debt security with a maturity of 10 years or more.

Treasury note (T-note)   A fixed-interest U.S. government debt security with a maturity of between 1 and 10 years.

Triple Witching Day   The third Friday in March, June, September, and December when U.S. options, index options, and futures contracts all expire simultaneously often resulting in massive trades.

type   The classification of an option contract as either a put or a call.

uncovered option   A short option position, also called a naked option, in which the writer does not own shares of underlying stock. This is a much riskier strategy than a covered option.

underlying instrument   A trading instrument subject to purchase upon exercise.

undervalued   A security selling below the value the market value analysts believe it is worth.

upside   The potential for prices to move up.

upside break-even   The upper price at which a trade breaks even.

variable delta   A delta that can change due to the change of an underlying asset or a change in time expiration of an option.

vega   The amount by which the price of an option changes when the volatility changes. Also referred to as volatility.

volatility   A measure of the amount by which an underlying asset is expected to fluctuate in a given period of time. Volatility is a primary determinant in the valuation of option premiums and time value. There are two basic kinds of volatility— implied and historical (statistical). Implied volatility is calculated by using an option pricing model (Black-Scholes for stocks and indexes and Black for futures). Historical volatility is calculated by using the standard deviation of underlying asset price changes from close to close of trading going back 21 to 23 days.

volatility skew   The theory that options that are deeply out-of-the-money tend to have higher implied volatility levels than at-the-money options. Volatility skew measures and accounts for the limitation found in most options pricing models and uses it to give the trader an edge in estimating an option's worth.

volume (vol)   The number of shares bought and sold on a stock exchange.

whipsaw   Losing money on both sides of a price swing.

wide opening   Refers to an unusually large spread between the bid and asked prices.

Wilshire 5000 Equity Index   A market index of approximately 7000 U.S. based equities traded on the American Stock Exchange, the New York Stock Exchange, and the NASDAQ stock market.

Witching Day   A day on which two or more classes of options and futures expire.

writer   An individual who sells an option.

Yellow Sheets   A daily publication of the National Quotation Bureau detailing bid and asked prices.

yield   The rate of return on an investment.

zeta   The percentage change in an option's price per 1 percent change in implied volatility.

Index

George Fontanills' Trading Package

$100 FREE GIFT!!!

Have George's latest trading ideas delivered to your home or office for FREE! As a special thank-you, George Fontanills would like to send you his latest trading secrets for FREE. Simply contact us to receive your FREE Trading Package worth $100.

Complete and mail to: Global Investment Management Corp.
P.O. Box 620238
Woodside, CA 94062-0238

Or FAX to: (650) 596-1142

$100 FREE
George Fontanills' Trading Package

☐ I would like to learn more about George's trading secrets and strategies. Please send me detailed information about his products and services.

Name: _____

Address: _____

City, State, Zip:_____

Phone: _____ Fax: _____

E-Mail: _____

I purchased this book from: _____

_____

Now that you've read George's book, wouldn't you like to keep up with his day-to-day trading strategies? We're going to make it easy to do by sending you a FREE Trading Package worth $100. Simply mail the attached reply card, fax (650) 596-1142, or call (888) 366-8264 today! Below is a sampling of George's wealth-building publications and videos!

Tradefinder Volatility Report
WealthWire Publications
Can't Lose Strategies Manual
Guide to Computerized Trading Videos
Maximize Your Profits Video
Creating the Optimal Trades for Explosive Trading Profits Video
High-Profit/Low-Risk Study Course and Live Seminars
OPTIONETICS Home Study Course

George's company, Global Investment Management Corp., is one of the leading publishing companies in the trading industry today. Global has grown to provide dozens of vital resources for futures and stock traders alike. Based on a simple yet effective philosophy of "continued education and personal attention," George and his team of traders strive for excellence in products as well as services.

If you have any comments or questions, do not hesitate to call. We want to hear from you. Please direct any inquiries to (888) 366-8264 or to (650) 596-1144 outside the United States. You may also reach us by fax at (650) 596-1142 or e-mail: george@globalinvestcorp.com.

Good luck in all of your trading endeavors.

Global Investment Management Corp.